"Building Like Moses with Jacobs in Mind"

In the series *Urban Life, Landscape, and Policy,*
edited by Zane L. Miller, David Stradling, and Larry Bennett

Also in this series:

Julia L. Foulkes, *To the City: Urban Photographs of the New Deal*

William Issel, *For Both Cross and Flag: Catholic Action, Anti-Catholicism, and National Security Politics in World War II San Francisco*

Lisa Hoffman, *Patriotic Professionalism in Urban China: Fostering Talent*

John D. Fairfield, *The Public and Its Possibilities: Triumphs and Tragedies in the American City*

Andrew Hurley, *Beyond Preservation: Using Public History to Revitalize Inner Cities*

SCOTT LARSON

"Building Like Moses with Jacobs in Mind"

CONTEMPORARY PLANNING IN NEW YORK CITY

TEMPLE UNIVERSITY PRESS
PHILADELPHIA

TEMPLE UNIVERSITY PRESS
Philadelphia, Pennsylvania 19122
www.temple.edu/tempress

Copyright © 2013 by Temple University
All rights reserved
Published 2013

Library of Congress Cataloging-in-Publication Data

Larson, Scott, 1961–
 "Building like Moses with Jacobs in mind" : contemporary planning in New York City / Scott Larson.
   p. cm. — (Urban life, landscape, and policy)
 Includes bibliographical references and index.
   ISBN 978-1-4399-0969-0 (cloth : alk. paper) —
ISBN 978-1-4399-0970-6 (pbk. : alk. paper) —
ISBN 978-1-4399-0971-3 (e-book) 1. City planning—New York (State)—New York. 2. Moses, Robert, 1888–1981.
3. Bloomberg, Michael. 4. Jacobs, Jane, 1916–2006. I. Title.
  HT168.N5L37 2013
  307.1′216097471—dc23
                                                         2012042291

Printed in the United States of America

031114P

Contents

Acknowledgments — vii

1 Jacobs versus Moses: A Fight for the City's Soul — 1
2 The "Patron Saint" and the "Git'r Done Man" — 15
3 The Bloomberg Practice — 33
4 Calls for a New Moses — 45
5 Planning and the Narrative of Threat — 59
6 The Armature for Development — 77
7 Ideas That Converge — 97
8 Ideas That Travel — 115
9 Design as Civic Virtue — 133
10 Building Like Moses with Jacobs in Mind — 145

Notes — 155
References — 167
Index — 181

Acknowledgments

While this book is the result of a very discrete interest, it is the product of a much longer and broader intellectual journey. In that regard, it would be futile to even try to acknowledge the contributions of every person who played a part in its realization. Still, it would be disingenuous not to acknowledge the invaluable contributions of a select and very important few. First, I offer my genuine thanks to Neil Smith, whose profound influence on my worldview resonates far beyond this current work. From those very first papers submitted as a new graduate student through the final manuscript draft, he was completely and always there. With much pride, and humility, I submit that this project never would have happened without him. Rest in peace, friend. I owe a lasting debt of gratitude to Michael Porter, who first suggested the cracks in Jane Jacobs's halo on a hike in the Shawangunk Mountains. And to Kareem Rabie, whose early enthusiasm and encouragement on that drive back to New York City from an Association of American Geographers annual meeting in Boston fortified my resolve. Likewise, considerable thanks go to Joshua Moses (no relation to Robert), Ted Powers, and especially Padmini Biswas, for commiseration and camaraderie during those alarming, empty moments when the words failed me and my thinking stalled.

I also owe sincere thanks to my fellow fellows and seminar participants at the Center for Place, Culture, and Politics, who over the course of a critical nine months, from 2009 to 2010, created such a stimulating space in which to engage. I would be doubly remiss if I did not acknowledge and thank David Harvey, Michael Sorkin, and, especially, Cindi

Katz. Their intellectual fingerprints are indelibly embedded in this book: David blazed a path the rest of us with like leanings can only hope to follow, Michael opened up new horizons, and Cindi made it all so meaningful and fun. Her early instigation gave this project life.

At the same time, I am extremely grateful to an anonymous outside reader whose piercing insights and invaluable suggestions helped shape and sharpen the final product. I wish I could tell this reviewer so in person. Of course, no one deserves more credit for sweating the ever-important details than Larry Bennett. Throughout the editing process, he was patient, calm, articulate, and exacting—in other words, exactly what every writer needs. Likewise, I am forever indebted to Mick Gusinde-Duffy for divining the latent value in my earliest manuscript.

Thanks go to my parents, Ken and Betty Larson. Without their unconditional support and remarkable capacity for understanding, I long ago would have settled for something far less. To Jamie—best friend, critic, muse—my unending gratitude and love. Not only did the seeds of this project take root on our runs on Riverside Drive, but they have since grown into a shared sense of purpose to build something better by aligning our worlds. This is every bit as much her achievement as mine. And finally, this book and any worthwhile ideas in it are dedicated to Annika. May you never stop fighting for *your* utopia.

"Building Like Moses with Jacobs in Mind"

1

Jacobs versus Moses

A Fight for the City's Soul

In October 2006 the Gotham Center for New York City History at the City University of New York hosted a public forum. Engaged in a spirited conversation was a select group of historians, architects, planners, community activists, developers, and political appointees. The group debated which of two urban visions dominates New York City's approach to city building today—that of Jane Jacobs, the legendary urbanist and writer who penned the now-classic attack on planning, *The Death and Life of Great American Cities*,[1] or her frequent antagonist, Robert Moses, the master builder of the mid-twentieth century.[2] Pointing to promotional posters that showed the pair posed as if ready for a modern-day gunfight at O.K. Corral, event moderator and Gotham Center director Mike Wallace suggested that the imagery was symbolic, indicative of "the ur status" Moses and Jacobs had achieved:

> They seem to have become almost iconic figures, touchstones with whom participants in contemporary debates on city building often seek to align themselves. In part, perhaps, this is because their clashes back in the '60s were so intensely dramatic. Yes, they each channeled and shaped forces far vaster than themselves, but their combat was also between two unique and powerful personalities. They really did detest each other, as far as I know, and what they believed the other stood for. (Wallace 2006)

Yet while Wallace and many of the gathered experts spoke as if Jane Jacobs and Robert Moses were truly physical combatants, metaphorical gun-slingers and ideological opposites, situated at the far ends of the urban planning spectrum, one of the evenings' featured speakers offered a starkly different view. Serving as New York City's representative on the panel, Amanda Burden, Mayor Michael Bloomberg's director of city planning and chair of the City Planning Commission, argued that the time had come to stop focusing on the ways in which Jacobs and Moses were at odds and to consider instead the ways in which their ideas could work together. Clearly, Burden acknowledged, the debate over the different ideologies of "these two icons" would continue, even as Jacobs had won greater influence among planners, urbanists, and elected officials. But, she added, the need to build additional housing, create jobs, and lay the foundation for New York City's future growth demanded the kind of leadership, ingenuity, and drive that Moses embodied (Burden 2006a).

At the time the administration was in the middle of a protracted battle to push through its own ambitious redevelopment agenda. Moses-like in scope and scale, it called for a massive city makeover, with plans that ranged from an effort to win the 2012 Summer Olympic Games and a proposed $4.4 billion conversion of Brooklyn's Atlantic Yards from an open-air rail yard into a mixed-use community of luxury condominiums, affordable housing, office towers, and a $1 billion basketball arena designed by noted architect Frank Gehry to an aggressive agenda for rezoning neighborhoods across all five boroughs and an ever-expanding and evolving proposal to transform midtown Manhattan's Far West Side into the city's "newest central business district" (Pinsky 2008). By the summer of 2009, more than ninety-four rezonings covering eight thousand city blocks had cleared the City Council, with fifteen more on the docket. Among the more prominent projects remaining on the administration's agenda were the development of an East River Science Park as "the flagship" of the city's effort to become a biotech hub (Pinsky 2008); the redevelopment of the industrial neighborhood of Willets Point in Queens from a "toxic wasteland to a green and renewable neighborhood"; the rezoning of seventy-five-acre Coney Island in Brooklyn; and the rezoning and redevelopment of Hunts Point along the East River in the Bronx (Pinsky 2008). Central to a number of the projects—including Atlantic Yards, Willets Point, and a proposed expansion of Columbia University in West Harlem—was the specter of the powers of eminent domain being invoked to clear the way for redevelopment.

"Big cities need big projects," Burden maintained, going on to say:

> Big projects are a necessary part of the diversity, competition, and growth that both Jacobs and Moses fought for. It is to the great credit of the mayor that we are building and rezoning today, once again, like Moses on an unprecedented scale but with Jane

Jacobs firmly in mind, invigorated in the belief that the process matters and that great things can be built through a focus on the details, on the street, for the people who live in this great city. (Burden 2006a)

To most readers of Jane Jacobs and admirers of Robert Moses, Burden's suggestion that it is possible, indeed desirable, to build like Moses with Jacobs in mind stretches all credibility. It certainly called into question many of the steadfast assumptions that for nearly five decades had cast the pair as fundamentally antagonistic, completely incompatible figures, even as it underscored the role their legacies continue to play in influencing broader debates in urban planning and the evolution of the built environment. It also said as much, if not more, about the contested nature in which those legacies can be read, remembered, and understood. Yet at another, perhaps far more fundamental level, Burden's invocation of the pair offered a window into the theoretical, ideological, and political context through which the Bloomberg administration pursued its redevelopment agenda.

This book aspires to force that window wide open. Its aim is to use the ongoing Moses-Jacobs debate as a means for examining and understanding the administration's redevelopment strategies and actions, and in so doing offer a critique of contemporary urban planning in New York City. These are among the questions it seeks to explore: How have the legacies of Robert Moses and Jane Jacobs been reinterpreted with the passing of time and evolution of urban space? In what ways have these legacies been mobilized in the service of particular redevelopment strategies—often in selective ways—reflecting the larger social and economic goals and agendas of those invoking them? And ultimately, what did the Bloomberg administration mean when it claimed to want to "build like Moses but with Jacobs in mind"?

That story begins with Jacobs and Moses themselves.

Larger-than-Life Rivals

In spite of the over-the-top characterization of the Gotham Center event, Jacobs and Moses had relatively few face-to-face encounters. Many of Moses's major projects were completed long before Jacobs came on the scene—his proposals for the construction of a highway across Lower Manhattan and the reconfiguring of Washington Square to make way for an extension of Fifth Avenue are among the more notable exceptions. In fact, while Jacobs clearly inveighs against Moses's approach to building—and her abhorrence of his authoritarian design lies at the heart of the activist bent in *The Death and Life of Great American Cities*—in the book she mentions her rival by name only seven times, preferring instead a more broad-brushed critique of the ideas and methods he so fully represents.³

As for Moses, did he ever publicly acknowledge Jacobs? More often he lumped her among an amorphous, nondescript crowd of naysayers, know-nothings, "malcontents" (Caro 1975, 1097), and "Beiunskis" (Moses 1944, 16) who stood in the way of progress and simply did not merit individual scorn. In fact, collective derision was a favorite weapon for Moses, one that for many years he wielded masterfully in minimizing and marginalizing opposition. One particularly representative example—almost joyfully recounted by Wallace to stoke the fires for the Gotham Center forum—came when, infuriated by efforts to derail his plans to run a road through Washington Square, Moses bellowed, "There is nobody against this. Nobody! Nobody but a bunch of . . . mothers!" Even in cases in which Jacobs, the mother of two sons and a daughter, was a clear target of his contempt, Moses avoided referencing her explicitly. In one instance—an especially acerbic letter written to her publisher characterizing *The Death and Life of Great American Cities* as "libelous junk"—Moses dismissed "the book" without referring to it by name and made no mention whatsoever of its author.⁴

Of course, that is not to say that the pair did not despise each other. Instead, it serves to illustrate how their duel, while between two powerful personalities at seemingly opposite sides of the debate over how best to plan and build cities, was and remains representative of things much larger. Jacobs was a thinker, an evocative writer. Her overarching goal was not to bring down Moses, though surely she reveled in his eventual demise. Her aim was to stop his projects: to derail the ramming of an expressway across Lower Manhattan and a thoroughfare through Washington Square Park, and to argue for a different way of thinking about, planning, and governing cities.⁵ Moses, meanwhile, was a doer. His projects are his texts, and he had little interest in Jacobs or in most people it seems. His overriding focus was on getting things built.

As a result, it has been largely left to others to flesh out the full oppositional nature of the Jacobs-Moses dialectic. Because they were such powerful personalities who engaged in big debates over broad ideals, the two have come to be viewed as the larger-than-life symbols of those debates, as well as figureheads for the subplots subsumed in them. Over time, they have evolved into poster material for all manner of principles and broadly defined, easy dichotomies—good versus evil, progress versus preservation, people versus the state, diversity and density versus chaos and overcrowding, the city ascendant versus the city in decline.

Yet partly because Moses and Jacobs have become strongly identified with so many things—though forever in relation to New York City and always in terms of their mutual opposition—their legacies remain works in progress, points of tension perpetually being reconstituted and reshaped by the ongoing spatial and temporal transformations of urban form. In a certain sense, Wallace hit the mark: their legacies have a remarkable and persistent way of participating in the shaping of urban processes.

Still, according to Burden, the Bloomberg administration's take on Moses and Jacobs suggests that what we think of these pivotal figures and their ideas at any given point in time seems to be fundamentally informed and wholly influenced by our image of the city at that particular moment. Urban thinkers and planners, after all, like the practice of planning and the ideas that guide it, build both literally and figuratively on the past, inheriting from bygone eras built environments and particular problems, as well as frameworks and conditions for thinking about potential solutions. Jacobs makes this point explicit in the often-cited introduction to *The Death and Life of Great American Cities*. In the span of nine pages, she traces and critiques the evolution of planning theory by connecting past theoretical paradigms—from Daniel Burnham's City Beautiful through Ebenezer Howard's Garden Cities to the utopian Radiant Cities of Le Corbusier—to their normalization within planning and design orthodoxy. It is from this context, of course, that she launches her withering "attack on current city planning and rebuilding" (Jacobs 1992, 1).

Moses and Modernism

At the heart of Jacobs's critique stands Moses's ability to marshal federal programs and the resources they represented as part of a broader modernist project prompted by visions of creating a new, more efficient and forward-looking society in the wake of World War II. On the eve of the war, New York City, like virtually all American cities, was heavily dependent on industry; it was the nation's largest industrial center, and nearly 40 percent of its workforce was still engaged in making things. Yet as early as the 1920s, groups like the Committee on a Regional Plan of New York and Its Environs[6] had begun arguing that the future of industry would lie outside the central city, and, in the years following the war, with the momentous socioeconomic shifts they would bring, the impetus turned to clearing the inner city of factories to make room for its postindustrial future.

At the same time, dilapidated housing, vast slums, and creeping blight framed the public's image of inner cities. In 1943, Charles Merriam, who had been a member of President Franklin Roosevelt's National Resources Board, suggested in a report titled "Make No Small Plans" that the country was "on the verge of a new era in city development," one in which a far broader and near-utopian focus would lead to programs and policies "for sounder urban living" (Merriam, quoted in Gelfand 1975, 105). The resulting modernist moment, grounded in a liberal reformist tradition but constrained by market forces and the perquisites of private property, sought not only to address urban ills, like slums and blight, but to set in motion wholesale transformations of urban built environments that would position cities for a more harmonious future. As Columbia University planning professor Robert Beauregard so concisely captured it, "As capitalism was tamed, the city organized and prosperity diffused socially and spatially, the lower classes would rise to affluence and take on the values and behaviors of the middle class" (Beauregard 1989, 387). Even though Moses balked at what he saw as the social engineering inherent in much of the liberal orientation of the modernist enterprise, he embraced the aspirational vision of the new, postindustrial city it inspired—as well as the vast resources and power it promised—and he eagerly framed ensuing fights in terms of what kind of city needed to be built for the public good.

Within this environment, federal programs such as Urban Renewal and the Title I projects intended to see it through were conceived to counter the rapid suburbanization and decentralization that were threatening American inner cities. In essence, the Title I program presumed that the physical attributes of dilapidated neighborhoods were to blame for the blighted conditions and social ills that inflicted many urban cores. Substandard housing, as well as incompatible land use, overcrowding, a dearth of recreational amenities, and transportation infrastructure unsuitable to the automobile age all contributed to the creation and maintenance of slums. As such, Title I offered a simple solution: improve the built environment and you improve quality of life.

On one hand, these federal programs were devised to eliminate slums. Moses also saw them as a means of forcing the city into the postindustrial future. His projects razed not only blighted neighborhoods but also manufacturing districts, on which he would build massive public-housing projects as well as educational institutions and government centers intended to reinvigorate investment in New York City's threatened downtown. But just as Moses aggressively pursued Title I projects as a means of inner-city rejuvenation, he every bit as tenaciously hatched schemes to build new highways that would—in his view—further strengthen city centers by connecting them with their growing suburbs. Ultimately, though, opposition to the destruction of existing urban neighborhoods in order to build highways through the heart of dense urban areas meant a limited number of such projects were built—the Cross-Bronx Expressway being one notable exception—even as networks of suburban and interstate highway systems were expanding. In a spectacular example of unintended consequences, Moses's support for the automobilization of the country fostered the forces that propelled people and businesses out of the city centers he was attempting to save. As Marshall Berman wrote in his groundbreaking critique of urban modernity, *All That Is Solid Melts into Air*, "The development of modernity has made the modern city itself old-fashioned, obsolete . . . by a fateful dialectic, because the city and the highway don't go together, the city must go" (Berman 1982, 307).

"The Kind of a Problem the City Is"

Jacobs, of course, would zero in on these destructive impulses within Moses's modernism and in response develop her own interpretation of what makes a city successful, prompting Marxist cultural theorist Fredric Jameson to assert that modernity "began to end the night Jane Jacobs delivered the first lecture in what was to become *The Death and Life of Great American Cities*" (Jameson 1996, 32). Yet while she is often portrayed as a revolutionary, radical thinker and an anti-planner, Jacobs's critique of planning emerged from a distinct historical lineage; a range of prominent earlier urbanists influenced her thinking. Among the more influential of these were members of an ecological tradition within early urbanism that included Camillo Sitte, the nineteenth-century Viennese writer and critic whose appreciation for the organic intricacy and complexity of the medieval city form inspired a critique of the technical aspects of planning, and Robert Morris, an influential eighteenth-century English writer and theorist who argued that the architect's overriding concern should be the interplay between design and nature. Like Sitte, Morris celebrated ancient built form and distinguished between organic—though not necessarily unplanned—cities and those conceived through more rigid applications of the grid.

Sitte, in particular, serves as a theoretical forerunner to Jacobs. Writing in the nineteenth century, at a time when enhancing the salability of subdivided property was paramount, he believed that the market alone, as a purely mechanical instrument, would not yield "good" urban design and artistic principles. Instead he argued that a limited form of planning focused on issues of relationship and proportion could produce more livable cities. He championed the curved, irregular layouts of Europe's medieval towns, the juxtaposition of varied buildings as a means of framing visual features, and the use of aesthetic and historical precedent to create human scale.[7]

These ideas, of course, would find purchase in Jacobs's own conceptualization of good urban form. In the introduction to *The Death and Life of Great American Cities*, Jacobs wrote of the "underlying order" and organized complexity of cities, and she argued that to approach understanding them as if they were simple problems involving one or two variables—housing or transportation, for instance—examined in isolation, only invited failure, as previous planning practice could attest (Jacobs 1992, 15). Instead, Jacobs advocated for thinking of cities as processes, unique and interrelated, but natural and observable, nonetheless: "The cities of human beings," she wrote "are as natural, being a product of one form of nature, as are the colonies of prairie dogs or the beds of oysters" (Jacobs 1992, 444). Through these close observations she would devise her precepts for making cities livable—a mix of uses, diversity, short blocks—and over time these would take hold as a set of planning and design principles that would come to serve almost as best practices within the field of urban design.

This tension between ecological and modernist visions of the city, however, provides still more background for the Jacobs-Moses divide. Decades before Moses lambasted Jacobs for her broadside against his version of the future, Le Corbusier, whose Radiant City towers-in-the-park would find material—if somewhat diminished expression—in Moses's superblock housing developments, mocked Sitte's views on medieval design, saying they were not only "based on the past" but "in fact WERE the past . . . a sentimental past . . . on a small and petty scale" representative of the "scatter-brained mentality of a donkey" (Le Corbusier, quoted in Lilley 1999, 435; emphasis in original). Such polemics quickly informed conceptions of "good" and "bad" urban form for succeeding generations of urbanists, serving as useful tools in ideological arguments over how best to plan and build cities. As the historical geographer Keith Lilley suggests, "What emerges from this is a complex picture in which the ideas of particular urbanists came to be misrepresented, or misunderstood, either deliberately or unintentionally, by their contemporaries," in a battle of ideas that is very much mirrored in the ongoing "gunfight" between Moses and Jacobs (Lilley 1999, 428).

It is this duality, then, this constant push and pull of cause and effect that continues to inspire the periodic revisitings and reassessments of Moses and Jacobs: a conference at Hofstra University in 1988 in celebration of the centennial of Moses's birth; another, "Ideas That Matter," in Toronto in 1997, which generated renewed public interest in Jacobs; then, of course, their deaths—Moses's in 1981, Jacobs's a quarter century later—which sparked further reflection on their ongoing influence on urban form. In between, occasional essays or opinion pieces in the print media, typically provoked by events or new ideas in planning and development, set off additional rounds of reengaging these figures and their pivotal roles.

More recently, the Bloomberg administration's ambitious plans to remake New York City, along with the rhetoric—loaded with references to both Jacobs and Moses—surrounding the resultant wave of redevelopment activity that washed over the city, rekindled interest in the pair and their ongoing influence. In early 2007, two Columbia University historians—Hilary Ballon and Kenneth Jackson—launched a Moses rehabilitation campaign with the opening of a three-part exhibition, *Robert Moses and the Modern City*, and the publication of a companion collection of essays of the same name along with the subtitle *The Transformation of New York*. Not to be outdone, that September, Jacobs's supporters gave her legacy its own shot in the arm with the opening of *Jane Jacobs and the Future of New York*, a three-month exhibit at the Municipal Art Society of New York.

Soon, a flood of books seeking new ways to add to and, in some cases, reinterpret the meanings of Jacob and Moses appeared. In the summer of 2009, Random House, the publisher of *The Death and Life of Great American Cities*, produced *Wrestling with Moses: How Jane Jacobs Took On New York's Master Builder and Transformed the American City*, in which Anthony Flint, an author and a journalist with the Lincoln Institute of Land Policy, recounts the "epic rivalry of Jacobs and Moses," a "thrilling David and Goliath story" of "the struggle for the soul of a city" (Flint 2009, back cover). Like an earlier, though largely overlooked, biography, *Jane Jacobs: Urban Visionary*, by journalist Alice Sparberg Alexiou, that appeared within weeks of Jacobs's passing, Flint's work is populist in tone and provides a running commentary on Jacobs's role in defying Moses's plans—a story that is conspicuously missing from Robert Caro's seminal Moses biography, *The Power Broker: Robert Moses and the Fall of New York*, which was first published in 1975. It also served as a rebuttal of sorts to Ballon and Jackson's Moses revisionism.

In early 2010 yet another journalist delivered an impassioned defense of Jacobs as a critical response to Ballon and Jackson's redemptive effort on behalf of Moses. Writing in *The Battle for Gotham: New York in the Shadow of Robert Moses and Jane Jacobs*, Roberta Brandes Gratz took up Jacobs's mantle as the feisty defender of small-scale dynamism and do-it-yourself neighborhood regeneration. Gratz, who describes herself as a friend and follower of Jacobs, draws on firsthand accounts to argue that Moses's fall, and the federal government's related abandonment of its urban renewal program, allowed for the type of "organic rejuvenation" that marks New York City today—a rejuvenation, of course, that was prescribed by Jacobs (Gratz 2010a). According to Gratz (2010b), and to Alexiou (2006) and Flint (2009), Jacobs had still won, and Moses had still nearly wrung the life out of New York City.

But is this the full story? After almost fifty years of debate, a handful of biographies, dozens of interpretive studies, and the seemingly perpetual reexamination of their "ur status" at opposing ends of the urban planning spectrum, have we fully explored and firmly fixed the nature of the Moses-Jacobs divide? Are the two and their ideas fundamentally incompatible? And what should we make of the Bloomberg administration's effort to knit them together?

For sure, there are many and very important differences—not to mention much acrimony—between Jacobs and Moses. If we think of the two in terms of urban renewal, the size and shape of city blocks, catastrophic money as opposed to gradual money, those differences do seem to make an imposing case for the incompatibility of their approaches to making cities better places. Moses's moment was made possible by an era of big government, and he enthusiastically served as an early proponent of the public-private model of redevelopment at a time when cities and their post–World War II middle classes were threatened by shifting socioeconomic currents. The expressways, bridges, cultural and civic institutions, housing developments, beaches, and parks that he built not only transformed New York City but thoroughly revolutionized the way midcentury America planned its urban spaces. Jacobs's opening, meanwhile, came at Moses's—and big government's—expense. With the activist state in withdrawal from the failure of modernist programs like urban renewal and the fiscal crisis of the early 1970s, her glorification of the democratic individualism of the street, informed by discernibly normative middle-class values, came to dominate the planning ethos.

Yet when viewed from a broader, more critical framework, one can argue that both figures espouse a distinctly class-based strategy for remaking the city, and it is here where they converge in contemporary New York City redevelopment politics. As Burden's (2006a) evocative characterization suggests, in devising its own vision of the city's future, the Bloomberg administration has culled from both Jacobs and Moses, faithfully adopting certain aspects of each figure's foundational ideas while reinterpreting others to fit the administration's view of the successful city in a twenty-first-century context. In this sense, while Moses's modernism appears to stand in stark contrast to Jacobs's localism, when synthesized within the Bloomberg administration's ambitious redevelopment plans, they converge in a call for disciplining space for capital accumulation and the building and rebuilding of the city at the expense of those of lesser class privilege.

This can be seen not only in the ways Moses's and Jacobs's ideas have been adopted, interpreted, and in certain cases bent to conform neatly to the purposes of others but also through the direct relationship between their precepts and the processes of gentrification. Moses's approach envisioned the clearance of slums and blight, the segregation of public housing, and the development of civic institutions, such as Lincoln Center and the United Nations. Jacobs's scheme involved a fix-it-up ethos and house-by-house, block-by-block rehabilitation of aspiring neighborhoods. In both cases, as well as in the selective incorporation of their ideas by the Bloomberg administration, real estate–based economic development within the context of an economically restructured postwar urbanism was trumpeted as the key to urban regeneration.

What follows is an exploration of how this could be true and what the resulting details look like.

To fully understand how the legacies of Jacobs and Moses have contributed to debates over urban form and the direction of urban redevelopment over time, this work examines the ways in which they have been mobilized at specific junctures in urban planning history. Chief among these are ongoing struggles over urban design, including the emergence of New Urbanism and the development of major projects that bear its mark; the ongoing evolution of New York City's planning infrastructure in general and its zoning regulations in particular; and the release by the Regional Plan Association in 1996 of its Third Regional Plan, *A Region at Risk*. Each of these critical junctures plays a significant role in the organization of this work, informing, and in certain cases framing, individual chapters.

Chapter 2 ("The 'Patron Saint' and the 'Git'r Done Man'") charts the evolutionary arc of the Moses and Jacobs legacies by exploring how perceptions of the pair have evolved over time. A particular emphasis of the chapter is on the ways those legacies have been read, reinterpreted, and at times mobilized in the service of specific planning ideologies, up to and including their appearance in contemporary debates over development policy in New York City. Ultimately, the chapter highlights the degree to which debates over Moses and Jacobs and their legacies increasingly hinge on conflicting and often competing interpretations, allowing them to be co-opted by mainstream forces within planning and development.

With revisionist elements of recent scholarship serving as the basis for both positive and negative comparisons between Moses and a Bloomberg administration intent on a revival of build-big urbanism, Chapter 3, "The Bloomberg Practice," offers a closer look at four of the megaprojects that have helped define redevelopment in New York City for much of the first decade of the twenty-first century: the effort to kick-start redevelopment of Manhattan's Far West Side by bringing the 2012 Summer Olympic Games to New York; the ambitious—and contentious—plans to redevelop the Hudson rail yards in Manhattan and the Atlantic rail yards in Brooklyn; and Columbia University's effort to expand by annexing seventeen acres of the Harlem neighborhood of Manhattanville in the face of significant community opposition. The chapter also introduces the administration's strategy of synthesizing Jacobs and Moses to win approval of specific projects and promote the city's overall development agenda.

Chapter 4, "Calls for a New Moses," turns to a closer examination of the campaign to incorporate enough of Jacobs to make the Moses-like aspects of the Bloomberg redevelopment agenda politically palatable and win over public opinion. As a means of contextualizing that discussion, the chapter provides a brief history of the collapse of planning and development in New York City that followed in part from Jacobs's crusading response to Moses-style top-down large-scale planning and projects.

Chapter 5, "Planning and the Narrative of Threat," further interrogates the power of rhetoric in planning and introduces a recurring theme in New York City planning history: the narrative of threat, which is explored in detail through a close reading of the Regional Plan Association's influential report, *A Region at Risk: The Third Regional Plan for the New York–New Jersey–Connecticut Metropolitan Area*. The chapter also explores the influence of Jacobs and Moses on this report. *A Region at Risk* came to serve as an important model for an emergent neoliberal form of urbanism as well as the Bloomberg administration's redevelopment agenda.

The administration's synthesis of Jacobs and Moses, however, goes beyond rhetoric. Chapter 6, "The Armature for Development," addresses administration efforts to incorporate selective aspects of each within its redevelopment strategy, most prominently through the aggressive rezoning of New York City. Once again, the legacies of Jacobs and Moses played a vital role in the evolution of zoning as a tool for city planning, and that history is recounted before the chapter turns to a detailed analysis of the Bloomberg administration's rezoning strategy. By recognizing the power of its land use decisions to drive development in "underutilized" neighborhoods even as it promotes middle- and upper-class qualities of life in other neighborhoods, the administration has mobilized zoning as the chief vehicle for remaking the city along class lines.

Chapter 7, "Ideas That Converge," takes up the call for a critical analysis of what the Bloomberg administration means when it talks of building like Moses with Jacobs in mind. It relies on a close reading of Jacobs's foundational concepts and a recounting of Moses's record as the master of modernist urbanism to make the case that the Bloomberg administration's synthesis of the two figures and their ideals is a selective usage that promotes gentrification.

Chapter 8, "Ideas That Travel," turns to the resonance of Jacobs's and Moses's ideals beyond New York City by mapping how, through the processes of policy mobility and best-practice production, the dialectic embodied by their legacies has traveled. In Jacobs's case this played out most directly in the planning discourse of Toronto, the Canadian city where she lived and worked for the last four decades of her life. There, against a backdrop of opposition to a Moses-like highway and housing projects, Jacobs's ideals have been repeatedly mobilized to justify real estate–oriented development, generating gentrification in the process. Whereas Jacobs's legacy is characterized by activism and ideals, Moses's imprint is physical: it can be seen in the parks, highways, and infrastructure that bear his mark, not only in New York City but also in Portland,

Oregon, where in the waning years of World War II he was invited to develop a plan for a postindustrial city. Of course, with Jacobs's "triumph," Moses would be banished to planning exile, and it would not be until the Bloomberg-inspired rehabilitation effort that his legacy would again be seen in a positive light and appeals to his ability to execute big projects become a recurring element in the rhetoric surrounding development projects across the United States.

Chapter 9, "Design as Civic Virtue," details how design—or what critics deride as a fixation on the way things look—also has emerged as a critical concept within the Bloomberg administration's distillation of Jacobs's and Moses's ideals. It examines how, under the direction of Amanda Burden, the administration's director of city planning, design has become a powerful means for enhancing real estate values and encouraging development that is reflective of a broader class-based planning ideology. It contends that the administration's articulation of design as a civic virtue and its constant celebration of the transformative potential of the parks, plazas, streetscapes, and buildings planned and constructed as part of the production of an "aspirational" city serve to naturalize and normalize the class-based values inherent in its larger redevelopment scheme.

Finally, Chapter 10, "Building Like Moses with Jacobs in Mind," problematizes the approach to urban redevelopment that emerges from the Bloomberg administration's synthesis of Jacobs and Moses within the context of recurring crises of global capitalism. It argues that the financial crisis that began in 2008 offers a valuable opportunity to examine the fallacies and limitations of real estate–driven redevelopment and to explore the relationship of Moses's and Jacobs's legacy to those processes. Ultimately, it makes the case that neither figure offers a meaningful model for addressing the stubborn problems—poverty, lack of affordable housing, and segregation along class and racial lines—that continue to vex today's cities. Within the redevelopment narrative created by the Bloomberg administration, building like Moses with Jacobs in mind becomes a mechanism for intentionally and artificially constraining the debate over urbanism to a narrow band that blindly accepts and promotes the logic of capital accumulation within contemporary urbanization.

Just as to varying degrees Robert Caro, Hilary Ballon and Kenneth Jackson, Anthony Flint, Roberta Brandes Gratz, the Bloomberg administration, and others have marshaled concepts and ideas—and in some senses ideology—to create narratives around Jacobs and Moses, this work is a narrative in its own right. As such, it is not intended to be passive. Rather, the intention is to focus a critical light on the limitations of the legacies of Robert Moses and Jane Jacobs and their relation to ongoing debates over urban form as well as to scrutinize the redevelopment agenda of the Bloomberg administration in New York City.

2

The "Patron Saint" and the "Git'r Done Man"

When Jane Jacobs died on April 25, 2006, she was widely viewed as the patron saint of urban dynamism, an irascible but venerable champion of street-level vitality and neighborhood diversity whose views "changed the way we think about livable cities" (Dreier 2006, 227). A mother and housewife, a sometime writer, and an activist, without any formal training in urban theory or design, Jacobs stood the planning world on its ear in 1961 by crafting what to many remains the seminal critique of mid-twentieth-century city planning orthodoxy, *The Death and Life of Great American Cities*.[1] In this book she challenged the top-down approach to planning and savaged the then widely accepted view that the best way to fix crowded cities and their aging, insufficient infrastructures was to bulldoze sections wholesale and rebuild anew. She derided massive, federally funded programs such as slum clearance, public housing, and highway construction as the products of so-called "experts" who knew nothing about the way cities actually worked. She then proposed her own prescriptions culled from personal observations of her own neighborhood, in New York City's Greenwich Village. To Jacobs, urban health was a process. Diversity, she declared, is the life blood of the successful city, and she laid out four recommendations for cultivating it: mixed land use, short blocks, buildings of various ages and conditions, and density of population.

Although Jacobs was far from the only voice to condemn the bulldoze-and-build approach to urban regeneration prevalent at the time or to expound on the instructive dynamism of the neighborhood, the vivid clarity of her message and its revolutionizing effect on the field of planning have made *The Death and Life of Great American Cities* a canon of urban literature. Likewise, its author has become an icon to subsequent generations of city thinkers and students. As a result, her death provoked an outpouring of tributes and remembrances (see, for example, Bernstein 2006 and Martin 2006). Within weeks, journalist Alice Sparberg Alexiou published *Jane Jacobs: Urban Visionary*, a glowing biography, while the American Sociological Association journal *City and Community* devoted a full edition to essays commemorating Jacobs's words and work. "Now the sorrowful and celebratory obituaries have been written," Herbert Gans wrote in that commemorative issue's introductory essay, "and we can begin to assess her contributions to urban studies and urban policy" (Gans 2006, 213). In that assessment, contributors painted Jacobs as a passionate proponent of the "joyous urban jumble" (Halle 2006, 237); an articulate voice against slum clearance, highways, and out-of-scale development; and a revolutionary thinker who "touted the role of cities as the engines of economic prosperity" (Dreier 2006, 228) and inspired a generation of activists to stand up for their communities. "Like William Whyte, C. Wright Mills, Betty Friedan, and other iconoclastic authors of the time," sociologist Sharon Zukin wrote in her contribution, "Jacobs indicted powerful elites and large-scale organizations for enforcing conformity—in her case, about principles of urban design—and stifling dissent" (Zukin 2006, 233). By the 1980s, Zukin recalled, Jacobs's ideals about urban design and what constitutes a livable city had become "firmly rooted" and her influence on community organization was widespread (2006).

Yet in 2006, that vision appeared to be under attack by a new wave of megaprojects that once again aimed to transform New York City on an enormous scale. Arguing that New York City was in a "competitive struggle" to maintain its position as a global financial capital, and drawing on population projections that predicted another one million people would live there by 2030, the administration of Mayor Michael Bloomberg had embarked on a massive city makeover that harkened back to the days of build-big urban renewal and Jacobs's longtime nemesis, New York City's "master builder," Robert Moses.

Although never elected to public office, Moses dominated urban redevelopment in New York City from 1934 until 1968, at one point holding twelve different city and state administrative positions, ranging from city parks commissioner and construction coordinator to chair of the Triborough Bridge and Tunnel Authority and the Mayor's Committee on Slum Clearance. Through those positions he created then controlled, with little to no oversight, public authorities that generated millions of dollars in revenue. He also proved particularly adept at leveraging federal monies, and, over the course of his career, he used the significant resources at his disposal to replace much of New York City's pre-twentieth-century infrastructure with an expanding network of roads, bridges, tunnels, parks, business and cultural centers, and housing and urban renewal projects.[2] The resulting era of redevelopment and the new urban landscape it produced made him a singular figure in the redevelopment history of New York City, as well as the face of urban planning that Jacobs so despised.

Sweeping in scope and therefore much in the Moses mold, the Bloomberg administration's proposed long-range redevelopment plan quickly engendered comparisons to that earlier era. It included creating scores of new parks and public spaces; thousands of units of new housing—both subsidized and market rate; and entire new business districts and neighborhoods. Miles of the city's largely abandoned working waterfront were to be transformed into residential and recreational enclaves, and new signature corporate office towers, many designed by the biggest names in the design world, were slated to rise in Brooklyn and Manhattan.

Yet at the same time the mayor's plan inspired images of a new Moses aggressively remaking the city, members of his administration were busy invoking Jacobs as the plan's true guiding light. In a November 2006 interview with the *Gotham Gazette*, Amanda Burden, New York City's director of city planning and chair of the City Planning Commission, insisted that while the city needed to build thousands of units of affordable housing, "reclaim and revitalize the waterfront," and "lay the foundations to support" future growth, "it is just not acceptable or wise, or even possible to undertake these challenges without espousing Jacobs' principles of city diversity, of the rich detail of urban life, to build in a way that nourishes complexity" (2006b).

That this rebirth of citywide urban engineering, fraught with allusions to two such seemingly antagonistic influences on urban form, coincided so closely with Jacobs's passing was surely coincidence. That it happened at all invited, if not required, a critical assessment of past planning practice in New York City. Within a year major retrospectives promising to reexamine the legacies of Jacobs and Moses—the three-part *Robert Moses and the Modern City* and *Jane Jacobs and the Future of New York*—were under way. As the writer Paul Goldberger noted in the *New Yorker*: "The notion of Moses as the evil genius of mid-twentieth-century urban design got a boost last spring in obituaries of and tributes to Jane Jacobs, a longtime antagonist" (Goldberger 2007a).

It is essential to note, however, that the dispute between, and continued assessments of Jacobs and Moses did not begin with the rhetoric surrounding the Bloomberg administration's redevelopment agenda. Over time, their legacies have been read in various and sometimes surprising ways. And while the pair typically is positioned at opposite and antagonistic ends of the spectrum of urban thought, impressions of their influence can and have been seen in a range of ideological lights, complicating their relationship to urban policy and those who make and interpret it. Each figure's legacy is far more complex than the boilerplate interpretations would lead one to believe.

To a large degree, Moses's urban agenda was in tune with a wider twentieth-century modernist movement that began reshaping society—from the visual arts and literature to engineering and science—in the wake of large-scale industrialization. Broadly speaking, the roots of this concept reach back to the nineteenth century and even to Enlightenment notions of marshaling objective science and accumulated human knowledge to build a better life. Until then, civilization had been viewed as following a continuous, effectively preordained course. But advances in science and technology brought about radical new conceptions of space and time, and with the onset of the Industrial Revolution, machine-based technologies enabled humans to significantly reshape both the natural environment and their own social order. Mass production led industries and governments to adopt methods of scientific management and organizational procedures that emphasized rationality, precision, and efficiency.[3]

In the realm of urban planning, the resulting modernist movement sought to attend to problems of blight, poverty, and overcrowding by harnessing these new technologies and materials and the soaring skyscrapers, fantastic bridges, and other feats of engineering they made possible to rationalize the chaotic city. Essentially, through the technical mastery of space, the modern city could be tuned to run with machinelike precision. To create this new world, however, the old one had to be destroyed through a process that the political economist Joseph Schumpeter recognized as capitalism's compulsion for creative destruction. Moses, of course, proved to be a particularly enthusiastic and unapologetic practitioner of the concept; in response to critics of the displacement caused by construction of the Cross-Bronx Expressway, he famously replied, "You can't make an omelet without breaking some eggs" (Caro 1975, 218).

The degree to which Moses transformed New York City and its region is unmistakable. Among his works are roads (from Harlem River Drive and the West Side Highway to miles of parkways and all of the region's major expressways) and seven bridges that help knit the city's five boroughs into an auto-oriented metropolis, as well as buildings (1,082 containing 148,000 units of public housing and the private housing developments of Stuyvesant Town, Peter Cooper Village, and Co-op City), 658 parks, more than a dozen beaches, and the string of cultural, educational, and political institutions (from the United Nations and Lincoln Center to Shea Stadium and campuses for Long Island University, Fordham University, and the Pratt Institute) that helped solidify New York City's status as the world's cultural and commercial capital.

Although Moses did not think of himself in such a way and at times was even highly critical of modernism's core concepts and leading figures, the scale of his projects and his emphasis on the machine age and functional efficiency cast him squarely in the modernist camp.[4] On a practical level, however, Moses was more opportunistic than ideologically partisan. He followed the programs prescribed by modernism's planners and politicians only so far as they granted steady access to resources. At any given time, he conformed his city-building efforts to the funds and associated stipulations that were available from state and federal agencies.

His legendary ability to force his vision on New York City aside, Moses was far from invincible, even at the height of his powers. In the late 1930s, for instance, the federal government thwarted plans to build a Battery Park Bridge connecting lower Manhattan to Brooklyn in spite of his vigorous advocacy, and in 1952 his plan to build a highway through Washington Square Park was derailed by unyielding local opposition. The later proposal earned Moses a sharp skewering from urban critic Lewis Mumford, who called it "an act of civic vandalism" (Mumford 1959, 185). In more general terms, Mumford steadfastly condemned Moses's far-reaching agenda to modernize the city through towers-in-the-park construction, the expansion of the high-speed freeways, and promotion of centralized urban planning.[5]

Mumford was hardly alone in his early criticism of Moses. Other prominent voices in planning and architecture joined in, including Charles Abrams, a Columbia University planning professor and expert on housing who created the New York City Housing Authority; Rexford Tugwell, who served as chair of the New York City Planning Commission from 1938 to 1941; and William H. Whyte, an urbanist, sociologist, and one-time editor at *Fortune* magazine who decried the banal redundancy and dehumanizing scale of modernist housing—be it a middle-class redevelopment such as Stuyvesant Town or the vast tracts of public housing that became known simply as the "projects."[6] Abrams, in particular, articulated the sense that far from improving the city, Moses and his top-down plans for automobilization, standardization, and demolition were destroying it.[7]

Still, before the opening of *Robert Moses and the Modern City* and *Jane Jacobs and the Future of New York* and the publication of a companion collection of essays, *Robert Moses and the Modern City: The Transformation of New York*, the prevailing view of Moses was that crafted by Robert Caro in his Pulitzer Prize–winning biography *The Power Broker: Robert Moses and the Fall of New York*. By Caro's account, published in 1975, Moses was imperious, exacting, and demanding, and for thirty-four years—spanning the administrations of six governors and five mayors—he "shaped a city and its sprawling suburbs and influenced the destiny of all the cities of twentieth-century America"

(Caro 1975, 5). Of course, the story of Moses as told by Caro is very much a two-sided tale. On the one side, there was "America's greatest builder," the "shaper of the greatest city in the world" (Caro 1975, 19). On the other stood a power-hungry apostle of urban modernity who "to build his highways . . . threw out of their homes . . . more people than lived in Albany or Chattanooga, or Spokane, Tacoma, Duluth, Akron, Baton Rouge, Mobile, Nashville or Sacramento"; "flooded the city with cars"; starved public transportation and skewed "city expenditures toward revenue-producing services" at the expense of programs for the poor (Caro 1975, 19–20). Thanks in no small part to this withering portrayal, for the better part of four decades, Moses, in the words of *Washington Post* culture critic Philip Kennicott, has been "synonymous with ugly and brutal city planning" (Kennicott 2007, NO1).

Together, however, the *Robert Moses and the Modern City* exhibit and its companion collection of essays, sought to reexamine Moses's controversial legacy from a broader perspective and, as the museum promotional material put it, in "the context of urban issues of his time" (Museum of the City of New York 2007).

Rehabilitating Robert Moses

Actually, the exhibits, conceived and curated by then-Columbia University architectural historian Hilary Ballon, and the companion book, which was edited by Ballon and her Columbia University colleague, history professor Kenneth Jackson, did far more than resurrect Moses in the twentieth century; they cast in relief the contested way in which we recall the past and contend with its spatial consequences. The exhibits featured previously unpublished renderings and archival and contemporary photographs and models, each beautiful in the abstract. For instance, in the exhibit *Remaking the Metropolis*, sketches show sleek, stylized cars whizzing down futuristic highways embedded within buildings, unperturbed by the productive intensity of the city, and vice versa. They and their inhabitants sped along an endless landscape of modernity carried forward by the transformative powers of the mobile age. Aerial images show projected highway arteries superimposed on the cityscape so as to make the requisite erasure of existing buildings, parks, streets, and human beings walking along them seem a foregone—and to some certainly terrifying—conclusion (see, for instance, Berman 1982). Of course, what was missing from this designer's view of Moses's dream city—and to a large extent from the exhibits themselves—were the people whose homes and businesses were to be wiped out by these fantastic schemes.

Indeed, this shoving aside of the era's destructive consequences appeared to be the point, for just as Moses's modernist project not only scrubbed the city of its blighted neighborhoods, obliterating the accumulated history of what Berman calls their "pre-modern" traditions and sensibilities (Berman 1982), Ballon and Jackson's revisionism relied on a parallel creative representational destruction: the privileging of the present at the expense of the past and the erasure of the intervening years in which Moses's works forcefully imposed a new and very particular future onto New York City's landscape and its people. While Caro argued for a good Moses–bad Moses and focused his descriptive powers on what—from the midst of the urban crisis of the 1970s—could surely be depicted as modernist planning's catastrophic contribution to the decline of cities, Ballon and Jackson countered that the passage of time provides a different perspective.

At the time Caro was writing, "New York City was in shambles," Ballon told alumni of the Masters of Urban Planning program at New York University (Ballon 2008). But, she added, when Moses was amassing his extraordinary powers in the 1930s and using them to reshape New York City over the course of the next three decades, "cities were endangered places," threatened by the gravitational pull of an emergent suburban nation. The publishing of *Robert Moses and the Modern City* and the conception of its offshoot exhibitions, Ballon asserted, were intended to "reprise the revisionist arguments"—originally made two decades earlier by Jackson and others at the conference "Robert Moses: Single-Minded Genius" at Hofstra University, which coincided with the centennial anniversary of Moses's birth[8]—to address the "imbalance" created by Caro's seminal *Power Broker* and to "historicize" the moment within which Moses operated (Ballon 2008).

Ballon claimed that Caro was guilty of making a "causal connection" between Moses's projects and the city's steady decline, from the immediate postwar period through the mid-1980s. Her goal, she explained, in a *New York Times* interview (Pogrebin 2007, 28), was to respond to elements of the Moses legacy that were left out or "underrepresented" in *The Power Broker*. From the vantage point of the first decade of the twentieth century, the Ballon and Jackson argument goes, Moses's projects "have been absorbed into the fabric of the city," and some of the urban problems he recognized, like "the vulnerable stake of the middle class," and many of the strategies he adopted for ameliorating them—including "the potential of art centers and universities to serve as engines of redevelopment"—remain current in projects such as Columbia University's proposed construction of a new research campus in West Harlem (Ballon 2007, 94). Having acknowledged the existence of Moses's "errant ways" (Ballon 2007, 94) and his "gross abuse of power" (Ballon 2007, 95), Ballon contends that Moses was far from an omnipotent autocrat. Rather, he was an alert opportunist in tune with the times, and his projects were "aligned with national policy" and "a manifestation of public policies" (Ballon 2008).

Contrary to Jacobs's localized focus on the neighborhood, Ballon maintains, Moses "thought about the city in relation to the region, the nation and world," and, with his legendary single-mindedness, he set out to define "a mission for New York in the post-industrial age" (Ballon 2008). In all of this, Ballon and Jackson—echoing arguments Jackson first made in 1988—contend that Moses marshaled federal policy to "shape the processes of the market through planning" (Ballon 2007, 96), with the ultimate goal to "modernize the metropolis and keep it strong" (Ballon and Jackson 2007a, 66).

In this sense, the revisionist reading moves from merely rehabilitative to redemptive: Moses was ahead of his time, reading broader trends in the evolution of postwar capitalism to anticipate what city officials and planners today see as the perquisites for urban health. Whatever his faults, then, this reasoning goes, Moses was ultimately and selflessly devoted to the public good, concerned only with positioning the city for a prosperous future. Jackson writes, "Had the city not undertaken a massive program of public works between 1924 and 1970 . . . had it not built an arterial highway system, and had it not relocated 200,000 people from old-law tenements to new public housing projects, New York would not have been able to claim in the 1990s that it was the capital of the twentieth century, the capital of capitalism, and the capital of the world" (Jackson 2007, 68).

Since the 1980s, Ballon and Jackson continue, Moses's reputation has been on the mend, "propelled" toward the positive by the sense that New York City is no longer capable of executing the types of ambitious projects required to maintain its elite status in the world because of "a multilayered process of citizen and government review" (Ballon and Jackson 2007a, 65).

Revisiting Jane Jacobs

In the fall of 2007, a little more than nine months after the Moses retrospective sought to recast the "power broker" in the public's eyes, riders on a number of the Metropolitan Transportation Authority's New York City buses were encouraged to "look outside" by advertisements for *Jane Jacobs and the Future of New York*, a three-month exhibit opening that September at the Municipal Art Society of New York. "The City is changing fast," the ads observed. "Is it moving in the right direction? Use your MetroCard to find out how a legendary activist changed New York in the 1960s and how you can shape the city today." The exhibit, as the show's literature explained, was designed to "inspire citizens to support and fight for the health of their own neighborhoods," and to encourage "city officials, developers, planners and architects to embrace and implement Jane Jacobs' teachings" (Municipal Art Society of New York 2007a).

Much like the story of Moses, however, Jacobs's tale is far from simple, and any effort to pin down her long-term legacy rapidly encounters multiple and at times competing interpretations of her influence. Like Moses, Jacobs certainly provoked her share of critical disdain. Some even came from an esteemed familiar source, if for dissimilar reasons. Among the planning luminaries Jacobs attacked in *The Death and Life of Great American Cities* was Mumford, whose book *The Culture of Cities* she blasted as "a morbid and biased catalog of ills" (Jacobs 1992, 20). Despite their shared contempt for the vast federally funded programs remaking America's mid-century cities, Jacobs took aim at Mumford and his fellow "Decentrists"—a group that included Catherine Bauer, Clarence Stein, and other later-day devotees of Ebenezer Howard's Garden City concept—for what she believed was a moribund, "incurious" analysis. She disparaged their views as having nothing "to do with understanding cities, or fostering successful large cities," but rather providing "reasons and means for jettisoning cities" (Jacobs 1992, 20).[9]

One year later, Mumford fired back in the *New Yorker*. In a detailed critique of *The Death and Life of Great American Cities* of more than thirty pages, he acknowledged that Jacobs's "criticism established her as a person to be reckoned with" and, in a backhanded compliment, a new kind of "expert" (Mumford 1962, 150). She was, he wrote, a "shrewd critic of dehumanized housing and faulty design" (154) and an accomplished observer of the great complexity of urban life. But, he asserted, Jacobs's dismissive attitude toward Howard showed that she lacked historical knowledge. Describing her book as a mix of "mature judgments and schoolgirl howlers" (173), Mumford accused Jacobs of a "preoccupation that is almost an obsession" with the prevention of criminal violence (158) and a myopic focus on big cities—New York City, in particular—even though her analysis was sharpest when aimed at the small scale, the neighborhood. He took her to task for demonizing great parks as the cause of crime rather than victims of it, and he exposed what he viewed as the central contradiction to her argument—the role of planning and architectural character in preserving her Greenwich Village neighborhood.

Jacobs, Mumford summarized, "gaily bulldozes out of existence every desirable innovation in urban planning during the last century and every competing idea, without a pretense of critical evaluation" (154).[10]

Even as a decidedly celebratory exercise, the exhibit *Jane Jacobs and the Future of New York* could not escape the complicated nature of her legacy. Beneath its seemingly coherent, focused message, the exhibit was the product of a behind-the-scenes tug of war among three vital forces in contemporary efforts to come to terms with Jacobs's lasting impact: the Rockefeller Foundation, which in 1958 had awarded Jacobs a grant for the research and writing of *The Death and Life of Great American Cities*;

the show's curator, Christopher Klemek, a professor of history at George Washington University who has written extensively about Jacobs; and the Municipal Art Society (MAS), an urban advocacy organization and the exhibit's host and chief sponsor. Each party, as it turns out, had its own ideas about Jacobs's lasting relevance and, as a result, the most appropriate direction for the exhibition to take.

Even before the Moses retrospective kick-started efforts to rehabilitate the "power broker," the Rockefeller Foundation had begun planning a commemorative exhibit that would celebrate its own affiliation with Jacobs's works and ideals.[11] Klemek, however, was interested in his own "scholarly, critical mission" of continuing to understand Jacobs and her ever-evolving relationship with historical context (Klemek 2008b; see also Klemek 2007, 2008a). The Municipal Art Society of New York, meanwhile, hoped to emphasize Jacobs's enduring impact on community organizing and urban form. The organization came late to the event, according to Kent Barwick, who twice served as the society's president before retiring in late 2008, entering into the planning just nine months before the exhibit was set to open. That late start prompted what Barwick deems a "crash-course submersion" in Jacobs, her accomplishments and her legacy, and led to the question "How would Jane Jacobs react to what is going on today?" According to Barwick, "What became clear was that Jane would say, 'Well, what do *you* think?'" (Barwick 2008b).

Klemek indicated that these three forces worked "in tension" to create "an open text, a conversation" that encouraged the exhibit's viewers to consider a number of implicit and explicit arguments about Jacobs, her life's work, and its impact on New York City (Klemek 2008b). With contemporary and controversial projects like the redevelopment of the Atlantic Yards and Columbia University's proposed expansion serving as a backdrop, the exhibit sought to reinvigorate Jacobs's relevance at a time when "the cards seem stacked against the individual in the neighborhood, through the use of eminent domain, for instance" (Barwick 2008b). As a result, the exhibition was conceived as two distinct but complementary halves of a whole. Literally split into two rooms, it celebrated Jacobs's lasting influence on contemporary community organizing in one, while highlighting her four foundational tenets of healthy neighborhoods in the other.

In the first room, photographs and text illustrated how Jacobs's ideas had served as inspiration for neighborhood organizations in "continuing to develop cutting edge tools to effect positive change and greater public participation" (Municipal Art Society of New York 2007a), or what Barwick calls a focus on the Jacobsian notion of giving "people confidence to make their own judgments about the world they live in . . . empowering a new generation to shape their own environment, not drawing directly from Jane Jacobs, necessarily, but from a tradition from Jacobs to Holly Whyte of getting people to stop and look" (Barwick 2008b).[12] One section of the room detailed the "human-scale" planning and grassroots organizing that helped Jacobs and her neighbors, in 1961, defeat proposals to wreck a fourteen-block portion of Greenwich Village via urban renewal.[13] Another section of the first room of the exhibit celebrated examples of Jacobs's contemporary ideological offspring, including Nos Quedamos, a grassroots planning group that successfully spearheaded community opposition to a redevelopment plan for Melrose Commons in the Bronx. "Today her example inspires new generations of activists," the exhibit's text declared, and *The Death and Life of Great American Cities* serves "as a bible for nascent grassroots movements to preserve and rehabilitate traditional urban neighborhoods" (Municipal Art Society of New York 2007a). "We wanted to show through example how citizens could change the outcome, that if you saw what happened at Melrose Commons, you would not shrink from trying," Barwick explained. "For MAS that was the goal—to give the visitor the sense that their impressions are as valid as any expert's" (Barwick, 2008b).

The exhibition's second room offered a different if complementary outlook on Jacobs's influence, focusing on the four principles of urban design—varied building ages, short blocks, density of population, and mixed land use—that made *The Death and Life of Great American Cities* an instant classic. "Jacobs's observations," the exhibit suggested, "and her willingness to act on them—remain critical to New York today as it is being reshaped by a private-development boom and, soon enough, by the goals outlined in the city's current plan for the future, PlaNYC 2030" (Municipal Art Society of New York 2007a).[14]

From Klemek's perspective, the exhibition also served as a response to the revisionist readings of Moses that had dominated discussions of the pair following the publication of *Robert Moses and the Modern City* and its companion exhibitions the previous spring. While Klemek readily agrees with Ballon and Jackson's notion that a more nuanced reading of Moses is necessary to counterbalance Caro's "sensationalized" treatment in *The Power Broker*, he contends that many of the efforts aimed at rehabilitating Moses too often come in relation to—if not at the expense of—Jacobs. In effect, Klemek argues, they serve to solidify the notion that if Moses was right on some issue or topic, Jacobs had to be wrong (Klemek 2008b).

Such reductionist dualisms, Klemek warns, threaten to overemphasize and inflate aspects of both figures' thinking beyond recognition, while downplaying others. In Jacobs's case, he contends, they have been used to paint her as, among other things, "the prophet of NIMBYISM" or an antigovernment elitist (Klemek 2008b; see, for example, Schwartz 2007).

Reinterpreting (or Misreading?) Recent Urban History

Are such connections necessarily revisionist and one-dimensional oversimplifications? Is any rehabilitation of Robert Moses intimately linked to a critical reappraisal of Jacobs? Does it require such a critical review? Such questions, and the range of answers they inspire, further underscore the complicated nature of the relationship between Jacobs and Moses. For example, at the Gotham Center forum, which was held six months after Jacobs died but before the Moses retrospective opened, *Robert Moses and the Modern City* coauthor Hilary Ballon argued that Moses believed in a decisive role for government in guiding urban development—an argument that can easily stand on its merits. She then, however, took aim at Jacobs, noting that in *The Death and Life of Great American Cities*, "government was seen as more likely to harm the community than advance it" (Ballon 2006). That notion of a pro-government Moses set in opposition to an anti-interventionist Jacobs, delivered by Ballon as the forum's lead-off speaker, served as a flash point and set the stage for one of the more engrossing subplots of the conversation that followed. Two speakers later, Brad Lander, then director of the Pratt Center for Community Development, the neighborhood advocacy and design organization,[15] picked up on the theme of planning and the government's role in the process. Lander suggested that early on, Jacobs's critique of state planning in the Moses style was understood as being "against planning all together" (Lander 2006). But by the late 1970s and 1980s, her ideals had evolved from broad prerequisites—like short blocks and mixed uses—for generating diversity into detailed sets of design precepts for fostering "successful" neighborhood development.

For example, in New York City's Battery Park City, the architects Alexander Cooper and Stanton Eckstut drew inspiration from Jacobs in devising a series of guidelines dictating the use of specific materials and architectural styles that could be found in the city's grand historic neighborhoods (Cooper 2009; Morrone 2008). On a broader scale, the concept of New Urbanism drew directly from Jacobs in linking diversity and fine-grain dynamism with design. Not only does one of its leading practitioners, the architect Andrés Duany, regularly invoke Jacobs, but the tenets laid out in its charter revolve around compact, pedestrian-friendly neighborhoods and safe, active streets seamlessly integrated into the surrounding city (Congress for the New Urbanism 2001). Jacobs the anti-planner, Lander noted at the forum, had emerged as the "patron saint" of urban design.

Yet at the same time, Jacobs's ideals also had begun to be used to "give intellectual, moral and aesthetic cover to right-wing efforts" (Rich, n.d.) "to drown the state in a bathtub" (Lander 2006) by attacking planning as a means of government regulation. To drive the point home, Lander cited conservative scholar Martin Anderson, whose *The Federal Bulldozer* critiques Jacobs and urban renewal, as well as the rhetoric and policies of conservative groups and figures from Ronald Reagan to the Institute for Justice, the Castle Coalition, and Americans for Limited Government.[16]

Lander, like the historian Christopher Klemek, rejects the suggestion that Jacobs was anti-interventionist, arguing instead that such a reading represents a selective and willful misuse of her ideals. Certainly, policy makers and proponents of government programs for reinvigorating cities in the wake of modernism's failed urban experiment found inspiration from her writing, as have a range of urbanists whose theories draw implicitly and explicitly from her work. These later thinkers were influenced not only by *Death and Life of Great American Cities*, which occupies a singular niche in terms of its lasting resonance among planners and designers, but by a later work, *The Economy of Cities*, in which many of Jacobs's earlier notions would reemerge, having evolved to form the intellectual basis for policies implemented in the United States and the United Kingdom during the Reagan-Thatcher years.

Writing in *The Economy of Cities*, Jacobs compared the English cities of Manchester, an advanced industrial city by the mid-nineteenth century, and Birmingham, which at that same time was home to a diverse range of small craft-oriented workshops. By the middle of the twentieth century, Jacobs noted, Manchester was in decline, its industries obsolete. Birmingham, meanwhile, had been more flexible, its small-scale entrepreneurs capable of adapting to the shifting economic tides (Jacobs 1969).[17]

To Jacobs, and the policy makers who shared her view, the lesson was clear, and from it were borne neoliberal programs, like urban enterprise zones—in which specific neighborhoods were targeted for economic revitalization through regulatory and tax relief—and subsidies for small craft and artisanal industries, the very enterprises Jacobs described as best suited for the inner city because of their adaptability and willingness to make do "operating in a basement, a disused warehouse, a garage, or even temporary buildings on a rubble-strewn lot" (Butler 1981, 82). These policy makers also picked up on Jacobs's notions of diversity, of eyes on the street and mixed land use, and her descriptions of the processes of unslumming and neighborhood regeneration to argue for an end to government-sponsored social welfare programs. In this scenario, informal networks of the kind Jacobs describes help to make communities self-reliant by providing services where government has failed.

Some two decades later, urban theorist Richard Florida would also draw from Jacobs in devising the notions of the "creative economy" and "creative class" (Florida 2002). To Florida, diversity serves as a key driver of innovation, therefore cities that not only foster diversity but cultivate it by providing the amenities that attract the best and brightest workers—the highly educated "creative workers" in the arts, design, fashion, and high technology—in a highly mobile, interconnected global marketplace are bound to be the most successful. Where those creative workers live, Florida reasons, economic growth and the accumulation of wealth will follow.

"Where Richard borrowed from Jane the most was diversity and inclusiveness, the idea that human capital is a flow and that people can and do move," says Kevin Stolarick, who worked closely with Florida in developing the creative class concept and served as the director of research for the Martin Prosperity Institute at the University of Toronto, where Florida was director. "The creative class knowledge worker will move around and will be willing to pick where to [move] by more than 'Do you have a job for me?' The idea of openness and diversity, the power of diversity to create innovation . . . Jane talked a lot about that" (Stolarick 2010).

To a certain extent, then, as Jackson and Ballon's revisionism focused renewed attention not only on Moses but on Jacobs as well, the emerging debate over Moses and Jacobs and their legacies increasingly hinged on conflicting and often competing interpretations of who those figures were and what they ultimately represented. In 2007 this in turn generated a further round of essays and events—including a March panel discussion at the Museum of the City of New York titled "Interpreting and Misinterpreting Jane Jacobs: New York and Beyond." There, Michael Sorkin, director of the Urban Design Program at the City College of New York, argued that Jacobs is often misread because of a tendency to focus on one aspect of her thinking rather than the interdependent ideals as captured by the Municipal Art Society exhibit—to "divorce Jane Jacobs the activist from Jane Jacobs the gifted observer of urban morphologies" (Sorkin, quoted in Haley 2007).

At the Gotham Center forum, the Pratt Center's Brad Lander went on to cite an unpublished essay, "Big Plans and Little People, or Who Has the Keys to the Federal Bulldozer?" in which Damon Rich, a planner for the city of Newark, New Jersey, and the founder of the Center for Urban Pedagogy, a Brooklyn-based organization that aims to develop innovative tools for teaching about cities, examines the role public narratives have played in forming and transforming public debates over urban renewal, with a particular emphasis on Jacobs and her efforts to defeat the proposed urban renewal of her neighborhood. This battle, as Rich points out, was not a showdown between Jacobs and Moses, and, by that time, Moses was no longer a member of the Committee on Slum Clearance. But decades later, it would be cast as just that in the award-winning 2001 television documentary series *New York: A Documentary Film*, produced by Ric Burns. The segment of the film that deals with the Jacobs-Moses rivalry—Episode 7: "The City and the World"—begins by documenting the early battle between the pair over Moses's intentions to ram an expressway through lower Manhattan (a project that came to be known as LOMEX). But it soon expands across the city and takes on an almost mythic tone, establishing Jacobs as a saint come to stand up against what Rich characterizes as the "inhuman, abstract, ugly icons of architectural modernism" for which Moses is easily made the poster boy (Rich, n.d., 15). In the end, of course, Moses is vanquished, done in by Jacobs's "endurance, wit and kooky grace" (Rich, n.d., 15).

To Rich, the Burns documentary can be seen as a widely viewed and influential example of the "mainstreaming of recent urban history," a flawed product of a legacy-building industry whose message hinges on a "misrepresentation" that "enables . . . the old-fashioned showdown between Jane Jacobs and Robert Moses" to continue (Rich, n.d., 14–15).[18] This narrative device can be traced to Caro's damning accounts in *The Power Broker* and Moses's name having over time become so synonymous with large-scale public housing projects promulgated under the urban renewal banner that history can easily be obscured. It is almost as if it does not really matter whether Moses had been involved in the urban renewal of the West Village or the bulldozing of a neighborhood for the construction of any particular public housing project. Those projects bear the unmistakable imprint of Moses's earlier actions and ideology, and, therefore, he might as well be held accountable.[19]

Quite ironically, Rich and others have noted that in addition to launching a populist revolution, Jacobs's ideals have been co-opted by mainstream forces within planning and development to promote large-scale redevelopment efforts she most certainly would have abhorred. By "mainstreaming" her terminology and popularizing her vocabulary, planners, developers, and real estate interests have reworked her invocation of words like *vibrant*, *human scale*, and *livable* to promote and market "large, top-down projects" (Shiffman 2007). Over time, her core conception of diversity has become planning's "moral watchword" (Kidder 2008, 260), and the principle of "mixed use" is no longer "a sharp-eyed writer's observation of what underlies a strong, organic urban fabric but a developer's mantra" (Goldberger, 2007b, 12). But also consider the view of sociologist David Halle, who writing in the commemorative issue of *City and Community*, argues that some critics have turned Jacobs "into a conservative opponent of modern architecture" (Halle 2006, 237), a devotee of the quaint and the small-scale, whose limited vision had paralyzed planning.

In effect, Jane Jacobs and Robert Moses have largely been reduced to characterizations, or more accurately, stand-ins for battles over big versus small, public versus private, the individual versus the state, competing notions of the "public good," and any number of good versus bad dualisms.

Mobilizing the Legacy Machine

Kent Barwick, of the Municipal Art Society, like historian Christopher Klemek, rejects such easy dichotomizing. "I thought the great trap was in them being seen as opposite poles," he says. "They probably agreed on a great many things. Both were certainly for a certain kind of development. Nevertheless, they became surrogates for points of view, monochromatic characters" (Barwick 2008b). To Barwick, Jacobs's true legacy is less tied to Moses and—while still centered on her principles of urban design and community organization—much more expansive than her legacy would suggest, spiraling outward as time passes and the city evolves to encompass the wide range of topics for programs that the Municipal Art Society sponsors, from Livable Neighborhood training workshops that "serve grassroots planners in their efforts to transform and revitalize their communities" (Municipal Art Society of New York, n.d. b) to an annual Jane Jacobs Forum (Municipal Art Society of New York, n.d. a).

And Moses?

As noted previously, with Jacobs's death—and the outpouring of remembrances and accolades, as well as calls for renewed attention to her ideals—came compelling reasons to revisit her old antagonist as well, and with the Moses exhibit and Ballon and Jackson's book serving as the spark, journalists, writers, and urban thinkers took up the call. A series of reviews appeared that, while not entirely embracing the idea of a rehabilitated Moses, celebrated the attempt to rethink the "power broker" from a new temporal and spatial perspective. For some, Moses's ability to command the creative destruction of entire city blocks seemed every bit as important as the resulting public housing complexes, highways, and cultural institutions. Urban design journalist John King notes, "If Moses wielded power with too heavy a hand, at least he got things done" (King 2007, E6), and *New York Times* architectural writer Nicolai Ouroussoff, in his comments at the Gotham Center forum, conjured up images of a New Orleans still devastated fourteen months after Hurricane Katrina's wrath to speak of "the tension" between the personas of Jacobs and Moses. As destructive as Moses was, Ouroussoff suggested, he still offers an "enticing sense of what can be done when government can mobilize itself" (Ouroussoff 2006b).

Such arguments prove particularly compelling in the current political-economic environment, one in which crumbling and inadequate infrastructures, economic restructuring, global climate change, and other issues are reshaping contemporary cities as well as the debates over what forms they should take. While King invokes the Moses legacy as a model for solving contemporary transportation problems in San Francisco, and Philip Kennicott (2007, NO1) argues in the *Washington Post* that its lessons about politics and power reverberated in contemporary battles over plans for extending Washington, D.C.'s Metro, Ballon, in her *New York Times* interview, waxes nostalgic for New York's return to a bygone era: "Living in New York, one is aware there has been no evident successor or successors to Moses. There are no master builders. Who is looking after the city? How do we build again for the future?" (Pogrebin 2007, 28).

Not surprisingly, these interpretations have been accompanied by calls for a new Moses to shepherd the contemporary city into the future (see, for example, Jackson 1989, 2007; see also King 2007, E6, and Kennicott 2007, NO1). Kenneth Jackson would be among the first who argued—making the claim as early as the 1988 Hofstra University conference celebrating the centennial of Moses's birth—that Moses essentially built the infrastructure for New York City's ascendance to a global financial and cultural capital and made possible its survival into the twenty-first century. "If another Robert Moses does not appear, however," he warned at the time, "New York is not likely to retain its exalted status in the face of fierce competition from Tokyo, Sao Paulo, Mexico City, and Los Angeles" (Jackson 1989).

And so the debate rages on, with Moses and Jacobs serving as foils representing opposing ends of the urban planning spectrum, as scholars, activists, journalists, and planners contest the nature of their legacies. As the recent array of reflective exercises—from the Gotham Center forum to the Moses and Jacobs retrospectives, dozens of retrospective and commemorative essays, a growing list of new books, and numerous round tables and panel discussions—so effectively underscores, that battle often is less about two historical figures and more about how they are perceived, interpreted, and perhaps misinterpreted at particular points in time. In some cases what Moses and Jacobs might have said, done, or believed is now almost secondary, mere background for forces that have adopted, even co-opted, their legacies to apply them to new purposes and broader ideological means. All the while, the pair frames—some might say haunts—any discussion over the future shape of the city. Referencing the Bloomberg administration's ambitious redevelopment agenda, with its reliance on the Moses-like mechanisms of massive public subsidies for essentially private projects and the specter of forced displacement through eminent domain, Brad Lander, at the Gotham Center forum, suggested that in spite of the prevailing picture of a triumphant Jacobs long ago vanquishing Caro's power broker, Moses-scale planning continues to threaten New York City neighborhoods. Regardless of the deification of Jacobs, he contended, "There are ways that we have not left Moses behind," and "contemporary urban development remains an elite set of bodies leading the public by the nose" (Lander 2006).

3

The Bloomberg Practice

From the moment Michael Bloomberg assumed the Mayor's Office in 2002, his administration sought to reshape New York City's built environment on a scale not seen since Robert Moses's build-big era. While some hailed the administration's ambitious plans as a rebirth of big ideas and a throwback to an age when leaders got things done (Ballon 2008; Goldberger 2007a), others questioned the redevelopment agenda's underlying long-term vision and economic rationale, and lamented the potential negative impacts of particular projects on neighboring communities as well as the autocratic means by which they were pursued (Lander 2006; Wells 2007). No sooner were the mayor's earliest proposals unveiled than they engendered comparisons with the worst aspects of Moses-like top-down planning (Angotti 2005, 2007; Sorkin 2007) and aroused opposition, from local neighborhood groups to members of the New York State Legislature. Four projects in particular exemplified the administration's aggressive agenda and underscored the contested nature of its plans.

NYC2012: Olympic Ambitions

For decades, Manhattan's Far West Side—a 360-acre swath of mixed light-industrial, residential, and transportation uses anchored by the Hudson Yards, which includes two below-grade Metropolitan Transportation Authority (MTA) railroad facilities spread over thirty-nine square blocks west of Ninth Avenue between Twenty-Eighth and Forty-First Streets—

has been viewed as an underutilized and underdeveloped remnant of New York City's industrial past, marking it, in the parlance of redevelopment advocates, the "last frontier" for development in an otherwise densely built borough (New York City Department of City Planning 2012c).[1] As early as the 1970s and then again in the late 1980s and early 1990s, the administrations of Mayor Ed Koch and his successor, David Dinkins, called for the redevelopment of the area from a "literal hole in the ground into a profitable development project" (Brash 2006, 64). In both cases, redevelopment efforts stalled, stymied in no small part by community opposition fueled by the lingering specter of the excesses of the Moses era. But in 1996, those efforts were reborn by the Giuliani administration, which pushed for the construction of a new stadium for the New York Yankees, the city's storied Major League Baseball franchise, and, simultaneously, explored the possibility of bidding to host the 2008 Summer Olympic Games. By the late 1990s a booming economy led by growth across the real estate, financial, media, and technology sectors generated talk of expanding the city's midtown business district westward.

Ultimately, New York City opted to bid for the Olympics in 2012, and the Yankee Stadium idea foundered, killed off by animosity between Giuliani and then-Govenor George Pataki, itself reinforced by Giuliani's own authoritarian tactics and stubbornness in the face of public opposition. But toward the end of Giuliani's tenure in 2001, New York City and NYC2012, the privately run, privately funded organization founded to oversee the city's Olympic effort, moved forward with separate but complementary plans to deck and redevelop Hudson Yards. First, in August 2001, NYC2012 published details of a hugely ambitious, $1.2 billion project that called for the existing Jacob Javits Convention Center to be expanded and joined with a domed 72,000-seat stadium that would serve as the main Olympic venue and, once the games were over, a new home for the National Football League's New York Jets. In addition, the proposal called for the construction of two large hotels, a new Madison Square Garden, and an eighty-story 1.2 million-square-foot media tower that would serve as "'a signature office building' anchoring commercial development on the rail yards," all complemented by an 8.5-acre plaza with green space, shopping arcades, and cafés (Brash 2006, 92).[2]

Developed under the leadership of Daniel Doctoroff, a former investment banker who, while at the private equity firm Oak Hill Partners in 1994, founded NYC2012; Alexander Garvin, an urban planner and former member of the New York City Planning Commission; and Jay Kriegel, a former senior vice president of CBS and one-time aide to Mayor John Lindsey, the proposal linked planning for the 2012 Olympic bid to midtown business district expansion, which in turn was to be fueled by the proposed extension of the No. 7 subway line west from Times Square to the to-be-expanded Jacob Javits Convention Center. Thus, the proposed redevelopment brought together real estate developers, planners, corporate executives, and politicians, uniting the city's pro-growth elites in an effort to overcome political opposition, which, to that point, had stymied attempts at transforming Hudson Yards. From the outset, Doctoroff would acknowledge, "the Olympic bid provided a patina of legitimacy to both individual development projects and the drive for a citywide campaign of urban development" (Brash 2006, 76).

Three months later, in November 2001, with the election of Bloomberg to the city's highest office, Doctoroff was tapped to become the new administration's deputy mayor for economic development and rebuilding, and the Department of City Planning detailed its proposal for rezoning the Far West Side in the report "Far West Midtown: A Framework for Development," which included a master plan for the city's vision of Hudson Yards redevelopment. Intent on seeing the proposal become reality, Bloomberg and Doctoroff sought to outflank potential opposition by sidestepping the New York State legislative process and courting business leaders and then pressing ahead with the rezoning, prompting the first of what over time would become a chorus of comparisons to Moses. "The opportunity to plan and design an entirely new district, encompassing a wide mix of uses, waterfront development, and the development of an open space network, awoke the Robert Moses or Baron Haussmann lying in the hearts of elite urban planners," writes urban anthropologist Julian Brash (2006, 113).

Still, New York State's partial ownership of the rail yards meant the administration would eventually need legislative support to move ahead. But even as it became obvious their strong-arm tactics had backfired, creating resentment among some lawmakers, Bloomberg officials continued to force the issue by delivering repeated threats, deadlines, and ultimatums. In the meantime, critics bashed the plan as an example of privatized planning, whereby a private organization was attempting to spur greater redevelopment in ways that ran counter to the local community's own desires and with very little public oversight or input, even though it would require significant public funding and the use of public land (Brash 2006).

All the while, and regardless of a concerted campaign by the city and NYC2012 to generate excitement around the bid, the residents of New York City remained largely indifferent to the idea of their town hosting the Olympics and building a mid-Manhattan stadium. As the administration's arbitrarily imposed deadline for action approached, a rival bid to redevelop Hudson Yards was submitted by Cablevision, a local cable television provider that viewed a new stadium as competition for Madison

Square Garden, the sports and event venue it owned. In early summer of 2005 Sheldon Silver, the speaker of the New York State Assembly, vetoed the stadium plan, and, weeks later, the 2012 Olympics was awarded to London. In the end, in spite of the administration's efforts to unite members of the city's elites, redevelopment of Hudson Yards was shelved.

Hudson Yards

However, plans for remaking the area would not die there. Even after the defeat of the Jets stadium proposal and the awarding of the Olympics to London, plans for the transformation of the Far West Side emerged yet again within another Bloomberg administration proposal to rezone and redevelop the site. Described by historic preservation consultant Laurie Beckelman as "the largest redevelopment scheme in New York since Rockefeller Center," the Hudson Yards proposal amounted to creating "a whole new neighborhood"—minus the stadium—with zoning providing the necessary conditions (Beckelman 2007). On November 23, 2004, the City Planning Commission approved a series of zoning changes to facilitate high-density office, residential, and commercial development on the eastern half of the twenty-six-acre site, and rezoning for the western portion was finalized on December 21, 2009 ("Mayor Bloomberg" 2009).

In October 2007 five companies submitted bids to develop Hudson Yards, and in March 2008 the MTA announced that real estate developer Tishman Speyer had been awarded the rights. But just six weeks later, Tishman Speyer backed out, citing an inability to reach a deal with the MTA to delay the start of the project until the western rezoning was finalized. The bid passed to the Related Companies (Bagli 2009a), which at various times could count three veterans of the earlier stadium battle among its senior leadership: Jay Kriegel, whom the *New York Times* referred to as Doctoroff's "right-hand man" in the unsuccessful Olympic effort and who in May 2007 was named a senior adviser to the company; Jay Cross, who as president of the New York Jets was a key public player in the failed effort to build the Jets stadium as part of the city's Olympic bid; and Vishaan Chakrabarti, who in 2002 was named by Amanda Burden, the director of the New York City Department of City Planning, to run the department's Manhattan office and in that capacity led the city's side of the stadium push. In July 2008 Chakrabarti joined Related Companies as its executive vice president of design and planning (Starita 2008).

Related Companies' vision for the site featured thirteen towers—including a hotel, office buildings, and as many as five thousand apartments—and a giant retail complex set on two massive platforms, each costing around $1 billion, all atop the rail cut. The total tab was $15 billion.

Initially, the project was to include a new corporate headquarters for Condé Nast, News Corp., and Morgan Stanley. But with the economy ailing, these featured corporate tenants pulled out, and in early 2009, with available financing in short supply, Related Companies sought and reached an agreement with the MTA to further delay closing on the project while the two sides worked out details of a ninety-nine-year $1 billion lease (Bagli 2009a). By late 2009 Related Companies had found a new corporate partner, Goldman Sachs, the powerful investment bank whose role in the sub-prime mortgage crisis led to its 2008 restructuring as a traditional bank holding company. But as Charles Bagli reported in the *New York Times*, in February 2010 Goldman Sachs "unexpectedly" backed out of the project, delaying it yet again (Bagli 2010).

Aside from the slowing economy, the project was plagued by the collapse or slow progress of the three big projects that had been expected to "kick-start" further West Side development (Sagalyn 2008): the $14 billion plan to move Madison Square Garden and replace it with a new rail terminus, to be called Moynihan Station; the No. 7 subway extension; and efforts to expand the Jacob Javits Convention Center. Eventually, the Bloomberg administration, through a specially created authority, issued $2.1 billion in debt to finance the extension of the No. 7 line (Pinsky 2008), projecting that the debt eventually would be paid from taxes generated by the new development. But with no development on the horizon, critics began warning that the city could be responsible for as much as $100 million a year in debt payments. A 2007 report from the New York City Bar Association said the Hudson Yards financing scheme "bears an eerie resemblance to the development of Battery Park City," which nearly defaulted and helped plunge the city into a fiscal crisis in the 1970s. Also, that report asked, if development of the West Side was inevitable, "why should costly artificial economic incentives be offered to encourage that development?" (New York City Bar Association, quoted in Buettner and Rivera 2009, A1).

Richard Ravitch, a former chair of the MTA who in July 2009 would be named lieutenant governor, offered his own withering critique at a January 2008 Museum of the City of New York panel discussion, "The Fate of the Far West Side." Arguing that "the full value of Hudson Yards won't be realized until the full development of Moynihan Station," Ravitch called the push to redevelop the site without concrete commitments for the subway extension or Moynihan Station "planning run amok" (Ravitch 2008). The project, he added, "raises serious questions about how we make decisions" regarding where growth will occur and how resources are allocated. Planning without a clear picture of who is going to pay," he concluded, "is an academic exercise."[3]

Atlantic Yards

Another of the more ambitious, and contentious, of the administration's early megaprojects was Atlantic Yards, a twenty-two-acre parcel of downtown Brooklyn that includes an eight-acre open rail cut—the Vanderbilt Rail Yards—also owned by the MTA. In 2002, the development firm Forest City Ratner announced its interest in redeveloping the site, which sits at the intersection of Atlantic and Flatbush Avenues where three of Brooklyn's neighborhoods—rapidly gentrifying Prospect Heights and Fort Greene and the already tony Park Slope—meet. It is also adjacent to two earlier Forest City projects: Metrotech, an eleven-building 5.7 million-square-foot commercial, academic, and office project on sixteen acres that was conceived during the Koch administration as part of a strategy to draw commercial and office development to the outer boroughs; and Atlantic Center, a twenty-four-acre $200 million retail and residential development built in the mid-1990s.

In 2003 Bloomberg and Forest City publicly announced plans for the company to develop Atlantic Yards in collaboration with Empire State Development Corporation (ESDC),[4] and in early 2005 the city and the developer signed a memorandum of understanding that paved the way for Forest City to buy the Vanderbilt Yards from the MTA for $100 million. Yet from the outset, the project was dogged by controversy and community opposition. Initial plans called for a Frank Gehry–designed village that included eight acres of public open space and sixteen mixed-use towers with more than one million square feet of residential, commercial (including 230,000 square feet of new retail and 600,000 square feet of offices), and hotel space, anchored by an 18,000-square-foot arena that would serve as the future home of the New Jersey Nets, the National Basketball Association franchise that Forest City CEO Bruce Ratner purchased in 2004 and planned to move to Brooklyn.[5] In addition to the arena—which was to be called the Barclays Center following the signing of a twenty-year deal that granted naming rights to Barclays Bank in exchange for $400 million—the architecturally ambitious project was to include four office towers and the soaring 620-foot mixed-use tower nicknamed Miss Brooklyn. As originally conceived, the complex of towers that defined the plan were touted by *New York Times* architecture critic Nicolai Ouroussoff as "striking," "resembling falling shards of glass," and Miss Brooklyn would have been the tallest building in Brooklyn, featuring thirteen hundred condominium and forty-five hundred rental units (Ouroussoff 2006a, C1).

Supporters hailed the project as a much-need injection of development capital capable of generating local jobs (Forest City claimed Atlantic Yards would provide fifteen thousand construction jobs and house six thousand office positions), tax revenue, and affordable housing. Proponents pointed to a community benefits agreement (BPA) negotiated between local community organizations and Forest City that promised 2,250 units—or 50 percent of the project's total number of residential rental units—would be designated affordable or middle income and that 30 percent of construction contracts would go to contractors run by minorities or women (Atlantic Yards, n.d.).

Opponents, meanwhile, argued the plan was ill-conceived and out of scale with the surrounding neighborhood and that it ultimately would require as much as $2 billion in government-backed funding, all for a privately owned project that would overwhelm existing roads, subway lines, and schools. As originally planned, Atlantic Yards would have produced the highest density census tract in the country. Opponents also challenged Forest City's proposed use of eminent domain to gain ownership of properties it could not acquire through more conventional means (Develop Don't Destroy Brooklyn 2009a). On December 8, 2006, the ESDC notified property owners and tenants in the Atlantic Yards footprint that the state would use its power of condemnation to clear the portion of the site not occupied by the rail cut, providing the impetus for the formation of a number of community coalitions to fight the proposal and setting off a series of protests and multiple court challenges (Moran 2006).

One lawsuit, *Goldstein v. Pataki*, filed in 2006, alleged that the transfer of private property to a private entity such as Forest City did not constitute public use and therefore did not meet the requirements for applying eminent domain as set forth in the United States Constitution or New York State law. After losing their original case and subsequent appeals (the plaintiffs appealed all the way to the United States Supreme Court, which declined to hear the case), property owners and tenants took a different tack, arguing in New York State Court (*Goldstein et al. v. Empire State Development Corporation*) that Atlantic Yards' use of eminent domain violated the state constitution because it proposed using public funds to underwrite an urban renewal project without restricting redevelopment to lower income occupants. While that claim was rejected, the State of New York Appeals Court agreed to hear the case. The subsequent appeal was dismissed on November 24, 2009 (Develop Don't Destroy Brooklyn 2010).

Still, community opposition, as well as rising costs, ultimately forced Forest City to repeatedly scale back aspects of the project. In 2007 local ire over the fact that Miss Brooklyn would tower over the nearby Williamsburg Savings Bank, a historic landmark and the tallest completed structure in Brooklyn, led the developer to reduce the building's height by more than 100 feet, rename it B1 (for Building One), and redesign it as strictly an office tower. That prompted another lawsuit on the grounds that since the scope of the project had changed, the existing environmental impact study was no longer valid. Then in March of 2008, with the credit crisis deepening and available lines of credit tightening, Forest City announced that initial construction would focus on building just two residential towers and the arena, leading community advocates to assert that the developer had reneged on promises regarding affordable housing and open spaces (Develop Don't Destroy Brooklyn 2009b). At the same time, the projected price tag for the arena ballooned, more than doubling to $1.1 billion, and in June 2009 Forest City announced that to save more than $200 million, Gehry's design was being dumped in favor a far more conventional one by Ellerbe Becket (Bagli 2009b). In response critics charged that elements essential to the original plan's approval had been abandoned in what amounted to a betrayal of the public trust, leading to the filing, on November 20, 2009, of yet another legal challenge (Bagli 2009c).

Even with Forest City's cost-cutting changes, state officials warned that overall development costs for Atlantic Yards could reach $4.9 billion—more than $1 billion beyond initially estimated—and in May 2009 the City of New York Independent Budget Office issued a revised cost benefit report. It suggested that far from providing benefits—in 2005 initial projections suggested the city might realize $500 million over thirty years—the project might actually cost the city $65 million over that span (City of New York Independent Budget Office 2009). The real estate consultant Karr Real Estate Group issued its own risk analysis, suggesting that a glut of high-end apartments in Brooklyn and the tough financing environment meant it would take twenty years to finish Atlantic Yards (Bagli 2009b). In the meantime, twenty-eight of fifty-three existing buildings scheduled for demolition to clear the way for the project had already been torn down.

In spite of delays and ongoing opposition, construction on the arena (the first phase of the project to be started) began on March 14, 2010, and that April the last residential holdout in the development footprint—Pacific Street building owner Daniel Goldstein—agreed to move out for a $3 million settlement.

Columbia University Expansion

Columbia University's proposed expansion is representative of the uncompromising nature of the planning process under the Bloomberg administration. Despite broad-based and sustained community opposition, the university sought and won the city's approval for plans to redevelop seventeen acres of gritty industrial land framed by 135th and 125th Streets and elevated stretches of the No. 1 subway line and Riverside Drive in the Harlem neighborhood of Manhattanville. The university contended that a lack of space for expansion at its existing campus less than one mile to the south put it at a competitive disadvantage. "With only a fraction of the space enjoyed by our leading peers across the country," a university website created to promote the proposed expansion asserted, "Columbia has had to face an especially critical need for space in a dense urban environment" (Columbia University, n.d.).

The $6.3 billion redevelopment—designed to make room for 6.8 million square feet of classrooms, research facilities, administrative offices, and university housing and parking—is scheduled to take place in two stages. The first, originally slated for completion by 2015, includes the construction of a medical research center and new homes for the Columbia Business School, School of International and Public Affairs, and School of the Arts. Phase 2, to be completed by 2030, would include additional classroom and research space, as well as housing for graduate students and faculty (Columbia University, n.d.).

Columbia's plan required the rezoning of the area—at the time home to a mix of self-storage warehouses, auto-repair shops, out-of-the-way restaurants, a bus depot, and 132 residential units—from manufacturing to mixed use, which the city council granted in December 2007. But as with all of the megaprojects proposed during the Bloomberg administration, Columbia's expansion plan engendered considerable controversy as it made its way through the New York City land use review process. In 2007 Columbia's proposal was rejected by the local community board, Manhattan CB9, which since 1991 had been preparing its own development plan for the area (Chan 2007). That alternative, crafted in partnership with the Pratt Center for Community Development, called for the expansion of light manufacturing uses and the provision of affordable housing and was submitted for review at the same time as Columbia's proposal. Despite the dramatic differences between the two plans, the City Planning Commission and the city council simultaneously approved both. Although the two plans were approved, the subsequent rezoning of the site rendered the Manhattan CB9 alternative obsolete, and Columbia's plan cleared an additional hurdle in May 2009 when the Public Authorities Control Board gave its stamp of approval (Bloomberg 2009).

Similar to Atlantic Yards, one of the major—and lasting—impediments to the Columbia plan was the proposed use of eminent domain to secure the necessary land for redevelopment. While Columbia was able to acquire sixty-one of the sixty-seven properties in the proposed expansion area through normal means, the owners of two gas stations and Nick Sprayregen, whose Tuck-It-Away storage business operated out of four buildings in the rezoned neighborhood, refused to sell. On July 17, 2008, the ESDC voted unanimously to declare the seventeen-acre site "blighted," paving the way for the powers of eminent domain to be invoked. However, in January 2009 the holdouts filed suit against the ESDC, arguing that the site was not blighted and therefore could not be subject to eminent domain. Among the criticisms articulated by opponents of the expansion were that a Columbia-funded consultant—the environmental planning and engineering firm, AKRF—conducted the study that deemed the area blighted and established the prices landowners were offered for their properties. Those critics also charged that AKRF came up with three values for each property—but that those were based on existing industrial zoning and not their worth once rezoned for mixed use—and offered the middle value to property owners (South 2007).

On December 3, 2009, the Appellate Division of the New York State Supreme Court ruled that the condemnation procedure was unconstitutional and that the state could not use eminent domain to acquire the remaining properties. On June 24, 2010, however, the New York Court of Appeals overturned that decision, ruling that the state's determination that the land was blighted held sway and that condemnation on behalf of a university constituted a public good. On December 13, 2010, the United States Supreme Court upheld that ruling, allowing the expansion to move ahead.

As in the case of other megaprojects initiated during the Bloomberg administration, Columbia's rationale for the use of eminent domain involved abstract notions of the greater good, best and highest use, and economic development. The university maintained that decades of construction required to build the new campus would generate twelve hundred construction jobs a year, and that once completed the expansion campus would represent six thousand university positions and solidify "Upper Manhattan as a world center for knowledge, creativity, and solutions for society's challenges" (Columbia University, n.d.). In addition, Columbia pointed to the creation of between fifty thousand and ninety-four thousand square feet of publicly accessible open space as well as retail amenities. Unappeased, the community formed the West Harlem Local Economic Development Corporation to press for additional concessions. While that group struggled to come to terms with Columbia on a community benefits agreement, it won the university's commitment to spend $150 million over twelve years on the establishment of a community-based K-8 public school administered by Columbia's Teachers College, as well as $20 million for affordable housing initiatives.

Expansion opponents and community residents, led by the neighborhood organization the Coalition to Preserve Community, also voiced concerns about the inevitable gentrification of surrounding areas, arguing that Columbia's plan would eliminate manufacturing jobs and result in rising rents as it cut into the stock of low-income housing in the area. To back those claims, the group pointed to 2007 rezoning documents in which the Department of City Planning acknowledged that 85 businesses with 880 employees and 219 residents would be displaced by the actual expansion, while rising rents would displace an additional 1,318 residents by 2030.

Overcoming the Past

Taken together, the early setbacks involving the Olympic bid and the effort to prompt further west-side development by building a new stadium at Hudson Yards proved in no uncertain terms that the Bloomberg administration would not be able to force its Moses-like redevelopment agenda on New York City. Fierce, ongoing opposition to continuing projects like Atlantic Yards and Columbia University's proposed expansion underscored the degree to which planning in general, and the prospect of megaprojects in particular, continues to conjure up images of Moses eager to bulldoze whole city blocks while Jacobs mobilizes the community in protest.

To be sure, the Bloomberg administration was running the city at a time when local concerns regarding its redevelopment plans were not easily ignored. Often bearing the banner of Jacobs's legacy, opposition to contemporary redevelopment projects had become more informed, engaged, and organized, if not always effective. Indeed, in cases in which projects initiated or backed by the administration were scaled down or slowed, the causes had more to do with difficulties related to private-sector development—mainly, the lack of access to credit and the overall economic slowdown brought about by the sub-prime mortgage crisis—than community opposition. Still, the administration came to realize early on that to accomplish its broader redevelopment goals, it would have to contend with planning's tarnished reputation and diminished stature as a government institution, the roots of which could be traced to the excesses of the Moses era and Jacobs's "spirited attack on the modernist concepts of master planning" in *The Death and Life of Great American Cities* (Muschamp 1998, E2).

4

Calls for a New Moses

While revisionist readings of Robert Moses were under way long before Jane Jacobs's death (Jackson 1989; Schwartz 1993), the resurgence of such thinking just months after her passing underscored the degree to which the two figures had become conjoined in the public imagination and further fanned the debates over their lasting legacies. But to Kent Barwick and others familiar with the politics behind the revisionist effort, "the whole Moses/Jacobs revisiting" was "provoked" by the Bloomberg administration, which came into office with a clear physical agenda and "conscious strategies" for how to implement it but was fully unprepared to contend with the unexpected obstacles (Barwick 2008a). "Moses would not have awakened six weeks before the Olympic selection committee was to make its decision to discover somebody named Sheldon Silver who could kill his project," Barwick contends. "Moses would have set up [approval of the proposed New York Jets stadium] 10 years ahead of time or written the legislation himself" (Barwick 2008a). Thus, far from complicating the administration's effort at promoting its ambitious redevelopment agenda, the memorializing of Jacobs and simultaneous rehabilitation of Moses would come to play a powerful role in informing and transforming public debate. Praising Jacobs and reenvisioning Moses fostered the sense that if New York City ever wanted to successfully build big again, it would have to confront and ultimately contend with the long-held negative connotations associated with the Moses legacy while at the same time making its build-big agenda amenable to Jacobs's notion of a livable city. In this way, the academic reengagement with Moses and Jacobs at the same time the administration was attempting to reinvigorate its redevelopment agenda following early defeats was no accident. Rather, it represented a strategic move by proponents of those plans to legitimize the administration's vision and actions.

Indeed, the revisionist readings of Moses and the flood of commemorations that accompanied Jacobs's death were soon followed by calls for a reconsideration of the two figures from Deputy Mayor Daniel Doctoroff and other powerful voices in New York City development and planning. They felt that this could be done in a way that would make the ideological case for a new era of building characterized by superprojects of a Moses-like nature but in sympathy with Jacobs's ideals of neighborhood diversity and dynamism. At "Learning from Moses," a panel discussion that kicked off the Moses exhibitions' three-month run, Doctoroff spoke of the lessons to be culled from Moses's mistakes—essentially the hazards of not listening to people—but, even more important, from his successes: his efficiency, "adeptness at harnessing public and private resources and negotiating bureaucratic tricks and traps" and ability to see "beyond the lived particularity of urban life and conceptualize the city as a whole" (Wells 2007). Not long after, Amanda Burden, the city's representative at the Gotham Center debate, would take the final step of fusing select aspects of the pairs' lasting legacies by arguing that under Mayor Bloomberg, New York City was building like Moses with Jacobs in mind.

In this regard, the administration, supported by academic reappraisals, had grown to conceive of the two figures less as antagonists and more as potential partners whose core notions, when updated to the present, could be complementary—Moses, the "git'r done man," capable of preparing the city to meet its future; Jacobs, whose small-scale devotion to mixed uses, diversity, and community represents the cure-all for local ills. Meld the two, this argument holds, and contemporary problems can be solved. In fact, this campaign for synthesis entered seamlessly into the administration's narrative of a new city ascendant, serving as a powerful justification for the desire to build big again. In a 2007 interview with the *New York Times*, Doctoroff echoed comments made by Hilary Ballon three months earlier at the Gotham Center forum. He suggested that New York City was now

> in a period of time when we have finally overcome a fear of overdevelopment that was in part the result of Moses' excesses. Part of the reason we haven't been able to do much is because people over-interpreted the lessons from that period of time. (Pogrebin 2007, 28)[1]

At this point, then, it becomes helpful to consider the role Moses's "excesses," to use Doctoroff's word, and Jacobs's crusading response played in the evolution of institutionalized planning in New York City, first by fostering the rejection of top-down, large-scale planning and projects and, then, in the rehabilitative twist to the Bloomberg administration's subsequent invocation of the tale, helping overcome the "fear of overdevelopment" that characterized and, at times, paralyzed the city's planning apparatus over the course of more than forty years.

The Collapse of Planning

Early in the twentieth century, New York City helped pioneer the notion of an active city government intent on shaping social and economic environments through physical planning. It adopted the nation's first zoning ordinance, in 1916, and the New York City Planning Commission held its first meeting in January 1938. That body soon reflected prevailing modernist wisdom—and Robert Moses's influence—by recommending in November 1938 that the steady demolition of slums was the only solution to intolerable urban conditions, and over the course of the next two decades, its role largely centered on overseeing local implementation of federal programs aimed at slum clearance and urban renewal. In 1960 the commission revamped the city's zoning resolution—its first real milestone of the modern era—and in 1969 produced its first comprehensive plan: a six-volume *Plan for New York City* that set an ambitious development agenda and in many ways prefigured issues that would continue to resonate for decades. But the plan had little long-term effect—virtually none of its proposals were ever seen through to completion—and twenty years later, as the Planning Commission turned fifty, in 1988, it was widely seen as a largely inconsequential body forced to share influence with local community boards, other government offices, and a politically charged Board of Estimate. Ordinary citizens, meanwhile, had come to associate planning with Moses and "the crude postwar urban-renewal projects" that Jacobs had "so cogently attacked" in *The Death and Life of Great American Cities* (Muschamp 1998, E2).

Worse still, with the completion of the World Trade Center towers and their ten million square feet of office space, and the deepening of the city's fiscal crisis in early 1970s, large-scale project development in New York City virtually ground to a halt. Suddenly, there was no market for office space—a glut of available units and declining demand sent rents tumbling. No new projects were under way in Lower Manhattan and successive schemes to launch the proposed development of Battery Park City—the ninety-two-acre mixed-use community slated to be built on the Hudson River using 1.2 million cubic feet of fill excavated from the World Trade Center site—foundered, including plans to finance the project's middle-income housing through the sale of housing revenue bonds. In 1974 Congress passed the Housing and Community Redevelopment Act and the Nixon administration ended federal payouts for funding low-income housing, putting an end to urban renewal as it was known. At the same time, New York City's luxury housing market collapsed, putting the brakes on private development. As a result, for the better part of two decades, the Planning Commission had "virtually no growth to orchestrate" (Dunlap 1988, B1), forcing it to concentrate instead on "workable" small-scale zoning and land-use issues rather than far-reaching master plans. "Planning itself," the *Times* intoned, "has been eclipsed by process—the Uniform Land Use Review Procedure, known as ULURP," the standardized multistep approval regimen adopted in 1975 during the administration of Mayor Abraham Beame as a means of limiting government power as "personified by Robert Moses," by increasing local participation in planning decisions (Dunlap 1988, B1). It would not be until the makeover of Times Square—a project with its roots in the Dinkins administration but realized during Mayor Giuliani's second term—that the city would be able once again to see a project of any meaningful scope through.

That is not to suggest that earlier administrations did not aspire to more aggressive large-scale planning as a means of reinvigorating the city. In 1982, under the direction of Mayor Ed Koch's first Planning Commission chair, Herbert Sturz, the city rezoned mid-Manhattan West to allow for increased building density, and in 1988 New York City's 578 miles of waterfront were the focus of potential, though still scattershot, redevelopment, with seven separate projects being "studied." At the time, virtually every zoning and land-use initiative was obliged to navigate ULURP, requiring a six-month review by local community boards—which were theoretically grounded on Jacobs's notion that local residents should have a voice in the planning process—and votes by the City Planning Commission (which was made up of seven members, all appointed by mayor) and the Board of Estimate. Viewed by many in the planning community and city government as overly burdensome, the resulting process was demonized as creating bureaucratic paralysis, and in 1989 a New York Charter Revision Commission was appointed to study its overhaul.

Initially, that commission proposed abolishing the Board of Estimate and giving expanded powers to a larger and conceivably less political City Planning Commission, suggesting that the city council "was not the appropriate body to decide questions such as precisely where to place city shelters and incinerators and whether to approve special zoning exemptions for individual private development projects" (Finder 1989, B3). It proposed replacing the existing seven-member planning board—all of whom were appointed by the mayor—with an eleven-member planning body, only four of whom served at the mayor's discretion. The planning community—including sitting and past Planning Commission chairs—objected, arguing that as the city's chief executive, the mayor, was ultimately responsible for providing direction for city planning and should have more say over who sat on that body. The charter commission then revised its proposal, boosting the Planning Commission's membership to twelve, with six appointed by the mayor, one by the president of the city council, and one by each borough president. The move was described as a means of balancing competing interests, but in effect, it would have given the mayor considerable leverage in battles over the Planning Commission's actions, as initiatives required seven votes to pass.

Following intense criticism from community, environmental, and housing groups, which wanted elected—not appointed—officials making planning decisions, the charter commission again shifted its stance, proposing that following Planning Commission review, initiatives involving zoning changes, urban renewal plans, and most city-owned residential property would go to the city council for a vote. In addition, certain Planning Commission decisions—including special zoning exemptions for private developers and the location of shelters and incinerators—could be appealed to the city council if the affected borough president and local community board objected. As a result, "almost every zoning and land-use proposal could, at least potentially, be reviewed by the Council" (Finder 1989, B3). The charter commission ultimately proposed a thirteen-member board, with seven members appointed by the mayor, one by the city council president, and one each by the five borough presidents. The proposal, which went before voters in a November 1989 referendum, would allow the mayor to veto land use matters approved by the city council, but the city council could override the veto with a two-thirds vote.

The lead up to the referendum featured vigorous debate, reflecting the extreme tensions over how best to balance the desire for community representation with the need for getting projects approved and built. While advocates of the charter commission's proposed changes argued the plan would produce a two-step process that would ensure elected officials a reasonable means for reviewing major or controversial land use proposals, opposition ranged from those who insisted that too many decisions would still be made by a panel of appointed officials—the majority of whom served at the whim of the mayor—to those who felt the mayor should have even more power so as to provide a broader citywide perspective to planning. The referendum ultimately passed, and in 1990 a larger, more politically diverse City Planning Commission retained its role as the main arbiter of zoning. Now, however, its decisions were subject to final review by the city council, not the Board of Estimate, which was disbanded, and the full ULURP process involved votes by the local community boards, the appropriate borough president, the borough planning board, the city council, the Department of City Planning, and the mayor.

Even with an overhauled planning commission and ULURP process in place, by the final years of the Giuliani administration, "planning had all but collapsed in New York City," amounting to a series of limited proposals—from moving Yankee Stadium from the Bronx to Manhattan's Upper West Side and building a casino on Governor's Island to rezoning waterfront manufacturing areas to make room for private residential development and giving Broadway theater owners expanded development rights (Muschamp 1998, E2). While large, these plans were reflective of Mayor Giuliani's preference for getting government out of the way and allowing the private market to determine what was to be built. The plans were roundly criticized as unimaginative in scope, "disconnected" ideas "floating in the void that city planning has become" (Muschamp 1998, E2). To some who wanted to see New York City begin to build again, Jacobs had almost single handedly, though perhaps inadvertently, crippled planning for almost four decades. While her critique may have been convincing when it was made in the early 1960s, these critics pointed out, the social, economic, and political underpinnings of urbanity had changed:

> That was 40 years ago. She probably did not foresee that planning would be substantially dismantled, or that its collapse would leave the public realm defenseless against market pressures. Nor could she have anticipated that the eyes on the street, the natural crime deterrent afforded by a vibrant street life, would need to be augmented by police surveillance cameras. . . . [T]he city's current mood of triumphalism has a hollow ring. . . . New York is back, but also backward. There's no overarching vision of the post-industrial metropolis the city could become. (Muschamp 1998, E2)

Shaping the City: A Strategic Blueprint for New York City

With Bloomberg installed as mayor in 2001, all of that would change. Despite the outgoing administration's pro-development bent but in keeping with its laissez-faire orientation, the Department of City Planning (DCP) under Giuliani had not been seen "as an economic development agency." Instead, it had been relegated to a relatively minor role within the same agency that oversaw "culture and schools," and its efforts were focused primarily on one borough: Manhattan (Burden 2008a). But in 2002—shortly after Bloomberg first took the oath of office—the DCP was placed under the direction of Daniel Doctoroff, the deputy mayor of economic development, marking an important shift in its role within

New York City government and a rebirth of comprehensive planning.[2] One of Doctoroff's first charges in the new administration was to produce a long-term strategic plan for the city. According to Doctoroff, what started as a simple land use plan borne of the city's challenges in finding space for basic government functions evolved rapidly into a future-oriented, long-term growth plan that established economic development as the fundamental goal, the driver of New York City's planning efforts. In the administration's view, "All the solutions" to all the city's physical problems were linked (Doctoroff 2009), and the resulting plan was developed as part of an emerging administration narrative that focused on the long-term sustainability of the city. Drawn up by a Sustainability Advisory Board, led by Doctoroff, it centered on six core principles, as outlined by Burden (2009, 2008a, 2007a):

1. That New York City do whatever is necessary to compete with Paris, London, Tokyo, Singapore, Shanghai, and other "global cities" in a rapidly evolving, hypercompetitive global economy.
2. That New York City grow in a sustainable, environmentally conscious manner—a concept that gave rise to a second plan within a plan: PlaNYC 2030, which was announced to much fanfare, symbolically, on Earth Day 2007. "What does sustainability mean?" Doctoroff would ask. "To us it means almost a sacred obligation to leave future generations a cleaner, healthier, more prosperous city than the one in which we inhabit today" (Doctoroff 2009).
3. That New York City is a city of neighborhoods—188 distinct neighborhoods whose unique characters are "to be protected," in keeping with the broadly accepted wisdom of Jane Jacobs.
4. That within its densely built environment, New York City should strive to create "signature sites" in order to "make great places." It would not engage in the piecemeal development of individual, isolated projects but build comprehensive, iconic places conceived of through master plans.
5. That the city "recapture" its vast waterfront—which historically has been given over to industrial uses—and "revitalize the street" through the development of public space—another very Jacobsian notion.[3]
6. That "design matters" and "architectural excellence is good economic development."

Ambitious in scope, the plan conjured up images of a bygone era, and Doctoroff, as the chief architect of the mayor's development agenda, emerged as the face of the new Moses (Wells 2007). According to Kent

Barwick, "The aggressive leadership of the Bloomberg administration and in particular Dan Doctoroff engendered comparisons between Doctoroff and Moses—in both admiration and disapproval—and that resulted in the inevitable invocation of Jane Jacobs" (Barwick 2008b).[4] Barwick went on to say that "while it may have secretly pleased [Doctoroff] to be compared to Moses, I don't think he had much time or interest in shaping academic discussion" (Barwick 2008b). Instead, like Moses, Doctoroff wanted projects built, and the rehabilitation of Moses was seen as an important if symbolic step in what the Bloomberg administration saw as "the emerging political battle over the next shape of the city" (Smith and Larson 2007).

While Doctoroff would pitch the administration's plans as visionary, in many ways their roots rested on strategies that had been pursued for years. The aim of securing New York's status as a leading world city through the postindustrial expansion of its business-friendly environment had become a recurring focus of successive mayoral administrations, beginning with the Koch administration, which in the late 1980s appointed a Commission on the Year 2000 to prepare "City Ascendant," its own long-range plan. In the early 1990s the Dinkins administration summed up this approach to planning policy by declaring that "the city's best prospects for expanding opportunity and combating poverty is to maintain its position as a global leader in finance and advanced business services, communications and the arts—the industries that drive the city's economy" (New York City Planning Commission 1993, 3).

Even earlier, the paralyzing effects of the fiscal crisis in the 1970s had created a "crucial turning point" in the formation of a local coalition of "real estate developers, conservative ideologues and corporate executives"—the very folks who controlled those sectors of the economy. Intent on restructuring New York "along lines more [to] their liking than those drawn by decades of liberalism and labor action" (Freeman 2000, 258)—and under the guise of ensuring the city's long-term competitiveness and economic growth—this development elite and globally integrated New York–based faction of what anthropologist Julian Brash called the "transnational capital class," sought to influence and rationalize urban development, transportation, infrastructure, and economic policy to "reshape the environments in which they find themselves" (Brash 2006, 39, 133). Essential to the success of this enterprise was the rationalization and normalization of their mission, and for that they relied on—much as Moses had for more than four decades—the rhetoric of the greater good:

> The ideological figure of the global executive legitimizes the increasing wealth and power of members of the [transnational capital class] by rooting their dominance in the natural order of things . . . even as it assures us we are in good hands: the use of

this enormous power will be governed by respect for cultural diversity and expertise and by a sense of social responsibility.

... [B]y acting to shape the city in accordance with this image, especially under the rubric of enhancing the ability of the city to compete for global investment, New York–based members of the TCC can claim to be pursuing the prosperity of the city as a whole, even as they enhance their own interests as the owners of the very global capital that is being wooed. (Brash 2006, 144, 145)

In a circular, self-perpetuating process that Brash contends results in the naturalization of the outcome, this attempt to remake the city was driven by the desire of coalition elites to consolidate power. The "relentless" recruitment of well-educated, highly paid professionals—the professional-managerial class (PMC)—to run global corporations in turn attracts additional "high-margin businesses in growth industries" and bestows on the PMC "a privileged role" in the formation of local economic and development policy (Brash 2006, 149–150). At the same time the efforts of the city's real estate-driven traditional growth coalition contributes to the expanding PMC population and its high profile, which in turn creates the continued impetus for urban development policies that are perceived to be in keeping with the group's preferences. This in turn deepens the postindustrial transformation of the city's economy and built environment, which enhances the position and visibility of the PMC even further (Brash 2006, 151). As Brash points out, these elites found a natural ally in Bloomberg—the corporate CEO billionaire turned politician whose private sector–inspired, technocratic approach to governance and economic development, in particular, was inherently linked to the city's shifting class structure. Within the administration, city government was seen as a corporation and the city as a product to be branded, at once "privileging the interests and experience of certain class factions at the expense of others" (Brash 2006, 7).

Abetted by this powerful ideological partner, New York City's development elite undertook place making on a scope and scale not seen since the Moses era. But by midsummer 2008, a little more than eighteen months before the end of his second—and at the time presumably last—term, these business leaders and corporate "titans" had begun searching for a replacement, arguing that the mayor's financial independence, lack of party affiliation, and corporate management style had ushered in a new era of prosperity and growth, and they wanted to see this continue. New York City's business leaders, Michael Barbaro wrote,

of course, have a vested interested in recruiting one of their own, like Mr. Bloomberg, to run for mayor. The Bloomberg administration is considered an ally to many corporations, especially developers. Rezoning projects under his watch have opened large swaths of the city to new construction. And Mr. Bloomberg, especially, travels in the same orbit as many of the city's elite; he goes to their functions and they to his; he gives to their causes and they reciprocate. (Barbaro 2008)

Fears of not being able to find such a successor—and of what a perceived return to partisan governance might bring—had some suggesting a movement to overturn laws limiting the mayor to two terms, arguing eight years was too short to implement Bloomberg's full redevelopment agenda. At the same time, citing a "keen awareness of time and the potential for future administrations to undo or derail many of his initiatives," the mayor and members of the administration "ramped up efforts to push some projects through and pass legislation to make it harder to undo his legacy," Barbaro wrote (Barbaro 2008). Developers, especially those of large projects that could span decades from conception to finish, and real estate moguls, whose wealth was contingent on the long-term prospects of property, were especially supportive of the notion. In early May 2008 the city council approved a bill that made permanent the Office of Long-Term Planning and Sustainability—the body created to devise and implement the administration's PlaNYC 2030 initiative—and mandated that it be updated every four years, ensuring sustainability would remain a future municipal priority, regardless of who became mayor (Doctoroff 2009). Eventually, with the support of this corporate elite, Bloomberg used the economic crisis of late 2008 to successfully make the case for overturning laws limiting the mayor to two terms, and in November 2009 he won reelection to a third term.

Breaking the Development Impasse

In sum, then, for nearly four decades and over the course of four different mayoral eras, conventional wisdom has held that a good business climate equals expansion of a postindustrial, office-based, and globally oriented New York City, in which city government best serves its citizens by fostering the necessary climate through tax breaks, zoning, and spending priorities, even as it scales back social programs at the expense of what little remains of an industrial economy and the working class (Brash 2006; Freeman 2000). Even during the budget-slashing days of the 1970s' fiscal crisis, for instance, successive administrations devised schemes for expanding the city's central business district by redeveloping the Far West Side of midtown Manhattan. Those efforts would reemerge in subsequent years, most boldly as a core component of the effort, borne by the Giuliani administration but pursued with single-mindedness by Bloomberg, to bring the 2012 Summer Olympic Games to New York.[5] Strategically, New York's pro-development elite saw the Olympics as "a forcing mechanism" or "new lease on life" for development projects that "would allow the imposition of an elite development agenda unable to win approval through normal democratic processes" (Brash 2006, 75). Even though these efforts foundered, the Bloomberg administration resuscitated the idea of redeveloping Hudson Yards and assimilated it into the administration's still-evolving land use plan, which was foreshadowed by two of the then-largest rezonings in the city's history—the waterfront in Greenpoint/Williamsburg in Brooklyn and Manhattan's Far West Side. Within the administration's narrative, those initial zoning changes, along with support for Atlantic Yards and other big development projects under way at the time, "were aimed at revitalizing underutilized land for economic development and expanding the city's property tax base." These were "accomplished, in part, by tying them to the city's timetable to apply for the 2012 Olympic Games" (Roberts 2006, 39).

In November 2006, Doctoroff told the *New York Times* that he viewed the Olympics "as a vehicle to drive the sort of longer-range planning in which local governments rarely have the resources, or the vision, to indulge" (quoted in Roberts 2006, 39). The ultimate aim of the bid, he admitted, was to create the conditions for the development of the West Side and portions of Queens, as well as the revitalization of New York City's transportation network, the need for which had been articulated several years before by a panel of business, political, and labor leaders known as the Group of 35, which was convened by Senator Chuck Schumer and Robert Rubin, former treasury secretary under Clinton. That group warned in 2001 that New York City's long-term economic growth would be limited by a severe lack of office space, and it advocated for breaking the development impasse through the use of condemnation and eminent domain, as well as the provision of tax breaks for developers, a call Schumer would repeat four years later:

> At the dawn of the last century, New York built a subway system and grand public works like Grand Central Station. In the late 1930s through the 1960s, we built a highway system, Lincoln Center and the World Trade Center. But there hasn't been a major public work built in the city for 50 years. Why? I believe a culture of inertia has set in. Criticism predominates over construction; critics are given more weight than those trying to build. (Schumer 2005)

The Group of 35 report—with its critical assessment of the political infighting and special-influence peddling that had dogged previous large-scale development efforts, including the creation of Battery Park City—would become a powerful influence on the Bloomberg administration's land use agenda (Burden 2007b). In some ways it also served as an important early salvo in the rehabilitation of Moses by making the case for a new era of big projects. Another key influence was the comprehensive master plan of 1969. To Bloomberg administration officials, that plan represented a "stirring" philosophy and set of ideas for transforming the city, and they drafted a number of its contributors—including Alexander Garvin, the architects Alexander Cooper (who with then-partner Stanton Eckstut produced the master plan for Battery Park City) and Jacquelin Robertson, and communications executive Jay Kriegel—to help orchestrate the NYC2012 Olympic bid and the Hudson Yards project. But the 1969 plan's failure to result in any progress of consequence—"Almost nothing in [the 1969 plan] that was proposed ever happened," Doctoroff said—offered a valuable lesson. As a result, the administration vowed not to make a "single proposal" that it "could not identify the funds for or actually implement" and to "begin implementation immediately after the project was announced" (Doctoroff 2009).

Almost immediately, however, this return to big planning conjured up images of the Moses era and inspired opposition, including some from a familiar and still formidable corner. As the city's proposal for rezoning the Greenpoint/Williamsburg waterfront went before the city council, Jane Jacobs weighed in by penning a letter addressed to Mayor Bloomberg, which was published in the local *Brooklyn Rail*. In it, Jacobs—who moved to Canada in 1968 and had been living in Toronto for nearly four decades—argued in support of the local community's alternative plan, maintaining it provided for affordable housing, schools, day care, and recreational facilities without violating the neighborhood's existing scale. It would encourage "the visual and economic" characteristics that attract artists and other live-work craftspeople and therefore initiate "spontaneous and self-organizing renewal" (Jacobs 2005).[6] After cataloging the various ways the community's alternative plan would not "destroy" the neighborhood's existing vital elements, the ever-acerbic Jacobs took aim at the administration's plan:

> The proposal put before you by city staff is an ambush containing all those destructive consequences, packaged very sneakily with visually tiresome, unimaginative and imitative luxury project towers. How weird, and how sad, that New York, which has demonstrated successes enlightening to so much of the world, seems unable to learn the lesson it needs for itself. I will make two predictions with utter confidence. 1) If you follow the community's plan you will harvest a success. 2) If you follow the proposal

before you today, you will maybe enrich a few heedless and ignorant developers, but at the cost of an ugly and intractable mistake. Even the presumed beneficiaries of this misuse of governmental powers, the developers and financiers of luxury towers, may not benefit; misused environments are not good long-term economic bets.

Come on, do the right thing. The community really does know best. (Jacobs 2005)

Barwick, who admits to a bad break with the administration over its plans for the rezoning and redevelopment of Greenpoint/Williamsburg, accuses the Bloomberg administration of consciously ignoring public input. Doctoroff, he contends, was able to hold over developers' heads access to city-owned land, threatening to shut them out if they did not concede to do the city's bidding (Barwick 2008b). Moreover, anticipating further political battles ahead, the city took a page directly from the Moses playbook and began a campaign to "de-legitimize opposition to particular development projects by ascribing it to knee-jerk emotional reaction rather than to rational analysis or thoughtful, political judgment" (Brash 2006, 56). Here the revisionist academic effort on behalf of Moses, with its suggestion that large-scale development—driven by a government that understood the city's long-term needs and possessed both the vision and means to work for a successful future—would dovetail nicely with the Bloomberg administration's ambitions. Indeed, the administration cultivated ties and relationships with like-minded figures in academia, in certain instances even recruiting urban scholars and intellectuals to help craft both redevelopment policies as well as the narratives underlying them.[7] An important part of that campaign would be to convince a wary populace to at least reconsider, if not embrace, the Moses legacy.

5

Planning and the Narrative of Threat

Planning, it has been suggested, is the creation of a master narrative about the future, "the construction of stories that describe the pattern of a desired world" (Mandelbaum 1991, 210) as a means of normalizing and rationalizing the logic behind proposed projects and redevelopment schemes (Dear 1989; Throgmorton 1992). From this position, planners become "authors who actively construct views of events" that others "read (construct and interpret)," though at times in "diverse and often conflicting ways" (Mandelbaum 1991, 211). As planning regularly confronts contested terrain in which a variety of counternarratives are forced to compete for legitimacy and support, a challenge for promoters of any particular plan is to convince the greater public, by producing superior narratives, that theirs is the preferred vision for the future. In a society whose structures are built on the asserted rigor of scientific reason, these generally emerge as empirical visions that rest on "the construction of a regime of facts," which lead inexorably to a single "Truth," as determined—we are assured—by dispassionate experts and authoritative processes (Mandelbaum 1991, 211). Indeed, planning as a practice can be "distilled to an exercise in the mechanics of persuasion" in which the goal is getting to yes or, in other words, arriving at a successful "professional encounter" (Dear 1989, 456). Nonplanners, or those not in a position to participate in the act of plan development or promotion, are told to "abandon control of their memories" to those who have assumed the role of "moral guardians" (Mandelbaum 1991, 212) and whose command of specialized knowledge entitles them to prescribe the right actions for the greater good and act in the name of an undefinable "public interest" (Dear 1989, 459).

Robert Moses, of course, was a particularly effective practitioner of such truth building, and if "good planning is persuasive storytelling about the future" (Throgmorton 1992, 17), he was an especially successful raconteur. He not only mobilized deception to clear "a path to power" (Kidder 2008, 257), but once enthroned as head of the various commissions he oversaw, he marshaled "experts" whose supposed scientific rigor not only embodied the modernist moment but helped sell its more utopian notions. In pushing his agenda, Moses leaned on specialists in the fields of real estate, finance, architecture, and engineering to create a masterful narrative, adorned with reams of inscrutable data in the form of "detailed plans, construction schedules, and financial calculations" that were then packaged in glossy marketing brochures (Ballon 2007, 99). Not surprisingly, the experts he chose—figures like General George Nold, former director of the Joint Construction Agency, part of the European Command—shared Moses's technical, engineering, and management-oriented approach to renewal (Ballon 2007, 108), and the narratives they helped create were designed to make Moses's projects—what Ballon calls "untested experiments in urbanism"—appear to be done deals, "irrefutable, routine projects" (Ballon 2007, 99). To a large degree the intended audience was not the public, which to Moses was largely irrelevant, but the city's political and business leaders, without whose buy-in his agenda would have gone nowhere (Ballon 2007, 100). The Moses method also featured liberal use of creative assumptions, delivered as facts, such as using projected property resale prices—which as Ballon notes were nothing more than "guesswork" (Ballon 2007, 100)—rather than market values to determine the write-down for assembled renewal sites.

In no small part because of Moses's mastery of planning narrative and the ultimate effectiveness of the Jacobsian moment in countering it, proponents of public works and other large construction projects in contemporary times face a gauntlet of regulatory red tape, budgetary pressure, and community input before being allowed to build. To overcome those hurdles and see projects proceed or long-range development schemes enacted, many developers, planners, politicians, and other growth coalition proponents have learned to engage in "Machiavellian" games of deception that rely heavily on Moses-like rhetorical constructions (Flyvberg 2005, 50). Armed with their own self-justifying narratives (what Flyvberg identifies as "a fantasy world of underestimated costs, overestimated revenues, overvalued local development effects, and underestimated environmental impacts"), they set out to establish the legitimacy and effectively sell the logic and value—even absolute necessity—of their projects (Flyvberg 2005, 50).

One particularly persistent tactic for attempting—though not always successfully—to overcome opposition in recent New York City planning history has been the assertion that the city's literal future depends on the successful implementation of specific projects or plans. At a July 2008 Museum of the City of New York panel discussion on Westway, a $2.1 billion Robert Moses scheme to submerge New York City's West Side Highway and build a park in its place, Albert Butzel, an attorney who fought for fourteen years to defeat the proposal, told of how the project was marketed as just such a city-changing public work. "It was said at the time that the city can't grow or be a great city without this project and the opposition was just marginalized," Butzel recalled (Butzel 2008). That argument is symptomatic of what Butzel defined as a tendency among New York City administrations and planning institutions past and present to promote projects as "absolutely essential" to the future, and warn that the city "would fall apart" if they were not built (Butzel 2008).[1]

Over time this narrative of threat has become a powerful theme—one that underscores a continuity in discourse that runs from Moses through even Jane Jacobs and Robert Caro to the Schumer Group of 35—of decisions to be made that have life-and-death ramifications for the city and its inhabitants. For Moses the threat came in the form of blight and backwardness, and as long as New Yorkers bought the notion that he had the city's—and their own—future best interests in mind, the "power broker" could plan and creatively destroy with impunity while all criticism was marginalized as the work of know-nothings and doubters. Ultimately, Jacobs was able to counter the Moses narrative with her assertion that it was Moses and other modernist planners meddling with the natural rhythms and designs of neighborhoods who were rendering cities unlivable. Soon Robert Caro, Marshall Berman, and additional critics followed suit, rewriting "the drama of Big Bob the Builder by casting him as the principal villain in their own production of 'The People versus the Planner'" (Fishman 2007, 123).

The fundamental premise of this narrative of threat—regardless of the era or the specific vision of urbanity from which it emanates—has always been that the city is under siege and its very ability to survive has been rendered uncertain by some combination of malevolent forces, bureaucratic incompetence, outdated ideas, economically induced inertia, and outright malaise that requires immediate, decisive action. Over time the direction from where these threats have appeared—as well as their intensity and the appropriate responses for dealing with them—has evolved. But the danger and subsequent demand for a response through planning always remains.

In 1996 this narrative of threat took on an especially explicit and geographically expansive form with the publication of *A Region at Risk: The Third Regional Plan for the New York–New Jersey–Connecticut*

Metropolitan Area, by Robert Yaro and Tony Hiss, for the Regional Plan Association (RPA), the not-for-profit planning organization whose mission, as described on the back cover of *A Region at Risk*, is "to improve the quality of life" and "economic competitiveness" of the region surrounding New York City (Yaro and Hiss 1996).[2] Using the economic recession of 1989–1992 and the long, slow process of recovery that followed as a backdrop, the framers of *A Region at Risk* drew heavily from both Jacobs and Moses in pushing for a new, postindustrial form of urbanism geared toward enhancing the region's competitiveness, given "new global trends [that have] fundamentally altered New York's national and global position" (Regional Plan Association 2012). Thus, *A Region at Risk* would serve as an important forerunner for the Bloomberg administration, influencing not only its approach for pushing forward with an ambitious redevelopment agenda but also its mobilization of Jacobs and Moses to that end.

A Region at Risk

With the lingering effects of the 1989–1992 recession prompting planners to reconsider certain of the assumptions that had guided previous attempts to shape urban environments, the authors of *A Region At Risk* surmised that "success is no longer guaranteed and that a new plan for the future of the region should not be about managing growth that is inevitable, but about finding new ways to stimulate growth that is uncertain" (Yaro and Hiss 1996, xix). To accomplish that, they concluded, would require nothing less than "a decade of region-shaping investments" (41) as a means of "building the region's economy in the new landscape of global competition" (xix).

Not surprisingly, the economic focus of this assessment resulted in a business-friendly plan that collectively represented a who's who of the region's corporate leaders and growth coalition members. A group of business leaders from eight key industry sectors was invited by the RPA to offer insights into how best to "address the dilemma of regional competitiveness in the global economy" (Yaro and Hiss 1996, 9). At the time the plan was created, the group's Executive Committee included Chair Gary C. Wendt, CEO of GE Capital; Vice Chair Aristides W. Georganas, CEO and chair of Chemical Bank, New Jersey; Bruce L. Warwick, executive vice president of the Galbreath Company, one of the nation's largest privately held real estate development firms; J. Christopher Daggett, managing director of the global merchant bank William E. Simon and Sons; and John L. Lahey, president of Quinnipiac University. Its full board of directors had fifty-four members representing a range of financial services, architectural entities, media outlets, real estate concerns, energy firms, and pharmaceutical companies, as well as the American Federation of State, County and Municipal Employees; the National Minority Supplier Development Council; the United Federation of Teachers; and representatives of six area academic institutions.

As the name suggests, the Third Regional Plan was not the RPA's first attempt at developing a long-range, comprehensive "blueprint" for the greater New York City metropolitan area (Regional Plan Association 2012). In 1929 the group, then called the Committee on the Regional Plan for New York and its Environs, proposed the "world's first long-range metropolitan plan" based on the premise that the New York metropolitan region's population would double—to twenty million inhabitants—by 1965 (Yaro and Hiss 1996, 1).[3] Its agenda, as the introduction to *A Region at Risk* points out, centered on the construction of highways, bridges, parkways, parks, and "proposals to create new kinds of urban and suburban communities"—and even though it spawned criticism from notable corners, it proved successful in providing the planning framework that allowed "master builders Robert Moses, Austin Tobin, and John D. Rockefeller, Jr.," to tap federal funds for their projects (Yaro and Hiss 1996, 2).[4]

In 1968 a second regional plan was completed, conceived in certain ways to deal with the consequences—suburban sprawl and urban decline, among them—fueled by the automobile-oriented aspects of the first.

The introduction to *A Region at Risk* also acknowledges the distinctive planning and political-economic environments in which each of the RPA's plans emerged. While those plans' broad frameworks—a regional focus on economic expansion and preserving green space during times of seismic demographic growth and cyclical economic crisis—drew inspiration from past planning paradigms and have remained fundamentally consistent, each grew out of geographically and historically specific contexts. This had important ramifications, not only in terms of the economic landscape but in political and planning dynamics as well.

As *A Region at Risk* details, the researchers and writers who crafted the Third Plan worked "in an era in which narrowly focused, one-issue-at-a-time strategic planning" predominated, and federal powers and funds were rapidly being transferred to states and regions as part of the greater shift toward neoliberal policies (Yaro and Hiss 1996, 2). "The current approach," the authors wrote, "presents the very real danger that the national government will abrogate responsibility for urban centers and the needs of the poor and elderly" (2). As a result, *A Region at Risk* represents what its authors believed to be "a radical departure" from the conventions of the day. By proposing a comprehensive, long-term approach to planning for the region's economy, equity, and environment—what they dubbed the "three *Es*"—the plan's drafters sought to reaffirm the region's "ability to chart its own course" in an age in which technological advances in communications and the rise of a global economy mean that "companies, and even whole industries that had been the mainstay of the regional economy, are no longer 'bolted down' here" (2–3) and in which—"in a post–Cold War, deregulated, Internet and inter-linked world"—those global businesses "can pack up shop any time and head for some place that has not already been fouled up" (9).

Yaro and Hiss warned that the threat from this looming storm was immediate and potentially catastrophic. Noting that the region lost 770,000 jobs and almost one-fourth "of its share of national output in key industry sectors, including business services, media and communications and advanced manufacturing" during the 1989–1992 recession, they suggested "that modest growth in the next few years could mark the beginning of a long, slow, and potentially irreversible and tragic decline" (Yaro and Hiss 1996, 5–7). Traffic congestion, environmental degradation, sprawl, inadequate infrastructure, and underinvestment in human capital all contributed to a growing inability to compete in the global economy, they maintained. Additional concerns included "fluid" economic conditions, "shifting employment prospects created by global competition, industry restructuring and immigration; growing disparities between poor central cities and inner suburbs and rich outer suburbs;" racial and social polarization; a decline in the number of low-skill employment opportunities; stagnant middle-class incomes; and gridlock, the "result of decentered, automobile-based growth" (11).

By emphasizing a wider geographic context, the RPA sought to tap into an emerging shift in planning orthodoxy regarding scale. In the last decade of the twentieth century, planners around the country maintained that given the linkages—economic, infrastructural, cultural—between older city centers and their surrounding suburbs, solutions to the ills of one or the other required integration and regional perspective (Fishman 2000). Without a resurgence of the type of metropolitan-wide "cooperation, competitiveness and investment" that Moses had championed decades earlier, the framers of *A Region at Risk* contended, the citizens of the greater New York City region faced a future of "declining growth and diminished prosperity" (Yaro and Hiss 1996, 6).

Yet by setting up a doomsday scenario, the authors also set the stage for potential salvation. A sustainable "alternative future is possible," they maintained, "because of new opportunities inherent in the transformed world economy" and the relative strengths of the New York City metropolitan region in seizing them (Yaro and Hiss 1996, 8). To "recapture the promise of the region," the authors wrote, it would be necessary to "reconnect" it to three basic and "interlocking" foundations—economy, equity, and environment—that together make up "the components of our quality of life" (6). The proposed solution would be to rebuild these three Es "through investments and policies that integrate and build on our advantages, rather than focusing on just one of the 'E's' to the detriment of the others" (6). At the time, the authors suggested, too much emphasis was being placed on economic development, leading to what amounted to "border warfare, as states within the region try to steal businesses from each other in what amounts to a zero-sum game" (6). Lost in that game, they asserted, was an effective approach to festering social ills, which were left to be addressed by a "bloated" system of welfare that failed to bring its recipients into the economic mainstream, or a meaningful, long-term plan to deal with increasingly worrisome environmental concerns (6).

Still, within the globalizing economy, New York City was, in their view, especially well positioned to leverage its existing strengths into building an infrastructure for the future: its cultural and arts institutions and universities and research centers "provide a foundation for continuing leadership in creativity-based industries, including advertising, broadcasting and publishing." Despite sprawl, the region remained "strongly centered, compactly developed," and at its economic heart was an expanding central business district that "takes in Downtown Brooklyn, Long Island City and the Jersey waterfront (Yaro and Hiss 1996, 8). "As markets have transformed in scope from a national to an international focus—tied together by global networks of information transmission, production, and distribution, and given new range by liberalized agreements on trade in goods and services," the authors wrote, "knowledge-based world cities have emerged as global capitals in design, management, and financial services for high value-added products" (27). The existing "concentration of globally oriented firms" in Manhattan—"the region's core"—served as a magnet for other international firms, they asserted, but global competitiveness requires highly skilled workers, and those workers "are attracted to a world city–region not solely by its economic opportunity, but also by its quality of life" (30).

To be sure, the city already had benefited greatly from this "structural transformation of the economy" and the resulting concentration of high-value industries at its heart. The study notes that between 1970 and 1989, the region's payroll employment jumped from 7.9 million to 9.5 million, with virtually all that growth coming after 1977 and 420,000 of the new jobs centered in New York City, reflecting the onset of "a period of rapid acceleration in international trade and the integration of global markets" (Yaro and Hiss 1996, 28). At the time of the plan's writing, the region accounted for some 50 percent of all securities traded, exceeding $3 trillion in 1994, and "more foreign companies were listed on the New York stock exchanges than in London or in Frankfurt, Paris and Tokyo, combined" (27). Twelve of the largest twenty international law firms and five of the six largest accounting firms of the day had their headquarters in New York City (27), and "advanced white collar skills"—executive, managerial, professional, and technical positions—accounted for three in every four net new jobs" created between 1980 and 1990 (30). In a cyclical process that fuels itself as well as the system it relies on, "technology elevates the level of skill required of the workforce and creates new demand for goods and services—by increasing productivity and therefore real incomes, and by generating new products of consumption" (30). In turn, the needs and whims of the sophisticated, highly compensated workforce that exhibits those skills can spin off ever greater demand for a range of "in-person" services—health care, personal care, entertainment—that cannot be outsourced or replaced through technology and therefore can provide additional jobs and income (33).

Yet because of that outsized reliance on Wall Street and downtown corporate functions for regional vigor, the city's economy and the quality of life it aspired to spawn remained especially susceptible to the volatility associated with the global economy, a susceptibility that in turn was passed on to the surrounding suburbs. Periodic recessions and global downturns routinely resulted in slashed incomes and fits of corporate downsizing and layoffs that rippled outwards from the region's epicenter. From 1989 to 1992, for instance, a "world-wide collapse of property and equity markets" meant the loss of 770,000, or 8 percent of the region's total, jobs; 42 percent of which were located in the city. A decline in old-economy manufacturing jobs, and what *A Region at Risk* refers to as a restructuring of "labor relations toward short-term employment contracts and performance-related pay," brought about by global drives to enhance cost competitiveness and shareholder value teamed with increased demand for "a highly skilled cadre of independent professionals who trade on knowledge, contacts, and virtual office technology" to help create an "hourglass economy," with middle-class incomes and opportunities squeezed by the same forces that beginning in the 1970s contributed to a widening divide between rich and poor (Yaro and Hiss 1996, 34). From 1979 to 1989, the wealthiest one-fifth of the region's households saw their incomes grow 40 percent while the poorest fifth saw theirs climb just 7 percent. The greatest impact on wages and employment, the study surmises, came from "technological change that displaces routine labor and increases the productivity and bargaining power of workers with higher cognitive and technical skills" (50). During the 1980s, the study continues, "over 1 million managers, professionals and technicians" were added to the region's payrolls, "while jobs that required primarily manuals skills . . . declined by 140,000" (51). As manufacturing jobs continued to fade, the study warned, "By continuing to lag behind national economic performance, the region is likely to forfeit 590,000 jobs it might otherwise have created by 2005" (32).

In an effort to better understand the region's relative strengths and weaknesses, the RPA and the economic consulting firm DRI/McGraw-Hill "engaged industry leaders" in financial, business, and media services; arts, culture, and tourism; biomedicine; transportation and distribution; advanced machinery and systems and fashion "in a collaborative process to determine industry priorities and to develop strategies to address competitive challenges" (Yaro and Hiss 1996, 35). Not surprisingly, this elite group of globally oriented, predominately white-collar industry leaders recommended plan prescriptions and strategies that prioritized their needs, from lowering regulatory barriers and upgrading workforce skills to retaining and attracting highly skilled professional talent, in part via the enhancement of the region's quality of life (36). "With the ability to attract and retain creative talent repeatedly cited as the major competitive issue for most of our leading industries, improvement in the region's quality of life is clearly a leading competitive priority," the authors noted (38). As for what constituted quality of life, the RPA turned to a Quinnipiac University Polling Institute survey of regional residents. That poll found that safe streets and strong communities and neighborhoods—notions at the core of Jane Jacobs's ongoing appeal—ranked highest, followed by strong financial institutions and good public schools (38). As a result, making the city safer and more appealing to "high-value industries" and their mostly white-collar potential workforces would become a central focus of the third regional plan, and its core strategies would be conceived to "underpin the region's quality of life and competitiveness" as a means of guiding "us to sustainable growth as we enter the 21st century" (13).

Quality of Life as Competitive Edge

Among the key proposals in this regard was what the RPA dubbed its "Greensward" initiative. Conceived as a third great round of "cityscaping and urban parks construction" (Yaro and Hiss 1996, 101) after the eras of Robert Moses and Frederick Law Olmsted, designer of New York City's Central and Prospect Parks, the Greensward effort served as equal parts urban environmentalism and economic development.[5] It featured three central components: the creation of eleven regional preserves; reinvestment in urban parks and public spaces, and the creation of a network of greenways, or linked open-space corridors; and within these, the potential to create "sensational new harborfront parks," including the Brooklyn Bridge Park (101). Within this initiative, limits would be set on future growth so as to "safeguard the region's green infrastructure of forests, watersheds, estuaries, and farms." Growth, instead of sprawling outward from New York City and the surrounding metropolitan region, would be focused inward, on existing employment and residential centers, augmented with improved mobility provided by complementary transit initiatives that would revitalize the region's transportation infrastructure in order to link those hubs.

Investments in workforce skills and training would fuel the region's economic dynamism and enable more of its residents to join the mainstream, while new forms of governance would energize and reorganize political and civil institutions. Well-designed "parks, playgrounds, and streetscapes" would help make urban areas "livable and attractive for residents and businesses" (Yaro and Hiss 1996, 14). "Abandoned and underutilized" waterfronts and leftover industrial sites and landfills—together accounting for fifty thousand acres of brownfield—would be redeveloped (15). "Transit friendly" initiatives, including proposals to develop an integrated regional rail network to smooth gaps and inefficiencies caused by seven separate systems operated by three distinct entities at the time, coupled with "civic design improvements in Manhattan's midtown and downtown districts" would reemphasize New York City's traditional business districts as the economic anchors of the region (16). Similarly, the central business district—essentially the downtown half of Manhattan from midtown south—would be strengthened by "coordinating transit initiatives to connect Lower Manhattan to regional rail with an effort to guarantee the district's role as a global financial center," extending public transportation across midtown (from the United Nations to the Hudson River and south past the Javits Center) and providing better public access to the Hudson River waterfront (120).

In keeping with the neoliberal orthodoxy of the times and its emphasis on increasingly shifting the responsibility for funding for federal programs to states and municipalities—what *A Region at Risk* refers to as "the newest federalism currently in vogue" (Yaro and Hiss 1996, 40)—the plan acknowledged a "universal disdain for big, distant government" leading the RPA to shy away from proposing the formation of a "general purpose metropolitan government" to oversee its proposed transformation.[6] Instead, it focused its government initiatives on ways to "rationalize the activities of existing authorities, 'right size' spending programs and encourage service sharing among municipal governments, and lend support to more effective state and regional land use planning programs" (17). The plan acknowledged that pursuing a new era of park expansion within such a resource-challenged environment made "innovative" strategies essential.[7] Among the options for funding and maintaining the urban parks it proposed were real estate transfer taxes and property tax surcharges linked to rises in property values and park improvement districts, as well as private funds—which the RPA credited with playing a vital role in the successful restoration efforts in Central Park, Brooklyn's Prospect Park, and Bryant Park in midtown Manhattan.

"As shown in Bryant Park, improvements paid for by [these] taxes can help pay for themselves by increasing property values and rents," the report reads, though it acknowledges that "these assessments are likely only to support parks in wealthier areas" (Yaro and Hiss 1996, 110). To fund parks in less wealthy areas, the plan suggested concessions and turning over swatches of public space to profit-seeking private enterprise. Waterfront parks and green spaces, for instance, should include "just enough water-related development, such as marinas and restaurants, to raise" the requisite operational funds (108). Similarly, in a section titled "Environment: Green Infrastructure under Siege," the plan argued that business should take the lead in addressing environmental issues, as part of a wider "shift from 'regulate the process' to 'set the standard for the outcome'" that was increasingly reflected in public policy. It suggested such business leadership could take the form of "collaborative pilot projects" and "incentive (but not subsidy) programs" (77).

"Nuance" and "Bold Strokes"

In spite of being shaped by such contemporary political economic trends, the Third Regional Plan is rife with influences from past planning paradigms, and Moses and Jacobs feature prominently, if not always explicitly, in its formulation. To Robert Yaro, the RPA's president and coauthor of *A Region at Risk*, "both traditions influenced us" (Yaro 2008). Jacobs's legacy, Yaro suggests, is "one of nuance," and by the time *A Region at Risk* was conceived, her "extraordinary" influence on urban design had been assimilated into the mainstream to become a fundamental element of the planning orthodoxy that shaped the RPA's plan. "She's St. Jane, and for good reason," Yaro says. "She's made a remarkable contribution" (Yaro 2008). In certain sections of *A Region at Risk*, the links to her are especially pronounced. At one point, the plan advises towns to adopt zoning ordinances to encourage high-density, mixed-use development in their centers; in another, in language evoking *The Death and Life of Great American Cities*, it argues for future development that would "fit the character of existing" neighborhoods (Yaro and Hiss 1996, 105). The plan also raises the specter of Jacobs when it proclaims that "involving neighborhood residents through community management strategies" can help secure park safety and contribute to maintenance in a time of shrinking municipal budgets. Much like Jacobs's celebrated notion of "eyes on the street," the RPA suggests that "maintaining an increased local presence in the park can also reduce vandalism and help make residents feel more secure when using parks" (110). It argues for incentivizing transit- and pedestrian-friendly development and advocates for the implementation of mixed-use planning and design principles (120).

Moses, on the other hand, represented "bold strokes, big moves, less nuance," and his shadow also loomed over the plan's ambitious scope and scale (Yaro 2008). According to Yaro, *A Region at Risk* built off of and, in a sense, served as a response to the elements of the region's built environment that Moses was responsible for. Within the plan, for instance, "there is a widespread recognition that there are few ways to expand the regional highway system, so we have to develop more efficient ways to make use of it" (Yaro 2008). Moses also cast a significant shadow over the plan's emphasis on regional integration, and the RPA undoubtedly had him in mind when it encouraged finding innovative ways of channeling federal money for local and regional projects.[8]

In a significant sense then, the Third Regional Plan, "splits the difference," incorporating elements of both Jacobs and Moses (Yaro 2008): at its heart, it is "a transit plan" that is regional in scope, making it consistent with Moses, with much in it about city planning and community design that is derived directly from Jacobs. The plan's "centers campaign," for instance, calls for "investing in the creation of 11 regional downtowns"—revitalizing "inner-city communities by reinforcing community-based organizations and linking them and the residents they serve with the regional economy" (Yaro and Hiss 1996, 117)—to absorb projected population growth and expand future economic opportunity. An important aspect of this campaign is what the RPA calls a revolution in design and the principals on which communities are planned. In postwar America, the RPA observes, "we built a new civilization around the interstate highways and the automobile and walked away from cities and older suburban neighborhoods" (Yaro and Hiss 1996, 118). In response, the plan promotes compact, mixed-use development in existing centers rather than new centers on the city edge, acknowledging a debt to New Urbanism, which also drew its inspiration from Jacobs. The plan calls on metropolitan governments to use all the resources at their disposal: "private initiative, community input, and the public tools of planning—zoning, incentives and master plans" (124).

Among the areas to be revitalized and transformed into new regional centers were Jamaica and Long Island City in Queens, and downtown Brooklyn, which, according to *A Region at Risk*, "has all the ingredients of a great downtown," defined by a distinctive melding of Jacobsian and Mosaic ideals:

> a ceremonial entrance, via the Brooklyn Bridge, to a civic park and an historic city hall; seven institutions of higher education; world-

class cultural institutions; an active pedestrian-oriented retail area; a state-of-the-art office and academic complex; headquarters of major government agencies and federal and state courts; a commuter rail system and excellent public transit access; a diverse population; and historic brownstone neighborhoods. (Yaro and Hiss 1996, 122)

Ultimately, however, the legacies of Moses and Jacobs converged in the Third Regional Plan as the promotion of an emergent form of urbanism in which planning *was* economic development. Virtually all of the RPA's proposals—from big projects, such as reinvigorated waterfront development, to small ones, like plans for planting street trees—were geared toward enhancing real estate values and attracting the sophisticated, highly compensated workers needed to keep New York City's information-based, globally oriented economy humming. The proposals were equally geared toward reworking the region's transportation networks or limiting sprawl and preserving its green spaces. Citing a 1992 Neighborhood Open Space Coalition publication, *The Value of Parks and Open Space*, by Tom Fox, the authors of *A Region at Risk* directly assert that "well-managed and attractive open space" is a vital element of redevelopment efforts as "numerous studies have clearly shown that adjacent parks, street trees and woodlots, and views of open space or water can significantly enhance rents, property value, and property taxes" (Yaro and Hiss 1996, 108).

Of course, this real estate orientation, together with an emphasis on enhancing New York City's competitive position while privatizing services and scaling back social services and social welfare was positioned as an effort to build a revitalized and resurgent New York City. But by striving to transform the city through quality-of-life initiatives aimed at making it more amenable to tourists, to a new class of workers, and to corporate and speculative real estate interests, *A Region at Risk* could also be read as a plan for its gentrification.

Gentrification as Urban Strategy

At the time Jacobs was crafting her conception of the successful city in *The Death and Life of Great American Cities*, gentrification had yet to appear as a recognizable process—even the term had yet to be coined. In the 1950s and 1960s, large-scale urban renewal as pursued by Moses and other city leaders was the widely accepted method for making central cities more amenable to the middle class. Jacobs, of course, was among the first and most influential voices to point out urban renewal's failures, and the fix-it-up ethos that she prescribed was welcomed as a small-scale, largely local, and thoroughly private initiative for addressing what previously had been a public concern: the dilapidated state of urban housing and the range of social ills that were associated with it. Even as the notion of buying existing, relatively low-cost housing and renovating it to increase its value became more commonplace, gentrification in its earliest and most basic form remained a sporadic, historically discreet phenomenon (Smith 1996). Only as the rapid—and federally subsidized—suburbanization of the United States after World War II set in motion large-scale shifts in urban land values that resulted in new rounds of slum creation did these physical manifestations of capital's tendency toward uneven development become ripe for large-scale reinvestment (Smith 1996).[9] Still, at the local level, gentrification remained the product of neighborhood housing markets, the seemingly quaint and somewhat "quixotic" rehabilitation and renovation of existing housing stock that occurred through the turning of tenements into historic brownstones, for instance (Smith 1996, 57).

Eventually, however, the process began to take shape as a central feature of the broader economic and social forces reshaping cities in the advanced capitalist world, prompting a critical shift in the scale and politics of gentrification.

With the loss of manufacturing jobs and the related growth in "producer services, professional employment, and the expansion of so-called 'FIRE' employment (Finance, Insurance, Real Estate)" that accompanied postwar economic restructuring came a "concomitant" restructuring of the processes shaping urban landscapes (Smith 1996, 38–39). In the United States and Europe, as well as in parts of the "developing" world, urbanization—through the establishment and promotion of private property rights and real estate markets intimately linked to the circuits of international capital connecting an emerging network of global cities (Harvey 1990a; Peck and Tickell 2002)—swiftly emerged as a critical vehicle for the absorption of surplus capital (Harvey 2008b). Local governments, eager to harness these forces and channel their productive capacities to their own advantage, increasingly turned to urban policies promoting the redevelopment of local areas deemed underutilized, underperforming, or otherwise blighted as a generalized strategy for reincorporating them into the local economy. These best practices of urban economic development soon were shared by an "emulative networking" of like-minded "policy peddlers and gurus" (Peck and Theodore 2010, 171).

Through the late 1970s and into the 1980s, neoliberal reforms aimed at deregulating markets, slashing public spending, and dismantling existing welfare states propelled these policies forward, transforming cities into "geographical targets and institutional laboratories" for a range of "policy experiments"—from place marketing and local tax abatements to urban development corporations and public-private partnerships. The ultimate aim, according to critics, was often the mobilization of "city space as an arena both for market-oriented economic growth and for elite consumption practices" (Brenner and Theodore 2002, 368). Within this increasingly global strategy, real estate development became a centerpiece of the urban economy, justified by appeals to jobs, taxes, and tourism and abetted by the privatization of planning, apiece with the subsequent "commodification" of planning functions and their "absorption" by the private sector (Dear 1989, 449). This "corporatist approach" to planning was granted even greater heft by local governments' need for private funds to help finance public projects, creating "a climate in which the necessity and wisdom of so-called 'public-private partnerships' go unchallenged" and the "rules of the development game are ceded in advance" (Dear 1989, 451–452). From this confluence of forces, a new form of urbanism, molded by economic development corporations, business improvement districts, and other forms of private encroachment on the public realm, took shape. The RPA's *A Region at Risk*, with its emphasis on public-private initiatives, represents one such plan.

Meanwhile, neoclassical economic explanations attributing gentrification to "gentrifiers' preferences" increasingly were critiqued as "excessively narrow" (Smith 1996, 39). Broader theories situated gentrification as an evolving process that unfolded in three discrete phases (Hackworth 2000, Smith 2002). The first phase, or wave, initially appeared in the 1950s and was marked by the small-scale, block-by-block form of neighborhood rehabilitation celebrated by Jacobs. It was followed in the 1970s and 1980s by a second, "anchoring" wave in which gentrification became more entwined with the broader real estate and redevelopment processes then remaking cities (Hackworth 2000). In the final wave, beginning in the 1990s, gentrification emerged as a calculated component of the intentional and methodical production of urban environments amenable to global corporations and their highly compensated workers. Whereas in the initial phase the principal actors were assumed to be middle- and upper-class individuals willing to pioneer the regeneration of rundown neighborhoods, the agents of the second and third waves were private developers and real estate interests and then systematic public-private partnerships between state planning agencies and corporate coalitions. As a result, over time the process of gentrification became less about the local "conversion of socially marginal and working class areas of the central city to middle-class residential use" (Zukin 1987, 129) and more a generalized recipe—in the 1990s fully state-supported and embedded within the larger logics of advanced capitalist urbanization—for remaking entire urban landscapes (Smith 2002).

In this third wave, in an evolved form of urban renewal practices from earlier decades, many local governments turned to the powers of eminent domain to carve out space for the construction of private housing, corporate office space, and cultural facilities as a means of repositioning themselves as global capitals and leaders in growth industries such as management, information, culture, and ideas. Abandoned and underutilized industrial spaces—from working waterfronts to entire manufacturing districts—were rezoned for "adaptive" reuses or slated for demolition and redevelopment. Privatized public spaces, including city squares, plazas, and waterfront promenades, became key components of this wholesale reconstruction of civic identity, intentionally possessing cultural and ideological attributes intended to signify affluence and attract investment and tourism. Cultural institutions—following the model of architect Frank Gehry's Guggenheim Museum in Bilbao, Spain—"become flagships for the redevelopment of whole quarters" (Miles 2000, 256), and enclaved neighborhoods, like Battery Park City, assumed positions as sites of affluence, symbolic "parts of a global city of electronic dealing in financial services and futures" within the greater city (257).

Design also took on new ideological force, serving to reify class relations and helping "secure the hegemony of certain groups" through the aesthetic preferences of local decision makers (Duncan and Duncan 2001, 393). This design imperative found expression in a number of material ways, often working in conjunction with local developers, real estate interests, architects, and local governments to produce iconic symbols of a city's cultural and economic capital. Spectacular architecture—striking and unconventional new buildings designed by famous and innovative architects, dubbed "starchitects"—became landmarks, prominent refuges for global elites, and physical manifestations of a city's global prestige. More than mere buildings, these attention-grabbing works of art were made conspicuous by design, "paradises for aesthetes" that served to draw tourists and boost nearby real estate values as a means of priming further development while simultaneously embodying the social, economic, and cultural shifts that fostered growing class divisions. Urbanism, as radical urban critic and activist Guy Debord had so presciently divined some forty years before, had become the production of spectacle, of capitalism remaking "the totality of space into its own setting" (Debord 1983, 169). Supported by what critics called "a concerted and systemic partnership of public planning with public and private capital" (Smith 2002, 441), this "third wave" of gentrification, as promoted by plans such as the Regional Plan Association's *A Region at Risk*, represented nothing less than the "retaking" of cities by the upper and middle classes (Harvey 2008a; Smith 1996, 2002; Smith and DeFilippis 1999).

The suggestion that at its heart *A Region at Risk* is such a proposal is one the RPA's Yaro both acknowledges and defends. "[Gentrification] is a real quandary. You preserve character and preserve the quality of life and people with money buy in, and people without are pushed out. How do you deal with that? Subsidies? Direct intervention? New York has had a housing crisis since the 1940s. [Gentrification] is one of the constants, one of the results of the success of the city" (Yaro 2008).

Continuities in Planning

Just as the Third Regional Plan drew from Moses and Jacobs—among others—it would come to serve as an influential model of gentrification through public policy for the Bloomberg administration, offering ideas that would reverberate through issues ranging from waterfront development and extending the No. 7 subway line west from Times Square to catalyze development on Manhattan's Far West Side to a new great era of park building. Indeed, much of the administration's redevelopment agenda reads as if it were plucked straight from the pages of the Third Regional Plan. While *A Region at Risk* suggested that "the reclamation of the region's urban waterfronts offers opportunities to create extraordinary new public spaces" (Yaro and Hiss 1996, 108), Bloomberg's director of city planning Amanda Burden would talk of "iconic public spaces" and "reclaiming the city's waterfront." In others ways, the Third Regional Plan presaged many of Bloomberg's signature initiatives, including the overt call for the provision of affordable housing options through "density bonuses" (Yaro and Hiss 1996, 105) and the focus on outer-borough development, including the RPA's call for regional central business districts. Under Bloomberg, redevelopment in Long Island City would be reconceived as a "revitalized Queens West waterfront" (123), and in Jamaica, the Queens neighborhood, the administration would produce one of its earliest "superior narratives" in pushing for a transit-oriented, mixed-use transformation of the neighborhood. In time, Bloomberg would also embrace the use of parks and open spaces to enhance real estate values, drive development, and raise issues of environmental sustainability and projected population growth to assert the need for immediate and decisive action. Like the RPA, the administration would steadfastly promote the privatization of public space as a way of covering the costs of redevelopment, focusing on supporting institutions—such as Columbia University in its fight to claim room for expansion—that contribute to the city's image as a global capital and embracing a class-based, value-laden definition of quality of life.

According to the RPA's Yaro, this nexus of ideas—from Moses and Jacobs through the Third Regional Plan to Bloomberg—was "no accident" (Yaro 2008). Having served on the sustainability advisory board that led to Bloomberg's PlaNYC 2030 and before that on Schumer's Group of 35, Yaro has been an influential member of the planning elite that has written New York City's redevelopment narrative for nearly three decades. "In the regional planning business," he notes, "things take time" (Yaro 2008).

While the resulting vision for transforming New York City's built environment harkens back to a time when, as the Municipal Art Society's Kent Barwick suggests, "we took for granted that our leaders had physical agendas" (Barwick 2008a), it stands in marked contrast to city leadership from the end of the Moses era, through the 1970s fiscal crisis, and up to September 11, 2001. As with many things, 9/11 changed the existing development landscape in New York City, ushering in a period of what Barwick calls "enormous optimism," when "we were in the mood for rebuilding in the wake of 9/11," and prompting calls for a development czar as well as spawning much discussion about what kind of city to rebuild. Into this build-friendly environment stepped the recently elected Bloomberg, with Dan Doctoroff as his "development guru" (Barwick 2008a).[10]

At the time, Barwick recalls, the Municipal Art Society was holding a series of workshops at which city residents were given the opportunity to express their views and "aspirations for Ground Zero" (Barwick 2008b). "There was recognition that you had to rebuild, but people wanted something to happen that addressed the problem—what led to the attack—a UN or a great university, something terrific. But you can't build cities for symbolic purposes. There has to be some economic underpinning. So when in trouble, reach for Bob Moses." With Doctoroff—who by then had engendered numerous comparisons to the power broker (see, for example, Flyvberg 2005), much as Moses had written about and been compared to Baron von Haussmann—serving as "the new Bob Moses" (Barwick 2008b), Bloomberg, using the specter of the attack on the World Trade Center and the city's precarious future as a "bully pulpit" (Pinsky 2008), would set his redevelopment agenda in motion.

6

The Armature for Development

For a Bloomberg administration bent on a neoliberal building spree and needing citizen buy-in to see it through, one of the essential challenges had been how to make the case for building on a scale not seen since the Moses era in a city still enamored of Jacobs. To be sure, by asserting, as New York City Planning Director Amanda Burden had, that the battle between Moses and Jacobs was over and Jacobs had won (Burden 2006a), the Bloomberg administration acknowledged a very important truth, one that no city agency or public entity claiming to represent the greater good could afford to ignore: in the wider court of public perception, Jacobs *is* triumphant and widely viewed as the champion of the livable city. She was a celebrity endorser, a veritable stamp of legitimacy for any author writing on urban design,[1] and even more than fifty years after the publication of her most influential work, *The Death and Life of Great American Cities*, her legacy continues to resonate with city dwellers and within planning theory.

In 2007 the Rockefeller Foundation established the annual Jane Jacobs Medal to reaffirm "the Foundation's Commitment to New York" and to recognize "those whose creative uses of the urban environment build a more diverse, dynamic and equitable city" (Rockefeller Foundation, n.d.). And in the fall of 2009, publication of *Wrestling with Moses* (by Anthony Flint, journalist and fellow of the Lincoln Institute of Land Policy) allowed Jacobs—for the moment at least—to reclaim her place atop the podium in her ever-evolving match of legacies with Moses. Earlier that summer, Jacobs was introduced to a new generation as the quintessentially rational and unproblematically nonideological heroine of a young-adult book, *Genius of Common Sense: Jane Jacobs and the Story of "The Death and Life of Great American Cities."*[2]

Meanwhile, prior to the revisionist efforts of Hilary Ballon and Kenneth Jackson, Moses had become frozen in ignominy, the perpetual evil villain of urban renewal and big plans whose underlying ideals and heavy-handed approach to process seemed to secure his fate as Jacobs's eternal dupe. Yet in virtually the same breath she used to assert Jacobs's victory, Amanda Burden embraced Moses's ability to build big by suggesting that under Mayor Bloomberg, New York City was building like Moses but with Jacobs's principles in mind.

In his discussion of storytelling strategies within planning, Seymour Mandelbaum argues that one of the more powerful means for resolving conflicting narratives is to synthesize their competing notions in a manner that "makes sense of the parochial difference in accounts and perspectives" (Mandelbaum 1991, 212). Much in the manner that the RPA drew from both Jacobs and Moses in drafting its Third Regional Plan, the Bloomberg administration incorporated select aspects of the pair's foundational precepts into its redevelopment agenda, as if through a reworking of those legacies to the purposes of the present, the individuals planning New York City's future could bury the Moses-Jacobs hatchet once and for all and provide a clear blueprint for—to incorporate a Jacobsian phrase—a truly successful city. Indeed, this effort at synthesis became a critical piece of the administration's planning rhetoric, an essential component in its strategy for legitimizing its redevelopment agenda. In speeches and frequent appearances at forums and urban policy discussions, former Deputy Mayor Dan Doctoroff, Burden, and other New York City officials took their case to the public, repeatedly offering a more tempered view of Moses, even as they described a rebirth of planning under the Bloomberg administration and argued for a very specific version of what the city should look like in the years to come.

"A Different Kind of Thinking"

At the July 2008 Museum of the City of New York panel discussion on Westway (see Chapter 5), for example, Adrian Benepe, the commissioner of the New York City Department of Parks and Recreation, spoke of the assorted "what ifs" and "give-and-take of whether something is a good idea" when it comes to planning. He suggested that while Westway and its associated park were defeated, a "successor park"—a series of connected Hudson River parks that were working their way up the western waterfront of Manhattan in increments—was "the right park for 2008," and represented "the will to continue to build waterfront parks"

(Benepe 2008b). Pointing to Springfield, Massachusetts, and Hartford, Connecticut, Benepe argued that in hindsight, "We now know . . . what it's like in cities with elevated highways running through downtown. It kills the downtown." But he also suggested that there was a time when the "Olmsted landscape"—a clear reference to New York City's Central and Prospect Parks—was not held in high regard and that Orchard Beach in the Bronx's Pelham Park—a wetlands when Moses proposed turning it into a public beach—"would never get built today" (Benepe 2008b).

Celebrating the Bloomberg administration's positive bent on Moses, he suggested that the eleven municipal swimming pools created by the Master Builder, through slum clearance, in the single summer of 1936, were representative of the "great challenges of can you build in the face of opposition? If you get bogged down in factionalism and infighting, you will never build the great parks and great public works—the city-changing public works—of the twenty-first century" (Benepe 2008b).

As Burden's (2007a) standard presentation of the administration's redevelopment agenda, "Shaping the City: A Strategic Blueprint for New York's Future," makes clear, the administration intended to avoid that fate by planning and building—much as Moses presumably would have—while preserving the fine-grain, block-by-block diversity that Jacobs argued gives the city its dynamism (see also Burden 2008a, 2009). Similarly, just as much of Moses's ability to build big was based on the effectiveness of his rhetoric regarding the threats to New York City's continued prosperity—and just as Jacobs crafted her response to the destructive effects of modernist urbanism as a literal life and death question and the RPA framed its Third Regional Plan as a response to the risks the greater metropolitan area faced at the end of the twentieth century—the Bloomberg administration generated its own narrative of imminent danger as the justification for a new era of aggressive planning. At the heart of this narrative, indeed the point on which it would pivot, was the sense that contemporary New York City faced a pair of new and distinctly twenty-first-century challenges to its future prosperity. The first, as articulated by Bloomberg in his 2008 state-of-the-city speech and routinely reiterated by administration officials, was that a densely built and bureaucratically hamstrung New York City was under siege in a high-stakes battle for prominence in the global economy:

> We are in a competitive struggle. And the stakes couldn't be higher. Over the past year, I've seen cities from London to Paris to Shanghai, pushing the frontiers of progress. They are doing everything they can to attract the best and the brightest in every field: medicine; engineering; construction and more. These cities are not putting up barriers; they're not looking inward or blaming

someone else. They're not afraid of the new or the different, and we shouldn't be either. If we are, we won't have a future. (Bloomberg 2008)

The second major threat stemmed from questions about the city's sustainability, given projections that its population would swell by one million inhabitants by 2030, even as its quality of life was assailed by "an increasingly unpredictable [natural] environment" and aging infrastructure (Bloomberg 2008).

The resulting redevelopment agenda, or "blueprint," as articulated by the planning department's Burden, represented a mix of the "git'r done" modernism and best-for-the-common-good justifications of Moses, along with the urban design emphasis and more capital-friendly elements of Jacobs's enduring appeal (Burden 2009, 2008a, 2007a). While the agenda stressed New York City's competitive relationship to other cities in a global economy, it nonetheless rested on the Jacobsian notion that healthy neighborhoods make for healthy cities, and just as Jacobs had a distinct, class-based notion of what healthy should entail, the Bloomberg administration prescribed its own formula for "protecting" the "unique character" of largely middle- and upper-class single-family residential neighborhoods while rezoning "underutilized," industrial, and working-class areas, like Willets Point and Manhattanville, to allow for more productive uses (Burden 2007a). Just as Jacobs saw a revitalized Lower Eastside waterfront catalyzing the economic development of nearby Manhattan neighborhoods by drawing residents, corporations, and tourists (Jacobs 1992, 159), the Bloomberg administration aggressively sought to reunite upland New York City with its historically industrial waterfront and "promote new uses" of "underutilized" land through the creation of parks and other public amenities in all five boroughs (New York City Department of City Planning 2012a). Throughout this redevelopment blueprint, and the series of individual initiatives it contained, regular references to "mixed use," density, reconnecting the waterfront to the rest of the city, and fostering dynamic street life (Burden 2009, 2008a, 2007a) underscored the administration's adoption of Jacobs's foundational ideas. Indeed, University of California, Los Angeles, sociologist David Halle, writing in the commemorative issue of *City and Community*, contends that it was Jacobs, through her call for locally oriented, market-based development, who left the more indelible imprint on the Bloomberg agenda: "In Jacobs' spirit, Bloomberg and his [Department of City Planning] see government's role as facilitating urban growth and density" by "fostering 'multiple downtowns' in Brooklyn, Queens and Staten Island, as well as on Manhattan's Far West Side . . . while also 'downzoning' certain neighborhoods to protect them from excessive development" (Halle 2006, 240).

Yet even as the physical manifestations of the Bloomberg agenda "represent[ed] an absorption of Jane Jacobs," and were "not Modernist in their physical forms, they [were Modernist] in their functionalist aims" (Fainstein 2005a, 2). Unlike Jacobs, who preached the self-healing powers of neighborhoods and embraced small-scale incremental change, the Bloomberg administration advocated an aggressive new round of creative destruction that harkened back to Moses and his methods, complete with a readiness to invoke eminent domain and to employ a creative blend of incentives, tax subsidies, and the blurring of public and private monies to secure developer participation (see Caro 1975, 321). This aggressiveness stemmed, in part, from the administration's belief that the only way to ensure that projects would be seen through to completion was to get them far enough along that they could not be sidelined or abandoned by future forces.

Admitting some "nostalgia for Moses" and his ability to get things built, Burden wrote in the *Gotham Gazette*, "With the limitation of a two-term mayoralty, it is an enormous challenge to get great new open spaces such as Fresh Kills, the East River Waterfront in Lower Manhattan, the High Line and the Greenpoint/Williamsburg waterfront approved, designed and built so that the initiative cannot be undone by subsequent administrations" (Burden 2006b). Similarly, Rohit Aggarwala, director of the New York City Office of Long-Term Planning and Sustainability, the department created for the express purpose of producing the long-term sustainability initiative that would become PlaNYC 2030, acknowledged "running as fast as possible" to impose as much of the sustainability agenda before Bloomberg was to leave office in 2009 so that the initiative would "live well past the Bloomberg administration" (Aggarwala 2007). Of course, reversal of the two-term limit and Bloomberg's reelection to a third term in 2009 gave the administration an additional four years to push its agenda.

Moses's lineage can also be found in the agenda's orientation of future development around existing or proposed transportation infrastructure—seen most keenly in efforts to extend the No. 7 subway line and replace the existing Penn Station with a new and expanded transportation hub, to be called Moynihan Station, as a means of opening Manhattan's Far West Side to redevelopment, as well as the creation of a new hub for business in the Jamaica neighborhood in Queens, where subway, regional rail, and AirTrain access to John F. Kennedy airport converge. Moses also resonated through the administration's focus on building and expanding cultural and educational institutions—including Columbia University's proposed expansion and a renovation of Lincoln Center for the Performing Arts, completed in 2009—and what administration officials liked to call the Third Great Era of park building and expansion in New York City history after the City Beautiful period, during which many of the city's playgrounds and monuments were built, and Moses's twenty-six-year tenure as the head of the city parks department, a period in which the acreage within the parks system tripled (Benepe 2007).

"Moses would build in six months or a year what it takes us three or four years to build," Benepe said in a 2008 interview in *Landscape Architecture* magazine. "He did not need to be nearly as accountable to the community as we do now" (Benepe 2008a, 55). Nonetheless, between 2001, when Bloomberg took office, and end-of-year 2007, New York City added 416 acres of new parkland. In 2007 the administration proposed spending an additional $3 billion over three years to develop eight regional parks and expand the city's network of green spaces so that no New Yorker was more than a ten-minute walk from a park or patch of grass (Benepe 2007). Plans for proposed waterfront redevelopments in Manhattan, Brooklyn, the Bronx, and Queens featured additional public open space, ensuring city residents access to the water while at the same time providing developers with nearby public amenities sure to enhance the value of their projects (Burden 2007a).

Inherent throughout the agenda, as well as in the narrative supporting it, was the notion that at the same time the administration was looking out for New York City's greater good, it was pursuing a thoroughly—if not the only—rational course for securing its physical and economic salvation. According to Aggarwala, planning for growth in an "old, mature American city" such as New York "requires a different kind of thinking," a discourse focused on "how to recover, not expand" (Aggarwala 2007). He and other administration officials routinely characterized this new approach as visionary, and even after his departure from the administration, former deputy mayor Dan Doctoroff continued to pitch the Bloomberg redevelopment agenda as "aspirational," "a detailed action plan . . . that embodies values specific to the city," and "a transformative vision" for "what we wanted the city to be, to stand for" (Doctoroff 2009). According to Doctoroff, ultimately what made the Bloomberg administration more effective than previous administrations in pressing its redevelopment agenda was a "lack of fear of addressing problems even when they [were] not politically—especially when they [were] not politically—palatable" (Doctoroff 2009).

Of course, unlike in the Moses era, the administration's grand notions largely transcended its ability to dictate the course of that future. After all, it was not the administration that would build big again, but private developers, who through tax incentives, subsidies, and favorable zoning changes largely were handed the reins to New York City's redevelopment (Angotti 2007; Wells 2007). In fact, the only concrete mechanisms the administration had for pursuing its agenda were the creation of specific master plans—which Burden described as "drawing what we want [spaces] to look like"—and the power to dictate land use by, in the language of its master narrative, providing "the armature for development" through zoning (Burden 2007a). As Burden admitted, "All we can really do is zone for the right height and for the right use and then let the market come" (Burden 2007a). Still, as the administration's preferred "tool of redevelopment," rezoning "opened the door to the type of development that private investors think will be most profitable while giving a nod of approval to Jane Jacobs' kind of authenticity" (Zukin 2010, 23). And by recognizing the power of its land use decisions to drive development in "underutilized" neighborhoods, even as these decisions protected single-family home values and middle- and upper-class qualities of life in others, the administration mobilized zoning as the chief vehicle for remaking the city along class lines.

At this point, once again it proves instructive to consider the influence Moses and Jacobs have had on specific aspects of the planning process, in this case the general evolution of zoning and, more specifically, the zoning standards that guided development in New York City for nearly a century.

Zoning: "A Mass of Contradictory Impulses"

From its very inception, zoning has been seen as a vehicle for social engineering, a way to protect public health, safety, morals, and general welfare—and promote certain activities while prohibiting others—through the regulation of land use (Wickersham 2001). As previously mentioned, New York City adopted the nation's first zoning ordinance, in 1916, as a means of controlling densities by encouraging the development of tall towers set in broad plazas. It also introduced restrictions on floor-area ratios (FARs)[3] and separated uses by dividing the city into residential, manufacturing, and commercial districts. The underlying assumptions of this "Euclidean" zoning were in line with the "functionalist" shift in planning during the 1920s, which itself was aligned with the Taylorist vision of the city as "a large and smoothly operating machine" (Wickersham 2001, 251). The core components of this functionalist view, including the separation of land uses, served as the framework for Moses-style modernism, with its superblocks and institutional campuses set off from surrounding neighborhoods. By 1926 all but five states had passed zoning acts, making zoning the default "template for the creation of new urban and suburban districts" (Wickersham 2001, 251).

Once in place, these comprehensive zoning standards would guide New York City's development for the next forty-five years, even as over time piecemeal exceptions—some twenty-five hundred by the late 1950s— added to the zoning law's bulk and complexity, and the lack of height limits led to fears that portions of midtown and downtown Manhattan would become a series of canyons, their streets and avenues running between rows of skyscraping towers. Civic groups and reformers pushed for a complete overhaul, and in 1961 the city responded by reducing FARs to 15, meaning that to reach higher, a building's footprint would have to cover a smaller portion of a lot. Included in those revisions was a shift away from across-the-board regulations in favor of a more flexible, case-by-case approach, as well as the introduction of the nation's first incentive zoning initiative as a means of creating new open spaces (Kayden 2000). This earliest form of incentive zoning allowed developers of buildings in districts zoned for commercial use to build higher in exchange for providing public amenities like plazas, atriums, gallerias, roof gardens and covered pedestrian walkways. For every square foot of public space produced, these developers earned the right to build an additional ten square feet of office space, effectively raising the allowable FAR on the building from 15 to 18. The only additional requirement was that the plazas had to be open to the public at all times. Developers embraced the incentives because greater densities meant higher profits, while communities initially welcomed the creation of new public amenities. The approach had the added benefit, from the city government's point of view, of boosting property assessments and enhancing tax receipts.

The results of the program, however, were decidedly mixed. An impressive amount of public space was created—some 3.5 million square feet from its inception until 2000 (Kayden 2000)—much of it in parts of the city with little access to such amenities. Yet while some spaces proved to be valuable public resources, others were inaccessible or devoid of features that attracted public use. According to a survey sponsored by the Municipal Art Society and the Department of City Planning, roughly 16 percent of the spaces served as regional destinations or neighborhood gathering spaces, while 21 percent were used as brief resting places, 18 percent were used as little more than shortcuts between two points, and 41 percent were deemed marginal (Kayden 2000; for a complete listing of the spaces surveyed and an explanation of the descriptions, see New York City Department of City Planning 2012d).[4] Almost immediately, critics charged that the plazas generated by the incentives were lifeless and "sterile," open expanses of concrete and stone suited to little more than walking across (Whyte 1989, 234). Jacobs, sensing the Radiant City influences at the heart of this "progressive zoning," was among the earliest opponents: "No matter how vulgarized or clumsy the design, how dreary and useless the open space, how dull the close-up view, an imitation of Le Corbusier shouts 'Look what I made!'" (Jacobs 1992, 23).[5] Indeed, zoning, with its traditional focus on the separation of uses, reduction of density, and privileging of automobiles over pedestrians, is historically at odds with Jacobs's most cherished ideals. Her "libertarian economic tendencies" (Wickersham 2001, 549) led her to conclude that zoning, by its nature, is "at odds with the needs of real life" (Jacobs 1992, 235). Still, her opposition was directed specifically at the mobilization of zoning in support of large-scale cataclysmic projects, dynamism-killing separation of uses, and what she surely saw as an unnatural suppression of the market. Jacobs's preference was for limited applications of public policy—what she referred to as moving chess pieces—"as an appropriate means of controlling the pace and nature of smaller-scale, more gradual changes in urban land uses" (Wickersham 2001, 550).[6]

Contributing to the clamor for further zoning revisions was the fiscal crisis of the 1970s. As construction activity collapsed in the middle of the decade—in 1973 12,260,000 square feet of office space were built; by 1976 that figure had shrunk to 360,000 square feet (Kayden 2000)—builders and developers advocated changes that would make it easier not only for them to build but also for them to build bigger on more desirable and therefore profitable sites closer to the existing business hub in midtown Manhattan. In May 1975, the New York City Board of Estimate (BOE), which at the time still held sway over the City Planning Commission, responded to the growing chorus by easing height restrictions, resulting in FARs in the 20s (developer Donald Trump's fifty-eight-story Trump Tower on the corner of Fifth Avenue and Fifty-Sixth Street, which was completed in 1983, maxed out at 21.6) and allowing new bonuses for through-block corridors, atriums, and shopping arcades (Kayden 2000). New restrictions, however, required that the plazas not only be open but also amenable to public use. To ensure that occurred, the BOE adopted a series of detailed design guidelines conceived by William "Holly" Whyte, the sociologist and urbanist whose observational studies sought to explain urban life by quantifying—often in extreme detail—how people use and interact with public spaces.

Like Jacobs, Whyte was an early skeptic of the city's incentive zoning bonuses and a critic of some of the public spaces they produced. In the early 1970s his Street Life Project set out to determine "what made good plazas work and bad plazas not work, and the reasons why" and to "translate" those findings "into tight guidelines" the City Planning Commission eventually incorporated into its zoning regulations in 1975 (Whyte 1989, 234). Included were formulas for determining the appropriate amount of seating—one linear foot for every thirty square feet of plaza—and a range of additional detailed prescriptions that critics contended amounted to top-down proclamations that "dictate[d] design by formula" (Whyte 1989, 235). Also in 1975, voters in New York City approved a new city charter that established the Uniform Land Use Review Procedure (ULURP), exposing proposed development projects to mandated additional layers of review. Developers chafed, arguing that such an onerous approval process would stall certain projects and possibly kill others, which in turn would lead to lost construction jobs and prompt corporations to move to the suburbs, where land and construction costs and building requirements were less restrictive. Although they failed in their effort to derail ULURP, developers soon became adept at skirting the guidelines by applying for special dispensations, and, by the late 1970s, so many of these "spot zoning" releases had been granted that the zoning code had swelled to two massive volumes.

Once again, Whyte would play an important role in the ever-evolving efforts to rationalize New York City's zoning regulations, employing time-lapse photography to study how plazas were used as part of the Planning Commission's Midtown Zoning Study in 1979. Whyte argued that bonuses for atriums and other inside spaces represented "an internalization of public space and a drain on the vitality of the street" (Whyte 1989, 248). One potential solution: off-site bonuses or the creation of nearby small urban parks, which were adopted in 1982 during a broader, sweeping revision of zoning in midtown. As a rule, FARs were reduced from 18 to 21.6 to 15 to 18, though on Manhattan's West Side, where the city was trying to drive development, higher ratios were left in place. Bonuses for everything but parks and plazas were eliminated, and instead of incentivizing amenities, the City Planning Commission began requiring them.

By 1992, scores of additional revisions and amendments again rendered existing zoning standards confusing and often contradictory, and with a new cycle of economic downturn putting the brakes on construction, the Dinkins administration saw the political opening to push for additional revisions that could pave the way for a new era of megaproject development. "Free from the pressures posed by intense construction," *New York Times* journalist David Dunlap wrote at the time, "planners have the chance to chart a fresh course in zoning, instead of incessantly fine-tuning a document that took effect 31 years ago, when New York was a much different city, before communities were given a formal role in land-use review" (Dunlap 1992, 101). Critics of the proposed revisions, however, including Peter Salins, then chair of the Urban Affairs and Planning Department at Hunter College and a senior fellow at the Manhattan Institute for Policy Research, argued that zoning regulations were created to prevent excessive density, the juxtaposition of incompatible uses, and visual offenses, not to serve as the basis for implementing comprehensive plans and pursuing "planning objectives of the moment" (Dunlap 1992, 101). Eventually, the ongoing "economic paralysis" led the Department of City Planning (DCP) to cut its staff by 25 percent between 1990 and 1992, and in the end opposition from the real estate industry buried the revision effort, as reported by Josh Barbanel (2004). At the time, Dunlap mused that New York City might never find the political will to rewrite its zoning rules, suggesting that if "zoning is the regulatory tool by which a comprehensive plan is shaped, some broadly held vision of New York's future would be a necessary precursor to a thoroughly revised ordinance" (Dunlap 1992, 101).

Zone, and Let the Market Come

A decade later, however, the Bloomberg administration would enter the picture with its renewed emphasis on Moses-scale planning, in which zoning would emerge as among the most powerful tools in New York City's planning "toolbox" (Burden 2007a). Once geared toward controlling dense, mixed-use development, zoning was now viewed as a mechanism for actively fostering density and mixed uses (Wickersham 2001), and on the surface at least it would be portrayed as a means of creating Jacobs's preconditions for diversity. In terms of scale, however, its intended effects more closely resembled Moses-style cataclysmic redevelopment, and soon the administration was well into the process of touting the wholesale transformation of the city. In early 2004, Burden took Josh Barbanel, a *New York Times* reporter, on a personal tour of an exhibit of the administration's plans at the Center for Architecture. Barbanel wrote:

> Flickering before Amanda M. Burden, the city planning commissioner, was a vision of New York City of the future. A computer animation showed the view from a car driving toward the Greenpoint waterfront in Brooklyn. The industrial buildings were gone, replaced by a stately procession of five- and six-story brick and stone apartment buildings, culminating in high-rise towers scattered along a wide landscaped promenade along the East River.
> Then she moved on to a cardboard and Lucite model showing a far West Side of offices and apartments in oddly shaped towers and spires rising along a midblock park between 10th and 11th Avenues stretching from 34th to 39th Streets, part of the Hudson Yards development.
> In another room was a view of the High Line, the long-abandoned elevated freight railway in West Chelsea, with a description of a complex plan to turn it into a landscaped promenade that could link up with the planned park in Hudson Yards. As part of the plan, owners of nearby properties would be able to sell air rights—enabling new structures to be larger than zoning would otherwise allow—to developers of new buildings.

Down the hall, she pointed out drawings and zoning maps for a planned office and residential center in a section of Downtown Brooklyn where height limitations and design guidelines were choreographed, sometimes building by building, to create what she called "a sense of place, a great place."

These plans . . . show a city transformed, but they are only a small fraction of the planning projects and zoning proposals under study or recently adopted across the city in a burst of activity not seen in many years, planners say. "We are creating the conditions for growth where the city can handle it," Commissioner Burden said, "while preserving the character of neighborhoods." (Barbanel 2004)

Indeed, over time, little in Burden's presentation of the administration's "strategic blueprint" changed other than the steady progression of the number of neighborhoods that had been rezoned. When Burden detailed the plan to Hunter College urban design and planning students on November 5, 2007, the DCP had completed seventy-eight rezonings, representing six thousand blocks—or one out of every six blocks in the five boroughs—in eighty-eight neighborhoods (Burden 2007a). By a May 26, 2009, presentation at the American Institute of Architects Center for Architecture, those numbers had climbed to ninety-four rezonings (eighty-one of which were outside of Manhattan) covering eight thousand blocks, including sixty-four downzonings to "protect neighborhood character," with another fifteen rezonings awaiting city council action (Burden 2009). At that point the presentation had also taken on a subtitle, the Five Borough Economic Opportunity Plan, a theme that had also found its way into Bloomberg's 2009 reelection campaign literature and had grown to include the assertion that the administration was committed to "zoning to improve people's lives" by addressing the disappearance of local grocery stores in low-income neighborhoods and expanding inclusionary housing bonuses to promote home ownership (Burden 2009).

While the city council had the ultimate say on all zoning changes—following advisory review local community boards, borough presidents, and the City Planning Commission—as of September 2009, none of the proposed zoning modifications put forward by the Bloomberg Department of City Planning had been rejected.

Within the administration's planning narrative, this invigorated approach to zoning represented what officials described as a customizable approach to land use, featuring regulations that varied neighborhood by neighborhood. In certain cases the DCP advocated for the use of "contextual" zoning—or what Burden called "fine-tuning" (Burden 2007a)—to limit the size and appearance of buildings on side streets while pushing higher densities and bigger buildings on avenues. In 2003, for example, one hundred blocks of East Harlem and Central Harlem around Frederick Douglass Boulevard were rezoned to direct development by allowing for the building of a new generation of twelve-story apartment houses on neighborhood avenues while protecting the row-house nature of side streets. In Brooklyn, Fulton Street in the Bedford-Stuyvesant neighborhood was proposed as another site for higher densities, and in Park Slope zoning was enacted that reduced development on side streets but allowed for twelve-story buildings on Fourth Avenue. As part of the latter deal, which was adopted in April 2003, the city guaranteed Park Slope several million dollars in city programs, offering subsidies to developers who produced below-market-rate housing.

As many of the rezonings were being contemplated, New York City was in the middle of a housing boom, reported Barbanel (2004). In the forty months leading up to year-end 2003, sixty thousand building permits were issued, a number greater than the total issued between 1990 through 1998, and the effort "followed the revitalization of the housing market" to the outer boroughs, where the DCP insisted it was "laying the groundwork for the next generation of office development and tens of thousands of new jobs too" (Barbanel 2004).

Indeed, a central focus of the rezoning effort was the creation of additional, less-expensive back-office space in Long Island City and Downtown Brooklyn to compete with New Jersey for those corporate functions. In Jamaica in Queens, city planners seized on the recently completed AirTrain link to John F. Kennedy Airport to call for the rezoning of four hundred blocks that would foster the creation of a new business district—replete with construction of new office buildings, hotels, retail space, and housing—while preserving the residential nature of nearby neighborhoods. But this burst of activity put extreme development pressure on low-density residential areas, pressure the administration had hoped to lessen by downzoning neighborhoods such as Clinton Hill and Bay Ridge in Brooklyn, Riverdale in the Bronx, and Richmond Hill in Queens, while upzoning to drive more dense residential development to communities with significant transit access, including Jamaica, Harlem, and Williamsburg/Greenpoint. As Barbanel points out, "much" of the proposed downzoning was taking place in neighborhoods that voted heavily for Bloomberg "and where he [was] working hard to rebuild support after the city adopted an 18.5 percent property tax increase." In certain instances, neighborhoods seized on the opportunity to be proactive in determining their futures by requesting downzoning as means of keeping out higher-density apartment buildings. "We are seeing six- to seven-story apartment buildings where there is a lot of detached housing, and that is of concern to us," Regina Meyer, the director of city planning for Brooklyn, told

Barbanel. "For the first time in decades neighborhoods like Bensonhurst have been asking us for rezonings" (Barbanel 2004).

Burden and other DPC representatives liked to present these downzonings as examples of administration planners working in consultation with local neighborhoods to promote and develop community-oriented plans. "If you wanted the public to buy in, you had to ask them first," former Deputy Mayor Dan Doctoroff insisted, referencing what he described—in the context of formulating PlaNYC 2030—as an "unprecedented outreach effort" that included an advisory board of "experts," the hosting of eleven town hall meetings and consultation with more than 150 advocacy groups in addition to mechanisms for website feedback (Doctoroff 2009; Aggarwala 2007). In terms of zoning, in general, Burden liked to tell the story of how she insisted that the city's planners attend community board meetings, walk the streets, and make sketches of what they observed, all the while keeping an appreciation of the community as the "backbone" of the neighborhood in mind (Washburn 2008a; Burden 2007a).

Manhattan's Community Board 4 (CB4), which represents the Clinton/Hell's Kitchen neighborhood directly north of Hudson Yards, provided a distinctly alternative take on the rezoning process, however. In December 2007, the City Planning Commission (CPC) presented its proposal for rezoning the neighborhood—bounded by Tenth Avenue and the Westside Highway and Forty-Third to Fifty-Fifth Street—to the community as part of the public outreach process required by ULURP. At that presentation, a group known as the Westside Neighborhood Alliance responded with its own list of concerns and development priorities, including the creation and preservation of affordable housing in the area. Six months later, CB4's Clinton/Hell's Kitchen Land Use Committee hosted a second meeting, at which Erika Sellke, a representative of the City Planning Commission, presented a revised draft of the rezoning proposal, noting that the CPC was "co-applicants with the Community Board in the process."[7] In her introductory remarks, however, CB4 Chair Anna Hayes Levin pointed out that even though the rezoning was "something [the CPC was] doing with us, not to us," the commission had to be "cajoled" before it "finally agreed to work with us." It did not take long before it became apparent that community members attending the meeting were not convinced. Following Sellke's technocratic, detail-oriented description of the revised plan's intentions—including encouraging residential and office development on the industrial-oriented west side of Eleventh Avenue and preserving the "typical Clinton walk-up" residential nature of street mid-blocks—a parade of area residents stepped up to an open microphone to voice their displeasure. Most were clearly frustrated and some turned emotional. One after another they argued for more than just rezoning. They asked for more hospitals and green spaces, for "affordable housing, not just residential housing." Finally, one mother burst into tears as she voiced her fears of ever finding a school for her daughter. "You're bringing in more residents," she stressed, "but no more schools."

Disappearing the Working Waterfront

Yet a third, and equally contentious, focus of the rezonings was the conversion of large tracts of land historically devoted to industry or manufacturing to office and residential use, especially along large waterfront properties, which the city deemed ideal for new—though primarily market-rate and in many cases luxury—housing (see, for example, Bloomberg 2007). Yet in spite of suggestions to the contrary, industry had not completely abandoned New York City by the end of the first decade of the twenty-first century. Although the nature of the goods produced had changed—from ships and textiles to niche segments, like specialty foods, high-end lighting, and sets for Broadway shows—and the overall number of jobs had dwindled to a fraction of former levels, by 2008 some 105,000 New Yorkers still made their living making things (Pratt Center for Community Development 2008). Equally important, the jobs that did remain generally offered higher wages—$49,000 per year, on average—than other blue-collar options, such as retail ($39,000) or food service (Pratt Center for Community Development 2008).

In 2005 the Office of Industrial and Manufacturing Business (OIMB) was created as part of the Bloomberg administration's "comprehensive industrial policy," which included efforts to promote industrial expansion and manage newly created industrial business zones (IBZs), ostensibly as a means of diversifying the city's economic base. Still, the city's own redevelopment policies and rezoning initiatives ran counter to whatever efforts were made toward industrial retention by fueling demand for space for alternative uses—residential, commercial, and mixed use—and thereby driving up real estate values. In 2002, 12,542 acres of land was zoned for manufacturing in New York City; by 2008 that number had shrunk 20 percent, to 10,746 acres, with another 1,800 acres slated to be converted to other uses by anticipated future rezoning (Pratt Center for Community Development 2009). Of the ninety-five rezonings approved from 2003 until the end of 2008, one-quarter converted manufacturing land to some other use, while none added to the amount of available industrial land (Pratt Center for Community Development 2009). "We only have any meaningful amount of manufacturing remaining in the city because we used the strong regulatory power of the state to require that in some areas that's what you can do with your property," the Pratt Center's Brad Lander pointed out during the Gotham Center forum. "There may have been a time when an economic mix of uses would have sustained itself, but the threat to our manufacturing spaces is the rents. Owners of those properties would like to convert them because they could make a lot more money if they were allowed to convert to residential development" (Lander 2006). Likewise, just because land had been zoned industrial, that offered no guarantee that it was used for manufacturing. New York City's zoning regulations allow big-box retail stores, shopping malls, hotels, and in some cases even office buildings—which Burden noted the administration was willing to incentivize "because that generates an enormous amount of jobs and tax revenue" (Burden 2006a)—to occupy land zoned for industrial uses.

Even the efforts of the OIMB suggest the administration was only serious about retaining a minimal level—and then of a certain kind—of manufacturing. Through 2008 the OIMB had created sixteen IBZs, covering forty-one hundred acres—or less than one-third the total land devoted to manufacturing in 2002 and less than half the remaining industrially zoned space—none of it in Manhattan. Most of the existing IBZs were run in partnership with local nonprofit development corporations and received city financial support—$17 million in direct funding and up to $9 million in tax credits through 2009—to assist in business relocation and provide grants for employee training and assistance. Still, that support paled in comparison to the massive public subsidies provided to any one of dozens of individual private redevelopment projects.[8]

Altogether, the conversion of industrial spaces to other uses factored into a wide range of the administration's proposed redevelopment projects, including many of the most high profile. Hudson Yards, where redevelopment, as conceived in 2004, was expected to play out over four decades and require $5 billion in development costs to be shared by the city and state, was among the most ambitious. Just to the south, portions of Tenth and Eleventh Avenues and some mid-block side streets in West Chelsea, historically the home of New York City's meatpacking district—were rezoned in 2004 to allow for loft apartments and commercial buildings. High-rise towers were allowed opposite Chelsea Piers, overlooking the Hudson River, and the owners of properties adjacent to the High Line were granted permission to sell their soon-to-be-more-valuable air rights for new and bigger buildings, including luxury housing, even as a nascent art gallery district was protected from redevelopment by preservation of its manufacturing zoning. Inclusionary zoning, or density, bonuses were offered to developers who agreed to include a certain percentage—typically 20 percent of the total—of low- and moderate-income housing on certain blocks. Earlier, portions of Long Island City in Queens, directly across the East River from Manhattan and the proposed hub of the Olympic Village for the 2012 Summer Games, had been rezoned from manufacturing to office and residential, and one and one-half miles of industrial waterfront in the Greenpoint and Williamsburg section of Brooklyn were rezoned to accommodate a public park and promenade surrounded by mostly luxury residential towers up to thirty-five stories tall.

In each instance, rezoning had the intended effect of raising the value of land as a means of encouraging redevelopment. In interviews, Burden spoke of the potential of proposed rezonings to "add value" (Vitullo-Martin 2008) and boost real estate prices, and Bloomberg in a keynote speech at the Manhattan Institute trumpeted rezoning as a mechanism to attract "private capital" (Bloomberg 2007). To the administration, this was part of an effort to allow market forces to "unlock the potential of the city's underused land" that would benefit the entire city, including existing community members (Bloomberg 2007). But in many cases rezonings only encouraged speculation, raising both housing prices and rents in neighborhoods that were increasingly growing too costly for the residents living there. In one instance, Burden proudly noted that by 2011 the price of apartments in a building in the rezoned neighborhood adjacent to the High Line had doubled to $2,000 a square foot since the first section of the park had opened in June 2009 (McGeehan 2011); in another, an Internet real estate blogger gushed about how the value of a property on Washington Street in the lower Manhattan neighborhood of TriBeCa soared from the "mid $5 million range" to $6.9 million following rezoning. "Smart buyers would be wise to track potential rezoning," the blogger, a real estate agent, advised. "If you have the patience to land bank, it can be very lucrative" (Nelson 2011). Similarly, a study released by New York University's Furman Center for Real Estate and Urban Policy concluded that rezonings oriented toward neighborhood preservation—or downzonings—were more likely to occur in census tracts with greater percentages of white residents and higher incomes, while upzonings designed to increase density occurred in census tracts with lower incomes and more black or Hispanic populations (Furman Center for Real Estate and Urban Policy 2010). As a result, community leaders and housing advocates in many neighborhoods targeted for rezoning pressed for requirements that developers provide below-market housing, but city officials argued the high cost of construction in many targeted areas, notably waterfront sites, would discourage developers from building.

The High Cost of Affordable Housing

Still, the administration did turn to zoning-related initiatives as a means of helping address New York City's affordable housing issue. Acknowledging that without some form of government intervention, the working poor and, increasingly, the middle class would be priced out of New York, the mayor unveiled a ten-year $7.5 billion New Housing

Marketplace Plan in December 2002. That initiative proposed to create ninety-two thousand units and preserve another seventy-three thousand units of low- to middle-income housing by 2013—enough, according to the administration, to house five hundred thousand New Yorkers (New York City Department of Housing Preservation and Development 2002). By rezoning "underutilized manufacturing districts" and "under-built avenues near transportation nodes" in neighborhoods such as Sherman Creek and Bedford-Stuyvesant, the administration argued it could foster the creation of "thousands" of new housing units (New York City Department of Housing Preservation and Development 2002). An estimated 68 percent of those units would be earmarked for families earning less than 80 percent of the area's median income (AMI), with the other 32 percent targeted at moderate and middle-income groups making from $50,000 to $100,000.[9] Included in the latter category were 435 units in rezoned sections of the Hudson Yards and West Chelsea neighborhoods.

Inclusionary zoning, or the offering of density bonuses in exchange for the provision of affordable housing units, served as another mechanism for mobilizing support of the initiative. Originally limited to the highest density districts in Manhattan, where it was specifically intended to address gentrification concerns, inclusionary zoning was extended to the outer boroughs and medium-density areas by the administration in 2005. All told, the tactic was expected to produce 6,000 new units of affordable housing, including 220 units in the 1,100-unit Studio City development as part of the massive Hudson Yards rezoning (New York City Department of Housing Preservation and Development 2002). In addition, the New York City Acquisition Fund, a $200 million public/private limited liability corporation established to provide acquisition and predevelopment loans to small developers and nonprofit groups for the creation or preservation of affordable housing in the city's five boroughs, was projected to generate 30,000 units of affordable housing. The Fund leveraged $40 million in city and foundation funding to attract an additional $160 million in private capital from "the City's largest banks and financial institutions" (New York City Department of Housing Preservation and Development 2002). A final source involved the establishment of the New York City Housing Trust Fund, including $70 million of Battery Park City revenues, which in conjunction with Low Income Housing Tax Credits was projected to create two thousand units for households earning less than 30 percent and between 60 percent and 80 percent of the area's median income. As of September 2008, the midway point in its expected life span, the New Housing Marketplace Plan had generated financing for 82,500 units—or half of its total target number.

But like so many of the city's projects, the New Housing Marketplace Plan relied on a combination of government subsidies and private-sector financing, and was tied to the willingness of private-sector lenders and developers to finance, acquire, and build affordable units. That in turn made the effort dependent on larger real estate dynamics, and in the fall of 2008, as the full effects of a global economic slowdown began to affect the price of the federal low-income housing credits used to finance low-income housing construction and lines of available credit for developers began to shrink, Bloomberg was forced to announce a one-year extension of the program because of the challenging economic climate.

Planning Director Amanda Burden contended that in spite of such setbacks, the administration's "aggressive" approach to rezoning represented an effective strategy for coaxing the private sector to participate in the provision of affordable housing. "You know this [is] the most aggressive affordable housing plan in the nation—$3 billion leveraging 168,000 units of affordable housing," she asserted in response to a question posed from the audience during the Gotham Center forum. "It is incredibly aggressive, and that is public sector initiatives. And yes, in each one of those initiatives we tried to leverage to the greatest maximum extent affordable housing and public space. . . . We really squeeze the private sector as hard as we can" (Burden 2006a).

To be sure, a wide-ranging coalition of voices—from housing advocates to city officials and even private developers—agreed that construction of affordable housing was among New York City's greatest needs. Many, however, questioned whether inclusionary zoning was the best solution, ultimately suggesting that the Bloomberg administration lacked the political will to realistically address the problem. At a Municipal Art Society forum, "The Oversuccessful City: Developers' Realities," held in November 2007, in conjunction with a series of events surrounding Jane Jacobs and the Future of New York, *New York Times* journalist Charles Bagli asked whether the city—as a result of the administration's aggressive rezoning—was not losing its "heterogeneous nature" and becoming "exclusively for the rich." The topic swung to inclusionary zoning and the affordable housing it was designed to generate, which the panelists—developers Douglas Durst of the Durst Organization, Carlton Brown of Full Spectrum New York, and Greg O'Connell of Kings Harbor View Associates, along with Eugenie Birch, professor of city and regional planning at the University of Pennsylvania—agreed should be made mandatory and permanent. But, Bagli wondered, was the existing ratio of 80 percent market-rate housing to 20 percent affordable enough? "Does that serve the need?" he asked. "Does that fulfill demand?" Brown noted that for the private sector to build affordable housing it required incentives—including cheap land and tax credits. But, he admitted, "80/20 hasn't solved all the needs." He and O'Connell also noted that affordable "means different things to different people," and Durst suggested that there was no reason the percentage of required affordable housing could not be higher. The administration, he argued, needs "to force developers to build less expensively" (Municipal Art Society of New York 2007b).

Even then, Bagli suggested, "is it possible to create neighborhoods that espouse the characteristics"—mixed uses—"espoused by Jacobs?" This time Birch answered. Referring to Jacobs as "a gentrifier," she argued that "if New York is to be a successful city, it must set the rules. Developers will follow rules, but you can't bargain bit by bit. New York [City] sits back and waits for the developer to come. The city is not proactive. It is reactive."

Other critics have pointed out that the cyclicality of housing markets and the inevitability of economic downturns underscore the flaws inherent in the administration's reliance on the private sector to participate in the provision of affordable housing, and it has been suggested that redirecting private real estate toward addressing the problem represents a neoliberal abdication of a necessary government function. In response to Burden's assertions at the Gotham Center forum, Michael Sorkin, director of the Urban Design Program at the City College of New York, suggested that New York City's experience creating "a city hospitable to all of its citizens" through direct public investment offered "a cautionary tale" (Sorkin 2006). "However welcome the city's inclusionary zoning initiatives . . . may be, they seem out of sync with the magnitude of what is nothing less than a housing crisis." Meanwhile, Brad Lander, then the director of the Pratt Center for Community Development, pointed to what he called a fundamental contradiction in the administration's policy for determining which neighborhoods qualify for downzoning to protect existing character and which qualify for upzoning to house future generations of New Yorkers and the office developments they conceivably would work in. He noted that local community groups had worked with the Pratt Center for Community Development regarding the redevelopment of the Greenpoint waterfront and had proposed provisions for lower-income housing in new developments and sought zoning that would further protect manufacturing. But when they put their alternatives forward, city officials responded that the market could not support them. "They embrace using zoning in an anti-market way on Staten Island for neighborhood preservation," Lander told Barbanel of the *New York Times*. "But they are not willing to use it for broader social and political purposes" (2004).

7

Ideas That Converge

As we have seen thus far, in various ways and at multiple levels, Jane Jacobs and Robert Moses continue to resonate in debates over urban form and redevelopment. At particular moments and in specific places, each has emerged as a foundational figure, an urban icon whose ideas inform the work of planning theorists and practitioners, and serve as cornerstones in ideological arguments over how best to plan and build cities. That in the New York City of the early twenty-first century, the Bloomberg administration would appeal to both at the same time attests to the lasting resonance of each figure's underlying message.

Yet growing criticism of the administration's redevelopment agenda toward the middle of the mayor's tenure called into question the suggestion that it is possible to build and rezone, "once again, like Moses . . . but with Jane Jacobs firmly in mind" (Burden 2006a). At the very least it argued for a clear explanation of exactly what that might mean in terms of redevelopment policy. After all, to most urban observers, such an assertion requires a fairly large leap of logic, especially in a city where negative reaction to Moses's excesses and generally positive associations with Jacobs's localism had dominated the debate over redevelopment for decades. But with Columbia University historians Kenneth Jackson and Hilary Ballon reopening the door by questioning the narrowness of the prevailing Jacobs-was-right, Moses-was-wrong dichotomy, a full-blown reappraisal of the pair seemed only natural.

Jane Jacobs Redux

Over the years it has become de rigueur to assert, as Amanda Burden did, that in the battle of urban ideas Jacobs has "prevailed" and that her "influence is much more deeply rooted and widely felt by urbanists, planners and elected officials" (Burden 2006a). Yet one could reasonably suggest that the passage of time and the stubborn persistence of urban poverty, inequality, lack of affordable housing, and segregation along class and racial lines argue for a new and more nuanced reading of Jacobs much as Ballon and Jackson's revisionism rests on the assertion that Moses should be judged from the perspective of today, not the immediate aftermath of the postwar period in which he operated. Jacobs's ideas, after all, were essentially a response to the logic of postwar urban renewal and large-scale planning as embodied by Moses, an era that has come and gone, giving way to a new form of globalized urbanism that rejects broad federal programs, large-scale public housing projects, and top-down planning in favor of public-private partnerships, vouchers for subsidized housing, and participatory planning (Brash 2006; Brenner and Theodore 2002; Harvey 2008a; Smith 2002; Peck and Tickell 2002). Whether Jacobs's principles regarding what constitutes a livable city still resonate when the old social, economic, and political logics underlying that city have shifted seems a question worth asking.

In her discussion of the value of short blocks in *The Death and Life of Great American Cities*, for instance, Jacobs takes her readers on a tour of the Upper West Side of Manhattan. She describes Columbus Avenue from Eightieth to Eighty-Ninth Street as "endless stores and a depressing predominance of commercial standardization," concentrated there because the street blocks are so long—eight hundred feet—that they keep area residents from forming "reasonably intricate pools of city cross use" (Jacobs 1992, 180, 181). Stretching "around about" are streets like Eighty-Eighth, between Columbus and Central Park West, dismally long strips of monotony and darkness—"the Great Blight of Dullness" and "stagnation"—that she argues typify "city failure" (Jacobs 1992, 180, 181).

To Jacobs, Manhattan's Upper West Side is "badly failed" (Jacobs 1992, 204).

Fast-forward fifty years, and the streets running perpendicular to Columbus Avenue in the West Eighties—at least in terms of their physical characteristics and use—look much the same. West Eighty-Eighth Street is still eight hundred feet long and lined with stoop after stoop, leading to four- to five-story residential buildings. No ground-floor retail. No mid-block tailor, locksmith, or café. Save for a school and the relatively recent addition of a high-rise condominium tower overlooking Central Park, in fact, the block and the buildings on it are just as Jacobs described.

How then does one account for the fact that this very same block is among the most desirable places to live in New York City, fetching some of the highest residential real estate values in the Manhattan?[1] For a badly failed block, West Eighty-Eighth occupies a special place among New York City's middle and upper classes. Which begs the initial question: Do Jacobs's prescriptive prerequisites for generating the diversity that she deemed essential to successful neighborhoods—the short blocks, blend of old and new buildings, mixed uses, and population density—still make as much sense in the first decade of the twenty-first century as they did almost five decades ago?

The short answer is that within the recent rounds of reassessment no shortage of voices has emerged to question the unproblematized embrace of Jacobs as winner in the battle of urban ideas. A number of critics have pointed out that the prescriptions presented in *Death and Life* offer few answers to the types of problems contemporary cities face (Ouroussoff 2006a; Perrine 2008; Zukin 2010). They note that in spite of the broad adoption of many of her principles by city planners, beginning in the late 1960s, cities in general and New York City in particular remain paralyzed by "intractable issues—traffic congestion, population growth, lack of affordable housing—that community organizing and gradual change do nothing to resolve" (Sorkin 2008). Others have argued that Jacobs's focus on the local misses the global nature of urbanization that exists in the twenty-first century (Fainstein 2005a, Harvey 2008a) and that her view of her Greenwich Village block is "a social construction" that was a "product of its time" (Zukin 2010, 15). Sociologist Sharon Zukin eventually takes Jacobs to task for failing to see that her prescriptions would lead to "a collective amnesia about the earlier eras of factory work and mass migration that made these neighborhoods come alive" (Zukin 2010, 23).

To be sure, Jacobs remains powerfully influential. As the exhibit *Jane Jacobs and the Future of New York* demonstrated, her efforts as a community organizer and activist remain a universally championed element of her legacy, and her views continue to inform conceptions of urbanism that conform to the normative logics of capital accumulation, even as aspects of her thinking appeal to alternative, even Marxist, formulations. Radical urbanist Henri Lefebvre, for instance, found common ground with Jacobs in a shared appreciation for the chaos and disorder of the street (Lefebvre 2003) and a keen sense of the city as "dynamic core . . . a vibrant, open public forum, full of lived moments and 'enchanting' encounters" (Merrifield 2006, 71). Unlike Jacobs, however, Lefebvre steadfastly believed that the essence of this dynamism was "disengaged from exchange value," not a fundamental contributor to it (Merrifield 2006, 71).

Similarly, the ecological framework that formed the basis for Jacobs's understanding of cities has remained a cornerstone of her appeal, spawning new generations of planners, urban theorists, and designers who embrace the notion that it is possible not only to identify but deliberately reproduce the physical conditions for successful neighborhoods. Over time, that ecological sensibility has even given rise to "a best-practices" approach for determining what works in "healthy urban 'ecosystems'" and incorporating those elements into new projects (Kidder 2008, 259). The architects Alexander Cooper and Stanton Eckstut based their design criteria for Battery Park City on such a practice, and the broad urban design themes Jacobs first articulated in her opus are now embedded in the principles of the Congress for the New Urbanism as well as in zoning regulations in cities across the country. Also, they inform the latest thinking of regional planning bodies, like the Regional Plan Association, and have become lynchpins of recent urban strategies for revitalizing economically underutilized city districts, as Richard Florida's conception of the creative class attests.

But while Jacobs was "an urban flâneur of the first order" who "reminded us that cities could only be fully understood with our eyes, feet and ears" (Ouroussoff 2006a, C1), she focused her observational powers primarily on neighborhoods like her own—devoting just two sentences in *Death and Life*, for example, to the Bronx (Perrine 2008)—and she saw her urban experience as the measuring stick for all urban experience (Montgomery 1998). Jacobs's model was Greenwich Village—and to an extent similar neighborhoods in Boston, Baltimore, Chicago, and Louisville—and her ideas were constrained by what she saw there (Berman 1982). So while she wrote of embracing chaos, in opposition to Moses's mission to impose order, her willingness to champion the jumble and diversity of urban life only went so far. To Jacobs, design might help "illuminate, clarify and explain the order of cities" (Jacobs 1992, 375), but she attacked rote formulas for making cities better places even as in her book she promoted prescriptions that tended to reinforce the values she found and cherished in her own neighborhood. Through the veil of the intervening years, one wonders whether, intentionally or not, Jacobs was a champion only for certain streets and communities, those whose well-worn features, brownstone buildings, rich cultural heritage, and dynamic character—or at least some simulation thereof—speak to the uprightness of their inhabitants and the latent real estate values of their buildings.

While Jacobs clearly advocated for mixed uses, a range of building ages and types, and frequent streets to break up blocks and foster interaction, her notion of neighborhood diversity was biased toward categories found in the physical environment. Indeed, she "gives physical differentiation a causal role in producing the other types" of diversity (Fainstein 2005a, 5), arguing that through the promotion of physical diversity, other forms—an expanded public realm, a diversity of active and empowered social groups, and a mixture of uses—will follow. As a result, in *Death and Life*, Jacobs mentions racial segregation just three times (Montgomery 1998), and the Greenwich Village streets she describes are ethnically homogenous (Berman 1982). In her neighborhood, residents not only know one another but look alike, share the same social values, and seem to live in a perfect bubble of shared expectation and natural harmony.

In an early manuscript, in which Jacobs explored the themes that would eventually make their way into her book, she marveled at the "balance between public and private life" that is made up of "many small, sensitively managed details, practiced and accepted by consensus, so casually they are utterly taken for granted" (Jacobs, n.d.). Here, local business owners and shopkeepers—folks like "Mr. Jaffe, whose formal business name is Bernie," the "proprietor of the candy and oddment store around the corner"—serve as de facto arbiters of neighborhood life, upstanding symbols of the small-scale, local enterprises that Jacobs believes not only provide the neighborhood with its economic vitality but establish its underlying norms and conventions (Jacobs, n.d.).[2] To Jacobs, Jaffe is representative of "the small business community of practical, law-abiding citizens devoted to 'free enterprise' and 'social mobility'" (Jacobs 1992, 190), and in this neighborhood, his most important job is to reinforce—and enforce—the normative behaviors that make the street safe for commerce and life as everybody knows it. Jaffe, of course, is more than willing to project onto the neighborhood these "taken for granted" norms of behavior, and he is just as likely to be seen lecturing kids trying to buy cigarettes and laying down the law to "rowdies" whose rowdy behavior is never described but nonetheless has been deemed detrimental to the street's sense of order (Jacobs, n.d.). In *Death and Life* this informal means of social control emerges as Jacobs's concept of "street eyes," and like so many of her ideas, it subsequently has been translated into generalized design standards, this time for making neighborhoods safe (Newman 1996).

In spite of Jacobs's inference that all of this—from self-policing by local residents to the market logics that provide the neighborhood with its economic underpinning—occurs as part of some "intricate, underlying order of cities," and in direct rebuttal to assertions that she was an antigovernment libertarian (Anderson 1964; Ballon 2006; Husock 1994), Jacobs argues that government plays an essential role in fostering functional neighborhoods. Public policy, she writes, can encourage diversity by moving the city's "chessmen"—primary land uses that serve as incubators for other uses—in concert to encourage mixed use (Jacobs 1992, 167). Diversity of other types, she indicates, "depends directly or indirectly" on "the presence of plentiful, convenient, diverse city commerce" (Jacobs 1992, 148). In short, Jacobs believed "public intervention was crucial to guaranteeing that the market would produce human and functional diversity that was for her so seminal for good cities" (Sorkin 2006). Today, such public intervention has taken the form of mixed-use zoning, and in New York City it is one of the most material ways that Jacobs's legacy lives on in the Bloomberg administration's redevelopment agenda.

Jacobs also had much to say about "failed" city districts, including those that she equates with "destructive" (Jacobs 1992, 230) or "low economic" (231) land uses—the junkyards and used-car lots that to her mean a certain slice of the city is not living up to its full economic potential. In her eyes these spaces are rundown and dismal not because such uses are located there. Instead, the inverse is true: those uses are attracted to unsuccessful spaces. This in her view is blight by definition. "Probably everyone (except possibly the owners of such objects) is agreed that this category of uses is blighting," she argues, and the only solution for salvaging the space "is to cultivate an economic environment which makes more vital uses of the land profitable and logical" (Jacobs 1992, 230, 231). Where, exactly, low-margin economic uses like auto-repair shops or storage facilities should ultimately operate, however, she does not say. Perhaps in the successful city she espouses these uses simply would not exist.

Where Jacobs and Moses Meet

At this point, then, the question becomes not whether Jacobs believed cities need activist governments intervening to shape the built environment to achieve certain purposes and address specific values but rather what she believed those purposes and values, which inform a city's ultimate shape, should be. In this sense, Jacobs shares much with Moses—something her supporters have not been entirely comfortable acknowledging. To return to our initial question, what might those similarities be?

To begin with, both Moses and Jacobs viewed the built environment as the root of the problem and therefore focused their efforts on spatial transformation rather than reimagining underlying social or economic processes to mitigate against what Lefebvre saw as "the brutal demands of economic growth and competition" (Lefebvre 1996, 149). In fact, these attempts at manipulating space served to conceal the full force of the processes at play and to pathologize space into "healthy and diseased spaces" that could then be diagnosed and reconceived as "harmonious social space, normal and normalizing" (Lefebvre 1996, 99). While Jacobs and Moses, as examples of what Lefebvre might call "physicians of space" (Lefebvre 1996, 99), viscerally disagreed on what the appropriate environment should look like in the material sense, they wholeheartedly embraced the notion that private enterprise with the occasional but highly prescribed assist from public policy offered the best means for reshaping space.

In Moses's case, both Title I slum clearance and later iterations of urban renewal were based on the notion that the best solution to the prevalence of slums, and the social problems associated with them, was wholesale clearance, not piecemeal rehabilitation of individual buildings or blocks, followed by replanning and ultimately private redevelopment of public housing.

For Jacobs, the preoccupation with physical form is an obvious reaction to what she and other critics of the age viewed as the social engineering aspects of Moses's modernist agenda. Whereas Moses and others framed blight and urban decline as a housing issue and advocated for large-scale slum clearance and neighborhood renewal, Jacobs offered a more organic, do-it-yourself revitalization based on the notion that active streets, a mix of old and new buildings, vibrant small enterprise, and plenty of eyes on the street were the keys to the successful city. She disparaged the type of renewal supported by the 1954 policy of conservation and rehabilitation that replaced slum clearance, arguing for a more gradual influx of money:

> Where rehabilitation occurs in cities, because a neighborhood population is staying there while its economic condition improves, instead of leaving, this rehabilitation does not occur all at once. One of the attractions of such a neighborhood is its population stability. But all the members of a stable population do not improve their economic lot at the same time, or to the same extent. Under the urban renewal concept of rehabilitation, everyone is supposed to be able to rehabilitate, or to support rehabilitation done for them more or less at once. Those who cannot do not fit into the plan. (Jacobs 1962, 2)

Her critique might have exposed the destructive power of mass rehabilitation's catastrophic money; however, it failed to foresee the power of the fix-it-up ethos to reverberate throughout the neighborhood in a manner that inherently displaces those who for whatever reason do not have the means to participate in the process. Gradual rehabilitation surely makes economic sense for those who own real estate or their homes and can enjoy their improving prospects as the value of their property appreciates. But in a city such as New York, where the vast majority of residents do not own their own homes, those who rent ultimately bear the brunt of the neighborhood's revival, through rising rental rates and in many cases displacement.[3]

Also central to the two figures' fetishization of the built environment is their faith in the private market—again, with select government intervention here and there—to solve urban housing woes. This embrace of free enterprise, in fact, is among the most important points of convergence for Jacobs and Moses. As Ballon notes, Moses was a firm believer in the ability of the private sector to solve the middle-class housing problem (Ballon 2007, 97). Likewise, Jacobs and her fellow "bohemians" in the West Village argued that "private enterprise could do the job of development . . . just fine, and without any publicly subsidized affordable housing" (Lander 2006). In her critique of the three forms of money that "finance and shape most of the changes that occur in residential and business properties in cities," Jacobs's touchstone for public funds are the public housing projects and clearance programs born of the Moses era and the suburb-building mortgage guarantees provided by the Federal Housing Administration and what was then the Veterans Administration (Jacobs 1992, 292). These programs are prone, she notes, to behave cataclysmically, "like manifestations of malevolent climates . . . affording either searing droughts or torrential, eroding floods" (Jacobs 1992, 293). The kind of money needed for nurturing healthy neighborhoods, she asserts, the kind that supports and encourages gradual change, is in short supply.

At the heart of this relationship between space and capital, then, is what both Jacobs and Moses see as the seeds of the real estate–based economic development serving as the key to urban regeneration. Moses's approach is through the clearance of slums and blight, the segregation of public housing, and the development of civic institutions such as Lincoln Center and the United Nations. Jacobs's envisioned the house-by-house, block-by-block rehabilitation of aspiring neighborhoods. The way Robert Caro told the story in his Pulitzer Prize–winning exposé, whether standing on a bluff overlooking the "filthy shanty town" of Marble Hill (Caro 1975, 534) or walking through the "valley of ashes" that was Flushing Meadow (1083), Moses simply could not be concerned with the systemic inequities and market failures that created New York City's Hoovervilles or the homeless who lived in them. Instead, he saw blight and wasted space and was driven to erase it. Indeed, this is a portion of Caro's narrative that Ballon willingly accepts. Moses, she contends,

> understood that the dynamics of New York City real estate and the housing market would not generate affordable middle-income housing. He warned that Manhattan would become a polarized city of rich and poor unless government intervened. And he used the Title I urban renewal program to build affordable housing for teachers, nurses, garment workers, municipal employees . . . the middle class. (Ballon 2006)

Jacobs, too, envisioned a city populated by the middle class—though now made up of office workers and artists—and those aspiring to reach it.

While she bemoaned the class-stratification of suburbs where, she claimed, the lack of public life meant opportunities for mixing do not exist, she was blind to the fact that just because those opportunities exist in cities, where folks do mix, they do not mean class differences go away or that that they do not matter in material ways. Today, poor kids from any of New York City's neighborhoods can play alongside rich kids in Greenwich Village playgrounds, but their working-class parents still struggle to pay the rent and do not have health insurance.

Jacobs is not completely antagonistic to the poor. In *Death and Life* she notes the paternalistic nature of slum clearance and urban renewal programs, arguing that fixing slums is "no simple matter of supplying better housing" (Jacobs 1992, 271). She even suggests that slum residents should not be seen as victims but people capable, should they choose, of improving their own lots in life. The reason slums persist, as she sees it, is once an area begins to unslum, too many people move out too fast. Citing census figures from Greenwich Village and Boston's North End, she argues that unslumming "did not represent a replacement of the old slum population by a new and different middle-class population; it represented much of the old population moving into the middle class" (Jacobs 1992, 281). In her view, then, successful unslumming depends on the retention of enough existing residents and businesses—just not those operating businesses that represent low-economic or ruinous uses—who over time will make "modest gains," thereby gradually raising the "threshold of success or ambition" and revitalizing the neighborhood little by little (Jacobs 1992, 230, 232).

Still, she offers no concrete mechanism for making that happen, no explanation for how those who stay make the leap up in class—just a vague endorsement of organic regeneration as a means of staving off the slippery slope to perpetual slumdom. "Cities," she asserts, "grow the middle class," which in turn is "a stabilizing force in the formation of a self-diversified population" (Jacobs 1992, 282). Jacobs acknowledges that as neighborhoods improve, newcomers seeking "a place to live which is fit for city life" will want to move in, but in her estimation they only add to the diversity and contribute to the neighborhood's new standards of success (Jacobs 1992, 283). Once the residential character of the neighborhood diversifies, commercial diversification will naturally follow, and in turn "visitors and cross-use" from other neighborhoods will occur in what she portrays as an ongoing and inevitable natural process.

As such, Jacobs's lessons on unslumming provide an anecdotal counterpoint to the effects of urban renewal but not a sense of the underlying political economic causes of poverty and the role of real estate markets in the uneven creation and distribution of wealth. In fact, her assumptions rest on an unproblematic embrace of the same socioeconomic myths—in which the fruits of generated wealth naturally filter down to those who work hard and aspire to own their own homes and to be faithful, productive members of a normative society based on the principles of the capitalist system.

"The processes that occur in unslumming," she writes, "depend on the fact that a metropolitan economy, if it is working well, is constantly transforming many poor people into middle-class people, many illiterates into skilled (or even educated) people, many greenhorns into competent citizens" (Jacobs 1992, 288).[4] Of course, those metropolitan economies did not always work well, as we are painfully reminded by the regular, periodic rounds of capital crisis in 1973, 1988, the early and late 1990s, and 2008, during the sub-prime mortgage–induced collapse. What to do in those cases is just one of many unanswered scenarios in Jacobs's equation.

Eventually, Jacobs even turns paternalistic in her own right. What she describes as "perpetual slums," or areas "which show no signs of social or economic improvement," are that way because those who are smart enough, ambitious enough, and enterprising enough have already left, leaving behind only the "apathetic" and "immigrating hillbillies" whose limited economic horizons doom them to the worst urban neighborhoods (Jacobs 1992, 272–274).[5] What ultimately is to become of them if and when their neighborhoods improve is never made clear. While Jacobs decries the "slum-shifting" endemic to slum clearance of the urban renewal model, she never accounts for anyone other than those capable of hauling themselves by their bootstraps into the middle class.

Clearly, the sense of spatial determinism that resides in Jacobs's views of slums and successful cities is at the core of more contemporary efforts to foster dynamism and diversity through the built environment. As noted previously, it provides the basis for Cooper and Eckstut's vision of Battery Park City—as well as Cooper's later work with NYC2012 and the Hudson Yards master plan—and it has become a foundational element in the New Urbanist agenda. While the charter for New Urbanism claims to "recognize that physical solutions by themselves will not solve social and economic problems," it maintains, clearly drawing from Jacobs, that "economic vitality, community stability and environmental health" cannot "be sustained without a coherent and supportive framework" (Congress for the New Urbanism 2001). And Battery Park City, with its planned-in mix of uses and simulated Main Street, was consciously designed with Jacobs's precepts for generating diversity in "the air" (Cooper 2009).

But these spaces have engendered criticism in their own right. Some have argued that among those guilty of distorting Jacobs's original ideals, New Urbanists are guiltiest, reducing "her vision of corner shops and busy streets to a superficial town formula that creates the illusion of urban diversity, but masks a stifling uniformity at its core" (Ouroussoff

2006a). Much as Jacobs ignores the very real issues of poverty by privileging spatial form over social processes, New Urbanism attempts to mask social inequality simply by designing a new physical environment (Harvey 1997). Battery Park City, meanwhile has been described as an early model for the "isolated, self-enclosed patches of development"—in this case stretching along Manhattan's "once-forgotten waterfront"—that serve as "postindustrial service centers planned to attract the young urban professionals and double-income childless couples increasingly populating the city" (Boyer 1992, 183–184).

Jacobs and Gentrification

While a clear—if contested—case can be made for the relationship between Jacobs's fix-it-up-ethos and the rehabilitation orientation of early neighborhood-scale gentrification, her ideas figure prominently in more recent manifestations of the process as well.[6] With the publication of *The Death and Life of Great American Cities*, Jacobs would add her voice to those who as early as the 1960s identified New York City's working waterfront as a "wasted asset" (Jacobs 1992, 159), and she called for its redevelopment as a means of diversifying and therefore catalyzing the economic development of Lower Manhattan. Pointing to the area's monochrome devotion to the financial and office sectors and a surrounding "ring of stagnation, decay and vacancies," Jacobs argued that a "great marine museum," complete with embarkation points for tour boats and seafood restaurants—"as glamorous and salty as art can make them"—would draw residents, corporations, and tourists (Jacobs 1992, 155). Further inland, she suggested a specialized marine library branch, free aquarium, and inexpensive opera and theater (Jacobs 1992, 159) would serve to attract visitors in the late afternoon and on weekends to counter the intensive day use generated by the denizens of the area's offices. As the district "livens up" during the off hours, Jacobs reasoned, new residential use would "appear spontaneously" (Jacobs 1992, 160).

A little over two decades later, Jacobs's prescription for the area would find expression in the creation of South Street Seaport, a private redevelopment project on the East River just north of Manhattan's Financial District. Here, early nineteenth-century counting houses were rehabilitated as museums, boutique shops, and restaurants, transforming a "leftover space of derelict structures" from New York City's mercantile days into an "upscale marketplace catering" to Wall Street workers, tourists, and urban adventurers (Boyer 1992, 181). Designated a historic district, complete with berths for renovated ships evoking the "city's maritime history," South Street Seaport was a further iteration of the Jacobs-inspired inner-city marketplace as originally conceived by shopping center developer James Rouse and previously implemented in Boston's Faneuil Hall Marketplace; South Street Market in nearby Waltham, Massachusetts; and Baltimore's Harbor Place. Marketed as "leisure-time zones combining shopping and entertainment with office and residential development" (Boyer 1992, 181), these antimodern urban renewal projects joined Battery Park City and the emerging New Urbanism movement in drawing from Jacobs's core precepts while appealing to a sense of nostalgia and referencing a perceived historic heyday to convey new urban aspirations.[7]

Whether they have proved successful, however, depends on one's point of view. To those inheritors of Jacobs's mantle who designed and planned these redevelopment schemes, successful neighborhoods could be defined by the quality of life they offered, and a good, or at least acceptable, quality of life was determined by a decidedly class-oriented notion of access to certain amenities—open space, restaurants, shops, cafés, and museums. Viewed from the angle of these designers and planners, such amenities represented Jacobs's prescription for a mix of diverse land uses, and in keeping with her logic they would attract a higher standard of potential residents, spurring additional investment. As planning historian David Gordon notes in his detailing of the story of the development of Battery Park City, public spaces were completed first, "in advance of private development in order to increase the value of the adjacent sites" and shape "the image of the project to the rest of the city and to potential private investors" (Gordon 1997, 81).[8]

These redevelopment projects also became central elements, weapons in a sense, in the competitive location game being played out between cities within the emerging form of global urbanism. If a city was to attract the finance, advertising, insurance, fashion, design, and art firms that ensured its membership in the network of select global cities, it had to market itself. And design codes and architectural patterns spoke the language of livability (Miles 2000). With local governments directing the nature of redevelopment through zoning regulations and design guidelines, "architects and artists" in places like Battery Park City, a refurbished Times Square, and South Street Seaport "focused their designs to appeal to the tastes of white-collar workers and upper-middle class consumers" (Boyer 1992, 193).

To critics, however, these redevelopment projects suggested simulacrums of authenticity (Fainstein 2005b) that romanticize the city's past even as they erase swaths of its working-class history and gloss over very real social issues by designing out socioeconomic—and by extension racial—diversity (Boyer 1992; Miles 2000). Just as the shops in South Street Seaport beckon to a certain class of clientele, in Battery Park City, which is owned and operated by a public-benefit corporation created by the state of New York, geography has been deployed in the creation and ongoing enforcement of a middle- and upper-class enclave. In a deal brokered to ensure the flow of private investment and development interest, the Battery Park City Authority (BPCA) was exempted from including any affordable housing in its development plans (Gordon 1997). Instead, the BPCA was permitted to use revenues—initially projected, eventually real—to finance the rehabilitation and/or construction of low-income housing in Harlem and the Bronx, those faraway, largely minority and low-income "neighborhoods with the greatest need" (Gordon 1997, 101).[9] As a result, by 2000, 74.4 percent of residents of Battery Park City were white, compared with 45 percent citywide (U.S. Bureau of the Census 2000a); the median family income was $136,950, compared with $41,887 for all of New York City; and 67 percent of annual family incomes were more than $100,000, compared with 15.3 percent for the city as a whole (U.S. Bureau of the Census 2000b).

Nonmembers of the middle and upper classes continue to feel the effects of Jacobs's influence on redevelopment in other, very concrete, ways as well. To Jacobs, reinvestment in a neighborhood by the business community was an essential element of the unslumming process and a critical driver of desired diversity. While in her day that reinvestment might have taken the form of small entrepreneurs—the barber, the hardware store owner, and the shoemaker celebrated in *Death and Life*—by the last decade of the twentieth century, it was more likely to appear in the form of chain retail stores and restaurants. Indeed, to many residents of economically marginalized neighborhoods long abandoned by investment capital, the arrival of a corner Starbuck's coffee house or neighborhood Dunkin' Donuts franchise signifies a rediscovery by the wider world. But while the inexorable spread of coffee houses whose familiar symbols—the commonplace logos, easily identifiable color schemes, and trademark designs that seem to be *everywhere*—certainly indicates an infusion of capital, it also serves as a forceful reminder that access to mainstream consumerism and its related retail amenities have become central to the American notion of quality of life (Sutton 2008). At the same time, the ubiquity and calculated sameness of chain expansion threatens to flatten the urban streetscape, rendering once ethnically and culturally iconic boulevards, such as 125th Street in Harlem, virtually indistinguishable from most other streets in most parts of any other city.

Presumably, given her elevation of diversity to a foundational characteristic of urban success, Jacobs would detest this creeping homogenization of the built environment as well as the ethnic, cultural, and culinary landscapes, even as she would applaud the arrival of new streams of investment. In fact, Jacobs acknowledged the potential for the "self-destruction of diversity" that unchecked neighborhood revitalization could create (Jacobs 1992, 331). In her later years she even seemed to recognize the direct relationship between the processes she advocated and the types of neighborhoods they produced, conceding that gentrification "can turn 'vicious and excessive' when demand for improved neighborhoods has outrun supply" (Rochon 2007, 42). As important as increasing the availability of desirable neighborhoods, she ultimately acknowledged, is a conscious and steadfast commitment to engendering class and racial diversity. Still, that recognition feels incomplete—arrived at in hindsight—and it suggests that Jacobs lacked "awareness of capital in the broadest sense" (Zukin 2010, 18) and only understood the destructive potential of her ideals once they were unleashed. Robert Yaro of the Regional Plan Association tells the story of attending a forum where he met Jacobs on what would be her last visit to New York before she died and asked her about the transformation of Greenwich Village. "I said the neighborhood has been protected but the characters haven't," Yaro recalled (Yaro 2008). "It gentrified. I asked her, 'How do you deal with that?' She said, 'Well, I don't think it will last.'"

Of course in a certain sense the issue is not whether Jacobs can be read as promoting gentrification. Perhaps a more relevant and compelling concern is that her views have been mobilized by others in ways that displace and marginalize the poor in the name of building a better city. To be fair, Jacobs cannot be held fully accountable for the ways her principles and ideals have been put into action. Some she clearly would not condone. Likewise, Jacobs never claimed to be all seeing or all knowing, and many others have shared her views about restoring cities. Still, her voice remains the most resonant, and looking back with the benefit of hindsight, it seems she was far more accurate in her critique of modernist planning than in her diagnosis of the nature of urban space. One of the things she clearly overlooked, or possibly just failed to foresee, was the dynamics of a speculative real estate market naturally inclined toward the accumulation of wealth. At any rate, in the end her ideals are inherent in contemporary forms of gentrification, propelling it forward in places like Battery Park City and in the principles of the creative class and New Urbanism.

Moses and the Middle-Class City

Less widely considered, though perhaps more cleanly outlined, is Moses's contribution to the historic evolution of gentrification. In many ways Moses can be regarded as the embodiment of the rhythms of capital as it restlessly remade the New York City landscape throughout the middle of the twentieth century, ripping out the old to make way for the new in a process that economist and political scientist Joseph Schumpeter had recognized—and others would further refine—as capitalism's compulsion toward creative destruction. In his essay "Between Space and Time: Reflections on the Geographical Imagination," geographer David Harvey reflects on how the civic planner Baron Haussmann sought to transform mid-nineteenth-century Paris into a cleaner, safer, and more easily controlled city by imposing "an entirely new conception of space into the fabric of the city" (Harvey 1990b, 426).

Driven—much like Moses would be a century later—to reengineer the city through a frenzy of construction that turned narrow streets into wide boulevards, reshaped existing parks, and erected new monumental public buildings, Haussmann pursued his plans with single-minded resolve, destroying much of the city's medieval character and uprooting its working class. To Harvey such projects can be seen as the inevitable hallmarks of capitalist expansion or more precisely as the temporal and spatial upheavals that entail "not only the destruction of ways of life and social practices built around preceding time-space systems, but the 'creative destruction' of a wide range of physical assets embedded in the landscape" (Harvey 1990b, 425). Indeed, within the inexorable advance of capitalist accumulation, "whole landscapes have had to be destroyed in order to make way for the creation of the new" (Harvey 1990b, 426). More recently, efforts such as urban renewal and regeneration have assumed major roles in the process as developers and financial institutions have fought for the means to, in Harvey's terms, "recolonize" what they view as declining but still strategic city centers (Harvey 1990b, 421).

To be sure, Moses's legacy was fashioned on its bearer's ability to creatively destroy on a spectacular scale, prompting some to liken him to his predecessor in Paris (see Jackson 2007; King 2007; and Harvey 1990a). Clearly, Moses saw much in Haussmann he admired—"Haussmann's great merit lay in the fact that he was both able and willing to grasp the entire problem," he wrote (Moses 1942, 58)—and in Haussmann he found inspiration for his own approach to modernizing the city and financing his schemes. As a particularly effective practitioner of the modernist project, Moses viewed the past as an impediment, its outdated buildings and insufficient infrastructure physical weights trapping the city in time, anchors to be transcended through progress. And like Haussmann, Moses possessed the political skills and imperturbable resolve to bend the city to his singular vision of the future. With federally funded Title I and other urban renewal programs emerging as predominant strategies for the absorption of surplus capital during the postwar period, Moses literally paved the way for a massive reshaping of New York City along class lines.[10]

At the heart of the Title I enterprise was a land subsidy known as the write-down. Through the write-down, the federal government would cover two-thirds of the losses a developer incurred in assembling and clearing land for private redevelopment. Cities picked up the other third under the assumption that they would recoup those moneys through higher tax revenues (Ballon 2007, 97). Through these write-downs, then, the state assembled properties "at a 'fair-market value'" and supplied them to developers at subsidized prices, making possible the "capital devalorization" that established the "broad conditions" for stimulating private market "redevelopment, rehabilitation and land use conversion" that marked urban renewal efforts (Smith 1996, 70).

While in certain ways Moses tried to link Title I dollars to the construction of public housing,[11] the program was explicitly conceived to promote private redevelopment of blighted areas. It was not intended as a means for providing housing for the displaced. And the real estate economics of the time—high construction costs, debt service payments, and taxes—ensured that the market-rate housing produced by Title I was "well beyond the reach of the middle class," not to mention those of lesser means (Ballon 2007, 97). As a result, existing residents of neighborhoods slated for Title I clearance rarely could afford the new apartments created where their homes once stood, and thus they were forced to move; in effect, Moses's Title I projects gentrified whole neighborhoods long before the term was even conceived (Ballon 2007, 102).

Similarly, the Housing Act of 1949, which initiated federal urban renewal legislation, did not mandate land use restrictions for sites of former residential slums and therefore did not require replacing existing housing with new housing. Moses would use this opening to mobilize federal funds for the clearance not only of slums but parts of the city devoted to manufacturing to make room for the civic institutions that he held were crucial to New York City's future as a preeminent global capital, even as it meant a net loss of lower-class housing and jobs (Ballon 2007, 108). From 1945 to 1955 along the East River alone, Moses's Title I projects cleared the way for the United Nations, Stuyvesant Town, Peter Cooper Village, NYU-Bellevue, public housing in Corlears Hook, and the Brooklyn Civic Center at the cost of at least 18,000 blue-collar jobs. While a relatively small percentage of the city's 3.5 million total jobs at the time, those lost jobs delivered "a body blow to the factory economy" (Schwartz 1993, 239).

The program also did not contribute funds for rehabilitating buildings and neighborhoods, privileging instead a "bulldoze and build" mentality (Ballon 2007, 102). Only passage of the 1954 amendment to Title I allowed cities to hatch alternative schemes and shift from urban redevelopment to urban renewal through rehabilitation (Ballon 2007, 109). Even though this new mass attack on slums also drew Jacobs's derision for its catastrophic potential, it did denote the end of the era of wholesale clearance and helped usher in a new, though at least to some equally destructive, approach more closely aligned with the notions of incremental change and "the self-healing powers" that Jacobs extolled (Ballon 2007, 112).

Furthermore, Moses fundamentally altered the very nature of urbanism, much as Haussmann had a century before, by seizing on the primacy of the urban property market as a means of "expanding the terrain of profitable capitalist activity" (Harvey 2008b, 28). By tapping into new financial institutions and tax arrangements to propel urban expansion, Moses helped pioneer debt-financing mechanisms that, while effective in assuaging the postwar capital absorption crisis, eventually and inevitably came home to haunt through the "bursting of the global property market bubble in 1973" and the subsequent fiscal bankruptcy of New York in 1975 (Harvey 2008b, 28), which amounted to a systematic meltdown of capitalist urbanism with global ramifications. Fast-forward, as Harvey suggests, to late 2008 and the rapid unraveling of the global economy following the sub-prime mortgage and housing asset-value crisis in the United States, and "the parallels with the 1970s are uncanny" (Harvey 2008b, 31).

As with planning in general, the characterizations that typically mark Jane Jacobs and Robert Moses revolve around questions of who benefits, and at whose expense? For the better part of fifty years this divide has been seen as one of dichotomizing extremes, of big versus small, of do something versus do nothing, and of Moses versus Jacobs for New York City's very soul. But those dichotomies are not anywhere as complete as we have been made to believe, and calls for a new Moses to guide New York City into the future have cast the pair in a new light, raising questions about many of the steadfast assumptions that for decades cemented Jacobs and Moses as ideological opposites. As the easy characterizations begin to fade, it becomes possible to see that those simplistic dualisms served to mask greater ideological agreements, and the insistent focus on their differences is exposed as a parochial position that makes sense only from within the naturalized, taken-for-granted logic of capital accumulation. As different as they were—and it is essential to reaffirm that in many aspects those differences were extreme as well as important—within the context of an emerging urbanism shaping cities in the wake of postwar economic restructuring, Jane Jacobs and Robert Moses found fundamental common ground in a shared ideology of building and rebuilding the city for people of greater rather than lesser means.

8

Ideas That Travel

Of course, New York City is not the only metropolis grappling with questions of urban transformation to have turned to Jane Jacobs and Robert Moses in search of ideas and inspiration. Indeed, many of the social, political, and economic forces that made New York a crucible of urban policy were at work in cities across the United States and Canada in the postwar years. So while the legacies of the two figures were cemented in New York, and their ideas about how best to build successful cities continue to resonate loudly in debates about redevelopment there, Jacobs and Moses have traveled, both literally and figuratively, influencing built environments and framing articulations of urban policy in other cities at specific times as well.

Facilitating the widespread adoption of their ideas in far-flung places has been a process of policy production and sharing originally conceived as fixed "policy transfer," or the wholesale implementation by one entity of successful strategies developed by another (Dolowitz and Marsh 1996). More recently, this notion of an efficient, one-way transfer of knowledge from producer-innovators to consumer-emulators has come to be viewed as overly simplistic, and a new formulation, characterized as "policy mobility" (Peck and Theodore 2010; McCann 2011), has emerged. In the urban sense, policy mobility can be defined as "socially produced and circulated forms of knowledge addressing how to design and govern cities that develop in, are conditioned by, travel through, connect, and shape spatial scales, networks, policy communities, and institutional contexts" (McCann 2011, 109). In this later formulation practitioners looking for answers to their own urban problems scour the globe, searching for "best practices to embrace, 'cutting edge' cities to emulate, and 'hot' experts from whom to learn" (McCann 2011, 114).

Within this view, the manner by which by policy makers adopt policies is not some simple transfer of favored models from point A to point B in a competitive marketplace of ideas. Instead, the sharing of models can be seen as the transmission of highly ideological and selective discourses imbedded with explicit sets of "rules, techniques and behaviors" (Peck and Theodore 2010, 170). These policies are often articulated as best practices that have emerged from the "right"—read ideologically sanctioned—sites by "policy peddlers and gurus" who traffic in "models that affirm and extend" "dominant paradigms" and existing power relations. These mobile policies are transmitted between "members of epistemic, expert and practice communities," but because of local variations in institutional, economic, and political contexts, they "rarely travel as complete packages" (Peck and Theodore 2010, 170–171). Instead, they arrive as "idealized abstractions" whose representational power is subject to translation, interpretation, and synthesis. In effect, such policies serve as "powerful political narratives" that legitimate and valorize existing development models (McCann 2011, 108).

The contemporary spread of neoliberal forms of urbanism—in which "creating livable and attractive environments for certain class factions as a central part of a wider economic development strategy" (McCann 2004, 1910)—has proven particularly amenable to the policy mobility idea. What urban geographers Jamie Peck and Nik Theodore describe as the "viral spread of creative city policies" offers one particularly illustrative example. As a favored policy fix of the early twenty-first century, the mobility idea was predicated on

> an array of supportive conditions and enabling networks, including: stylized, but ground-truthed claims about the underlying causes of innovation-rich growth in cities like Austin, TX and San Francisco; Richard Florida's brand of guru performativity; the easy manualization of creative-city policy techniques by consultants and other policy intermediaries; and, not least, the competitive anxieties and fiscal constraints of cities around the world. (Peck and Theodore 2010, 171)

The fact that the concept draws from ideas first articulated by Jane Jacobs certainly did not hurt, either. Still, long before Jacobs's notions of diversity and dynamism found a new home in Florida's conception of the creative city, city leaders and planners were looking to her—and her arch nemesis, Moses—for urban best practices to adopt, emulate, and adapt.[1]

Thus, Jacobs and Moses continue to stand out as particularly resonant experts from whom leaders of urban transformation have chosen to learn.

Moses in Portland: "A Shot in the Arm"

For Moses, no city outside of New York bears his physical imprint more than Portland, Oregon, where a familiar pattern of plans enacted to contend with the consequences of the past includes a mid-twentieth-century fling with Moses-style build-big modernism. In 1943, with the end of World War II on the horizon and a concomitant slowing of industrial expansion brought about by the war effort, Portland Mayor Earl Riley asked his chief planner, William Bowes, chair of the Metropolitan Planning Commission, to appoint a Portland Area Postwar Development Committee to assess the region's long-term prospects. Made up of forty-seven members drawn from the ranks of Portland's city government, banks, utilities, large retailers, manufacturers, labor unions, and real estate and construction interests, the committee's stated mission was "to study and recommend action on the problems of postwar planning for employment and healthy urban growth" (Bowes, quoted in Abbott 1983, 137).

Prior to the war, Portland had been a large city but not an especially dynamic magnet for growth. In 1940 the city's population stood at 305,000, roughly the same as it had been a decade before. Yet by 1943 the number of people living within the city limits swelled to 380,000 and over that same three-year span the greater Portland metropolitan area ballooned from 355,000 to 470,000 residents, as workers poured into the region to provide labor for its wartime industries. Shipbuilding, in particular, was a major draw. All told, Portland-area shipyards received $2.4 billion in wartime contracts, pitching "Portland headfirst into prosperity" and employing most of the area's 140,000 war-related workers in the production of more than 1,000 cargo ships, carriers, tankers, and Liberty ships (Abbott 1983, 126). At first the workers came from nearby, mainly the rural counties of Oregon and Washington. But over time, what started as a trickle became a steady stream, and local industries recruited labor from the Northwest, the plains states, and the Midwest—and eventually as far afield as Chicago and New York (Abbott 1983).

It was this influx, and the specter of all of those newcomers eventually deciding to stay, that led to the creation of the Postwar Development Committee, in February 1943. High on the committee's list of concerns was the realization that the end of the war would likely result in massive layoffs that could lead to a labor surplus of as many as seventy thousand unemployed workers and prompt a postwar recession that could result in "social stress and public burdens equated with the worst years of the Depression" (Abbott 1983, 136). Despite the seriousness and scope of those potential problems, the group spent its first seven months mired in bureaucratic dawdling before, in August, committee member Edgar Kaiser—whose three area shipyards alone supplied jobs to some one hundred thousand workers—took matters into his own hands and invited Robert Moses to give Portland "a shot in the arm" (Abbott 2010c). "These are people who know the larger ones in Washington," Bowes later recalled of the decision to call in Moses. "They know where the money is available" (Abbott 2010c).[2]

Moses, who at that point was at the height of his powers in New York, was offered $100,000 to prepare "a general report and recommendations" (Moses 1943, 7), and he and a team of "consultants"—highway, bridge, and infrastructure engineers—arrived in Portland in September. They spent only a week in the city, but the plan they produced, dubbed *Portland Improvement*, was released just two months later, and it would help set Portland's planning agenda for the following twenty-five years.

In typical Moses fashion, *Portland Improvement* was what urban historian Carl Abbott characterized on his website, the Urban West, "an infrastructure plan," a massive public works effort designed to position the city to be "economically competitive in the postwar world" (Abbott 2010c). As Moses wrote in the Director's Report to the document, the plan's recommendations were oriented toward the "expediting of needed and desirable public works to afford employment, stimulate business and help bridge the gap between the end of the war and the full resumption of private business" (Moses 1943, 7). Even at the time, with nearly two years of fighting in Europe and the Pacific still ahead, Moses foresaw a postwar world in which an increasingly global economy would shift the balance of industrial power away from the United States to newly industrializing nations. He also pinpointed the resulting degree to which surviving American industries would need to be "ruthlessly overhauled and cut down" to compete with countries that had "a much lower wage and living standard" (Moses 1943, 9). Just as important, however, he recognized the vast potential for new infrastructure projects not only to absorb the army of workers sure to be cast adrift by inevitable demobilization but also to aggressively reshape the city for its role in what he foresaw as the emerging urbanization of the economy. Warning that the plan he proposed did not constitute work relief or a return to the "boondoggling, leaf raking and desert projects" executed by "various alphabetical agencies" during the Depression, he insisted that it represented a limited and temporary government intervention that would create the conditions for a reinvigorated private sphere (Moses 1943, 19). "The program we propose," he intoned in the Director's Report, "does not represent mere enthusiasm for public construction. It is no substitute for private enterprise" (Moses 1943, 16). Still, it called for a $60 million construction program employing up to twenty thousand workers for up to two years.

At the plan's heart, in keeping with Moses's notion of an auto-oriented "Great City" at the center of the urban future, was the "road, whether it be a highway, a parkway or a bridge" (Bianco 2001, 102), and it focused on rationalizing traffic flow and contending with congestion through the construction of a series of limited-access freeways and widened and improved bridges. The price tag included $20 million for a new downtown freeway loop that would encircle the central business district, more than $5 million for improving city streets, and $8 million for highways outside the city. It also proposed $20 million in sanitation, public buildings, port and school construction, and sewer upgrades, including $10 million for a sewage disposal system to reduce pollution of the Willamette River. Moses's signature commitment to parks was evident as well, and here *Portland Improvement* drew on a long, though largely unrealized, lineage of previous planning efforts. Included in the $6.2 million *Portland Improvement* earmarked for expanding the city's public parks were new green spaces on the city's blighted industrial waterfront—first called for in a 1932 plan drafted by Harland Bartholomew, a planning consultant from St. Louis—and a "Forest Park" on the steep hillsides of the city's western border that was originally proposed in 1903 by John Charles Olmsted, the nephew and adopted son of Frederick Law Olmsted.

In fact, between 1903 and 1938 a handful of outside consultants were brought to Portland to produce plans for beautifying and otherwise enhancing the city's built environment. Ultimately, though, each of these recommendations was deemed too expensive or radical, and all were shelved by the city's traditionally conservative civic leadership. Olmsted's 1903 plan, which, in the tradition of his famous uncle, proposed "a network of open spaces that vary in use and is connected by a system of parkways and boulevards" (City of Portland Bureau of Planning 2008, 62), was followed in 1912 with a proposal by Daniel Burnham's protégé, Edward Bennett. This plan was based on projections that the city would one day grow to two million residents. Drawing from the preoccupations of the City Beautiful Movement, it called for the construction of new civic centers, parks, and rail and water terminals. Next, in 1921 came the Cheney Plan, a more limited and pragmatic effort conceived by World War I housing expert Charles Cheney to address the difficulties in implementing the more expensive aspects of the Bennett Plan. It in turn, was followed the Bartholomew Report, with its waterfront revitalization initiative.

Then in 1938, a group known as the Northwest Regional Council, "a private advocacy group dedicated to the dissemination of information about the social, economic and governmental problems of the Northwest," invited the urban thinker and social commentator Lewis Mumford to

Portland "in order to observe and critically appraise the growth and development of the region" (Mumford, quoted in Bianco 2001, 96). One year later Mumford produced the report *Regional Planning in the Pacific Northwest*, which outlined his philosophy of planning at that time. It contained few specific recommendations or concrete plans, though it did call for the creation of a Columbia River Planning Authority to transcend the "artificial division" separating Portland from nearby communities in Washington State and coordinate planning on a regional scale. Among the proposed Planning Authority's charges would be overseeing growth through planned greenbelt towns (Bianco 2001, 98). In the end, though, these proposals proved too vague and Mumford's approach lacked enough clear, tangible benefits to win over the city's cautious leaders.

Clearly aware of Portlanders history of commissioning plans "but rarely acting on the advice of consultants they brought to town" (Bianco 2001, 99), Moses employed a trusted tactic to convince city leaders to embrace *Portland Improvement*: the creation of a master narrative laced with intimations of potential threats to the city's future prospects should his proposals go unrealized. Portland, he argued, was not the only city facing a postwar employment problem. But, he emphasized, failure to undertake the massive construction program his team had proposed, "while there is still time" (Moses 1943, 8), would mean that Portland "must face the threat" of "the long arm of the federal government" reaching out from Washington, D.C., at the expense of private enterprise. He played on still-fresh memories of immense Depression-era federal employment programs and emerging fears of state-sponsored socialism to warn of government control of the fruits of individual initiative and hard work. "Make no mistake about it," Moses wrote:

> Th[e] alternative is just straight work relief with home relief for those who can't work at all, in a volume and with a concentration never attempted before even in the depth of the depression, together with a tremendous expansion of social security, especially unemployment insurance and large bonuses for veterans. It is hardly necessary to say that every sane person wants to avoid a repetition of the relief system which began with the CWA in the fall of 1933 and lasted in one manifestation or another . . . for the better part of seven years. (Moses 1943, 19)

Suggesting that it was "astonishing" that such a "progressive" community as Portland "should allow the unregulated mixture of all sorts of commercial, industrial, residential and recreational uses," and cautioning that all the other proposed improvements would fail within Portland's existing land use regimen, Moses also called for "sounder and stricter zoning regulations," in part as a means of safeguarding property values and securing municipal tax revenues (Moses 1943, 12).

In May 1944 Portlanders took those warnings to heart and overwhelmingly approved $19 million in bonds to raise the revenues for many of the projects proposed in the *Portland Improvement* report. Ultimately, they embraced nearly all of Moses's recommendations, although they did not tackle, much less complete, most of them for decades. The inner beltway was built, but it was not finished until the construction of the I-5 and I-405 freeway loops in the 1970s. Likewise, the massive 902-foot-long, 6,000-ton Fremont Bridge across the Willamette River was finished in 1973. The conversion of a portion of Portland's industrial waterfront into green space was realized with the opening of Tom McCall Waterfront Park in the 1970s, and sewer improvements, bridge improvements, new schools, bus and train stations, and a civic center housing the Multnomah County Justice Center, the Portland Building, and City Hall all followed as well. One project completed in a more timely fashion was Forest Park, which was dedicated in 1948.

It is important to keep in mind, however, that Moses was not just about any one, or even any combination, of individual projects. Rather, he was far more concerned about their cumulative effect, and his goal was to shape the course of the future through a transformation of the built environment. Moses did not impose modernist planning on Portland. The city had created a housing authority that began planning for public housing in 1941 and was actively engaged in urban renewal by the early 1940s. Furthermore, the automobile was already so central to the city's emerging form that by the mid-1930s its planners defined their jobs as "traffic engineering" (Abbott 1983, 122). What Moses did was encourage Portlanders with his modernist discourse, assuring them that they were "prepared . . . to face the future with unclouded vision and with a determination to meet the challenge" (Moses 1943, 7). Of course, this new urban vision would have profound economic and social ramifications well beyond Portland— or even New York City—and the highways and urban infrastructure that Moses built or promoted. As geographer David Harvey points out, by focusing on redeveloping the region, rather than just the city, Moses forever changed the scale of urbanization:

> Through a system of debt-financed highways and total re-engineering (using new construction technologies pioneered during the war) not just of the city but of the whole metropolitan region, he defined a way to absorb the capital and labour surpluses profitably. This process of suburbanisation, when taken nationwide through the geographical expansion of capitalist development into the American south and west, played a crucial role

in the stabilization of not only the U.S. economy but also U.S.-centered global capitalism after the war. (Harvey 2010, 169)

Where, Harvey asks, "would the capital surplus have gone" had it not been for the transformation of metropolitan regions—from New York City to Chicago, Los Angeles, and other cities of that "ilk"—after 1945 (Harvey 2010, 169)?

With *Portland Improvement*, Moses helped set Portland on this same path, and by the turn of the twenty-first century it had emerged as the dynamic heart of a thriving, economically diverse region.[3] In the process, however, the old Portland had to go, just as the old New York City had gone before it, and many of the projects within *Portland Improvement* resulted in cleansing the city of poor and immigrant neighborhoods. The I-205 portion of the inner freeway loop swung south of downtown, displacing Jewish and Italian residents in South Portland neighborhoods adjacent to areas that had already been cleared by urban renewal. On the east side of the Willamette River, a section of I-5 knifed through an African American neighborhood that was designated for slum clearance to make way for the Memorial Coliseum and Emanuel Hospital (Abbott 2010b).

In the end, Portland's mid-century civic leaders were every bit as amenable to Moses's road map to the future as their colleagues in New York. They enthusiastically embraced many of his projects because they saw them as crucial to the revitalization of Portland's downtown as well as the growth of the greater metropolitan area. Indeed, as Abbott has written, Moses gave Portland's wartime civic leadership exactly what it wanted (Abbott 2010c). Echoing arguments—though not the redemptive claims—made by Ballon and Jackson in relation to the rehabilitation of Moses in New York City, Abbott points out that most contemporary Portlanders would find it hard to imagine how their city would function without the roads, bridges, parks, and infrastructural improvements that Moses said would be so crucial to its postwar success (Abbott 2010a). Others in the Portland planning sphere largely share that tempered view, expressing little of the outright acrimony that the debate over Moses's lasting legacy produces in New York.

Chet Orloff, an urban historian and a one-time member of the Portland Planning Commission, says, "To give Robert Moses credit, he did get Portlanders thinking and, ultimately, acting big, even though we ended up building some extremely damaging roads." Orloff goes on to say:

> He also got Portlanders, who were very conservative going into WWII, to begin to think about the need for more public infrastructure (parks, schools, bridges, roads) at a time when the prevailing attitude was to hope that all the people who had moved

here in the early '40s would move back to Arkansas [or wherever else they had come from]. He advised Portland's leaders to be realistic and plan for these people to stay. (Orloff 2010)

Over time, however, Portlanders—in step with urbanists and city dwellers across the country—would turn their backs on the modernist paradigm in planning to embrace a more organic, "neotraditional" model of city building. Originally espoused by Mumford, the resulting planning "ethos," according to Abbott, represented a rejection of large-scale, Moses-style highway and infrastructure projects (Abbott 2010a), and, from the 1960s onward, Portland, in effect, would become a laboratory for an emerging new urbanism and civic activism that in many ways is reflective of Jacobs and the precepts for a successful city that she so effectively set forth in *The Death and Life of Great American Cities*.

"We (meaning most planning-savvy or political leftish Portlanders) are extremely proud of removing one 1940s expressway (Harbor Drive) and killing new freeway construction after the early 1970s, including the so-called Mount Hood Freeway through close-in neighborhoods in SE Portland in the 1970s and the proposed Westside Bypass in the western suburbs more recently," Abbott explains (2010a).

But even with the victory of this new form of thinking about the city, what Abbott describes as "Jacobsian," and in spite of Portlanders' rejection of—and according to Abbott, near amnesia regarding—his influence, Moses continued to resonate in Portland's planning politics (Abbott 2010a). As Orloff contends, perhaps Moses's greatest "contribution" was "as a foil," his plans and proposals invigorating debate and helping produce the more neighborhood-based approach that holds sway today (Orloff 2010). Indeed, aspects of the Jacobs versus Moses dialectic continued to inform urban planning in Portland, though there they were held stridently at bay, de-personified and just below the surface by the complete triumph of an evolved, community-oriented, and forward-thinking brand of urbanism that features light rail systems, bike lanes, no-growth boundaries, and progressive politics. In Portland today, according to a 2010 promotional brochure, members of the creative class, with their artistic and entrepreneurial energies, are "migrating here to craft the American Dream by hand" (Portland State University College of Urban and Public Affairs 2010). Whether drawing from Jacobs directly or interpreting and adapting her views to fit contemporary conditions, Portland has become the image of the livable city-region, a "walkable, sustainable, green, cool, micro-entrepreneurial city" (Abbott 2010a) whose view of itself is captured in bumper stickers proclaiming "KEEP PORTLAND WEIRD."

"More generally, people in Portland think that what we do best is to accumulate a series of smaller scale success stories that build up to a livable everyday environment," Abbott explains. "Whether we live up to our reputation is an entirely different question, of course, but that's how we present ourselves" (2010a).

To be sure, in spite of that carefully crafted image, Portlanders have found themselves facing some of the same intransigent twenty-first-century problems as many other urban areas. Oregon's adoption of statewide urban growth regulations in 1973, for instance, has put a premium on land within designated urban growth boundaries. The resulting development stresses, in conjunction with the influx of the creative classes and increasing strain on employment and wages, has exerted tremendous upward pressure on land values, rents, and real estate prices (Nelson et al. 2002). As a result, poorer residents have been pushed to the periphery, out of Portland proper and into the older suburbs (Abbott 2010b). A 2007 study of equity conditions conducted by the Coalition for a Livable Future, a Portland-based research, advocacy, and education organization, found, for instance, that only eight of 225 metropolitan neighborhoods examined were "'affordable' to households making no more than the region's median income" (Coalition for a Livable Future 2007, 97). Rising housing costs, the study also found, affected more than just home buyers. Adjusting for inflation, the median rent for the region rose 16.5 percent between 1990 and 2000, and by 2000, 40 percent of area households were spending at least 30 percent of their incomes on housing (Coalition for a Livable Future 2007, 97). The incidence of child poverty, meanwhile, had moved beyond Portland's city limits and was now concentrated in Southeast Portland and East Multnomah County (Coalition for a Livable Future 2007, 97). Being hip and trendy comes at a price, and gentrification, Abbott contends, "is certainly a concern" (2010b).

Portlanders were also discovering the limits of the small-scale approach for dealing with issues of regional reach. In 2010 one ongoing development debate embroiling the greater-Portland area concerned a proposed $3.6 billion I-5 Columbia River Crossing project to replace two aging Moses-conceived bridges that connect Portland to nearby Vancouver, Washington, with a single twelve-lane automobile and light rail span. After more than a decade of discussion, political wrangling, and near-constant refinement, the project continued to be bedeviled by questions of cost, design, scale, environmental impact, and ultimately who was in charge of shepherding the project through the morass of competing claims to completion. "Should it be Moses-sized as favored by the two state transportation departments, or more modest?" Abbott asked, referencing a multiagency, cross-state, and distinctly un-Moses-like decision-making process disparaged by some as management by committee. But while some Portlanders pined for a Moses-like figure, one who would be able to cut through layers of bureaucracy and the mélange of competing interests to build the bridge and deal with the area's other pressing problems,[4] Moses himself remained "in the doghouse among Portland planners. I don't think anyone would try/dare to invoke R[obert] M[oses] in favor of the big project" (Abbott 2010a).

Elsewhere, though, influential voices in planning and urban design were doing exactly that, wistfully appealing to Moses's legacy in regard to stalled or stymied projects and redevelopment plans. In the spring of 2007, with the Moses exhibits and Ballon and Jackson's book generating renewed attention to the power broker's legacy, *San Francisco Chronicle* urban design critic John King encouraged readers trying to "understand the renewed respect" for "the long-detested planning czar of mid-century New York" to look no further than the Bay Area's own Bay Bridge. Heavily damaged in the Loma Prieta earthquake in 1989, a section of the bridge between Oakland and Yerba Buena had for years been slated for replacement. But, King reminded his readers, "Bay Area politicians and activists demanded a full-blown public process." Add a meddling state bureaucracy, King continued, and almost two decades later the price tag for the project had grown to $5 billion and best-case scenarios had it opening in 2013, more than eight years behind schedule. "From this perspective, in which it seems that everyone has veto power and no one is in charge," King concluded, "Moses can no longer be seen as the neighborhood wrecker portrayed in Robert Caro's 1974 classic, 'The Power Broker: Robert Moses and the Fall of New York'" (King 2007, E6).

In a similar vein, culture critic Philip Kennicott referred to long-running debates over expansion of the Washington, D.C., Metro system in his review of the Moses exhibition. Characterizing Moses as the classic "git'r done man," Kennicott reelevated him to membership in a select club of power brokers "whose lesser children include political figures as disparate as Donald Rumsfeld, Mitt Romney and Eliot Spitzer." Today's cities, Kennicott continued, "need massive new kinds of infrastructure, built quickly. . . . And very likely, cities like New York will need a new Robert Moses" (Kennicott 2007, NO1).

Once seemingly banished for good to planning exile, Moses was making a twenty-first-century comeback.

Mother Jacobs and Liberal Urbanism in Toronto

If mid-1940s Portland represents Robert Moses's non–New York moment, then late-twentieth-century Toronto is Jane Jacobs's. There, against a backdrop of Moses-scale proposals and projects, Jacobs picked up where she left off when she and her family moved from New York City in 1968.

As in New York and Portland, civic leaders in postwar metropolitan Toronto were preoccupied with economic expansion, and in their case, at least, "growth was the unquestioned goal" (Klemek 2008a, 319). In 1943 the city adopted a Master Plan, its first, in which leaders recognized that future expansion would have to occur outside the built city's existing limits. To overcome opposition from the surrounding suburbs, which had their own interests in mind, a metropolitan government—the Municipality of Metropolitan Toronto, or Metro Toronto as it came to be known—was established in 1953. Individual municipalities retained control over services such as police and fire departments, libraries, and public health, while Metro Toronto took charge of regional planning, public transportation, housing, metropolitan parks, and major infrastructural projects. Throughout the 1950s and 1960s, Metro Toronto's planners focused on modernizing the city's transportation system, extending its freeways, building parks, and increasing the available housing stock, including the construction of towers-in-the-park public projects. Like Portland, Toronto was a relatively small city at the outbreak of World War II, but by the late 1960s the metropolitan region was experiencing its own modernist overhaul, with its own Robert Moses—Frederick Gardiner, the Metro Toronto Council's first chair—in charge.

Almost immediately upon arriving in Toronto, Jacobs—armed with what historian Christopher Klemek calls her already "well-honed antiexpressway arguments"—joined the battle against this highway-oriented "urban renewal order," most famously through opposition to the construction of the Spadina Expressway, a proposed six-lane freeway that was slated to slice through her adopted neighborhood, the Annex (Klemek 2008a, 320). With Jacobs helping lead the charge, the Spadina scheme was defeated in 1971, and soon she was a celebrity in her new home: In 1972 the *Toronto Citizen* ran a photo of her shopping for green peppers at the Karma Co-op, and in 1988 she was pictured in the *Toronto Star* taking a harbor tour alongside Queen Beatrix of the Netherlands and Toronto Mayor Art Eggleton. Over the course of three decades, she would become, in the words of the online magazine *Torontoist*, "something of a mother-figure to the city of Toronto," her precepts indelibly etched in its built environment and her ideas permeating the city's take on itself (Dotan 2009). In 2008, May 4 was officially set aside as Jane Jacobs Day in celebration of her birth.

Still, Jacobs did not so much revolutionize planning in Toronto as she gave voice and intellectual stature to what many there already believed in and were already fighting for. The grassroots effort she helped organize in opposition to the Spadina Expressway served to propel a liberal reform movement to political power in 1972, but by the early 1970s she had moved on from writing about the failures of central planning and urban form to exploring the city's growing role in the larger economy.[5]

Even so, Jacobs would become a direct and influential force in Metro Toronto's post-Gardiner approach to the built environment even though she never held public office or served in any official planning capacity. Her initial, and perhaps most-lasting, contribution came during the administration of Mayor David Crombie, a reformer who held office from 1972 to 1978. In 1972, in response to earlier plans to bulldoze a portion of downtown Toronto to make way for office projects, shopping malls, and high-rise, high-density apartment complexes, Crombie's administration produced a Central Area Plan that mirrored many of the antimodernist prescriptions Jacobs's had proposed in *Death and Life*. The plan promoted public transportation instead of new highways, encouraged community input in local decisions, and featured a moratorium on megaproject development, including a forty-foot height limit on new buildings.

Another signature moment in the reform movement's approach to the built environment came with plans for the redevelopment of St. Lawrence, a former industrial area adjacent to downtown Toronto. Originally slated for wholesale renewal, in the mid-1970s the Crombie administration devised an alternative redevelopment proposal that also drew directly from the precepts for urban livability that Jacobs had identified a decade earlier—small blocks, active public spaces, mixed use, and diversity. It called for reconnecting the district with the rest of the city by creating a new, mixed-use, but predominately residential neighborhood modeled on the aesthetics of nineteenth-century Toronto. "It was really creating a new piece of the city fabric," says Ken Greenberg, a Toronto architect and former director of Toronto's Urban Design Department from 1977 to 1987 (Greenberg 2010). It also promoted the creation of mixed-income neighborhoods—"socially mixed public housing," in the local parlance—instead of isolating the poor in vast low-income housing projects (August 2008).

Even after the reform period ended, Jacobs would continue to exert a powerful pull on Toronto's urban landscape. In the late 1990s she again played a firsthand role in a major city project by helping shape conditions for the redevelopment of the King West and East neighborhoods, two downtown districts that together formed a four-hundred-acre swath of leftover industrial land that had been largely abandoned as local industry gave in to the forces of globalization. At the time, city zoning regulations called for keeping the area industrial, but Jacobs and others, including Greenberg, argued for eliminating land-use restrictions altogether. "We took a page straight from *Death and Life*," Greenberg says. "We said, 'Let's get out of the land-use zoning business.' It was pure Jane, allowing things to happen" (Greenberg 2010). With zoning restrictions removed, market forces were freed to steer the resulting redevelopment, and by the turn of the twenty-first century, King West and East had emerged as "highly desirable urban lifestyle communities" of converted loft-style condos, upscale shopping, and entertainment (City of Toronto 2002).

Over time, Jacobs's prescriptions for converting such remnants of Toronto's industrial past into socially mixed, multiuse neighborhoods have became entrenched in the city's larger redevelopment agenda, including its approach to overhauling Toronto's vast public housing system. In the wake of her critique of urban renewal, high-rise housing became anathema to city planners. In response, planners in Toronto began to explore ways of weaving the massive, single-use housing projects into the fabric of the city, a strategy that would be dubbed the "Toronto approach" and elsewhere eventually give rise to New Urbanist–inspired redevelopment. By the summer of 2010, the same Jacobsian principles that found expression in St. Lawrence and King West and East were being applied in Toronto's Regent Park, a sixty-nine-acre former public housing complex that was being demolished and rebuilt as a mixed-use, mixed-income residential neighborhood of mostly privately owned condominiums and rental properties. Simple in nature, the six-phase fifteen-year plan called for running new roads through the project as a means of reconnecting it with the surrounding city's street grid and as a way of filling the barren gaps between individual buildings with additional housing, amenities, and commercial spaces.

Eventually, Jacobs's basic precepts for building a successful city became formalized within Toronto's overall planning agenda. In 2002 the Toronto City Council produced an "Official Plan" that outlined what would be the city's antisprawl, transportation-oriented, and human-scale approach to development for the following thirty years. At the time of the plan's passage, an eighty-six-year-old Jacobs, who was confined to a wheelchair, was on hand "to bestow her blessing" (Hess 2010). One year later, Toronto's city council adopted a ten-year "Culture Plan for the Creative City" that outlined sixty-three recommendations for "positioning Toronto as an international culture capital" with "culture at the heart of the city's economic and social agenda" (City of Toronto 2003). Drawing directly from Richard Florida's concept of the creative city—and by extension the Jacobsian precepts that he adopted—the plan focused on marshaling public and private resources to enhance cultural dynamism and diversity, preserve Toronto's built heritage, and attract the "right type" of residents: "the young, cool, educated, high-value-added worker of the knowledge economy" (Boudreau, Keil, and Young 2009, 183). Taken together, the two plans represented a Jacobs-inspired urbanism that prized diversity as the city's defining characteristic and valued mixed-use urban spaces, citizen participation, active parks and public spaces, and culturally vibrant neighborhoods as a means of marketing Toronto as a world-class city (Garber and Imbroscio 1996; Boudreau, Keil, and Young 2009).

As a result, contemporary Toronto was following much the same redevelopment path prescribed by the Regional Plan Association in *A Region at Risk* and pursued with particular gusto by New York City. Not surprisingly, the resulting focus on quality of life as a competitive asset has produced a number of prominent development parallels between the two cities. Just as in New York, Toronto has placed a particular emphasis on reconnecting the city to its waterfront through a variety of public-private projects built on the site of former industrial harbor lands. In addition to fourteen new public spaces—including a beach known as Sugar Beach, named for its proximity to the still-functional Redpath Sugar refinery—plans called for the creation of a series of mixed-use residential projects along a revitalized harbor. In the summer of 2010, some thirteen thousand residential units were planned for the initial phase of waterfront development—which encompasses Toronto's East Bayfront and West Don Lands areas—with another twenty-seven thousand units expected over the following decade in those areas as well as the planning of another development known as North Keating.

Likewise, design had taken on a prominent role in Toronto's redevelopment agenda. In pursuit of their own "signature" developments, one waterfront park plan employed an artist, whereas another, a mixed residential, commercial, and office complex called Parkside, featured designs by noted architect Moshe Safdie. At one point in early 2010, some boosters were suggesting that New York's High Line could serve as a model for converting a section of Toronto's Gardiner Expressway into an elevated $700 million "Green Ribbon." That particular plan called for erecting a steel and concrete platform over the existing roadway, and covering it with plants and paths.

Toronto was also attempting to leverage its status as host of the 2015 Pan American Games to attract private investment and drive broader redevelopment goals, many of them centered on the waterfront, including the construction of new stadiums, arenas, housing, and infrastructure. When Toronto was awarded the Games, an existing twenty-five-year development plan was compressed into five years.

Throughout this expansive and aggressive makeover plan, Jacobs was regularly invoked through frequent references to mixed-use communities, people not cars, and the neighborhood scale. Waterfront plans called for converting an existing three-kilometer stretch of Queens Quay, a busy east-west artery deemed "the backbone of Toronto's waterfront revitalization plans" (Winsa 2010), from four lanes to two and turning it into what the *Globe and Mail* called a "signature," "tree-lined" boulevard, "one of the best pedestrian streets in the world" (Grant 2010). Other pedestrian-friendly initiatives include expanding the city's inventory of bicycle lanes.

But in Toronto, as in New York City and Portland, Jacobs's ideals were being co-opted by developers and real estate interests as a means for driving up property values. Her ideals were likewise being used as marketing tools for selling Toronto as a regional merchant in the competitive global marketplace. While the rhetoric was about creating a holistic approach to development by building livable, people-focused, mixed-use neighborhoods dotted with vibrant parks and access to transit, the bulk of redevelopment was geared toward "luxury condo living for the hip, fit and green," as reported in the *National Post* (Wintrob 2010). That summer, plans called for at least 20 percent of the new housing in East Bayfront, the West Don Lands, and North Keating to be affordable housing and another 20 percent to remain rental. Still, the initial phases of those developments featured almost exclusively for-sale luxury residential units. In one development, River City in West Don Lands, phase one of a five- to seven-year plan to build nine hundred loft-style condos, penthouses, and townhomes consisted of two high-rise buildings totaling 348 units and selling at $239,900 to $750,000, with occupancy scheduled for late 2012. A development known as Oakville, meanwhile, was described as "a quintessential boutique condominium," and its suites ranged in price from $1.2 million to more than $2.5 million. "Waterfront land is a commodity," one developer explained, "and in urban areas such as the [Greater Toronto Area], it's a scarce commodity. That makes it a sound investment and something people take great pride in owning" (Wintrob 2010).

To that end, in Toronto, just as in New York City and Portland, Jacobs's ideals for how to build a better city were mobilized to foster a real estate redevelopment agenda, one that the Metro Council enabled and encouraged through its land use policies and commitment to social mixing.

Critics, including University of Toronto geographer Paul Hess, point to the degree to which these redevelopment projects featured the privatization of what had been public resources—both housing and land—and in the name of social mix and greater income diversity, an overall reduction in the number of affordable housing units (Hess 2010). In Regent Park, for instance, more than two thousand units of public housing were to be torn down, but only 1,357—or roughly 65 percent of the original—were to be replaced. The balance of these public-assistance units was to be shifted elsewhere in east downtown through a practice known as "off-site replacement housing." Meanwhile, of a total of 5,100 new and replacement units being built on site, as little as 27 percent would be subsidized. The rest would be available at market prices, prompting critics to raise the specter of gentrification (August 2008).

Among the earliest of these voices was James Lemon, another University of Toronto geographer, now retired, who in *Liberal Dreams and Nature's Limits* suggested that the liberal urbanism of Toronto's reform movement and subsequent political periods inevitably resulted in displacement, if for no other reason than it privileged private property at the expense of the "public corporation" (Lemon 1996, 23–24). Pointing out that certain people have more choices than others, Lemon argued that:

> Jacobs' position is seriously flawed because she picked the wrong targets. . . . To blame planners—and Jacobs is still attacking them today in Toronto—is to miss the mark: behind the planners have been the developers, their bankers, the chambers of commerce, and politicians who were desperate to overcome decay. (Lemon 1996, 21)

Greenberg, the architect who engaged with Jacobs in the St. Lawrence redevelopment and was a prime player in Regent Park, rejected the suggestion that Jacobs could be saddled with the charge of being a gentrifier, even if her ideas have been used in ways that continue to push the poor out of central cities. "A lot of the derivative stuff that others attribute to her is shallow, fixated on cozy images that don't do justice to her thinking," he maintained in a not-so-subtle jab at New Urbanism. "What we had after the Second World War was this incredible exodus. As cities emptied out they became places where the poor ended up living. Two and a half generations later, as cities became the locus of where people wanted to be, what we have is inevitable displacement. To blame Jane Jacobs is kind of absurd" (Greenberg 2010).

Still, Greenberg acknowledged that even as one intention in redeveloping neighborhoods like St. Lawrence and Regent Park had been "a full gradation of incomes," supporting and maintaining that mix of social classes had become a struggle, and he decried Toronto's "neoliberalization" for taking the teeth out of policies intended to guard against displacement. As in New York City, for instance, Toronto has adopted inclusionary housing—although it is not referred to in those terms—as the affordable housing element of its redevelopment agenda. Toronto's approach even takes the same ratio, 20 percent, of affordable housing to market rate as its goal. Toronto originally adopted this particular approach in 2004, when the city council approved a five-year target of building one thousand units of affordable housing annually through 2009. At year's-end 2009, some twenty-six hundred residents moved into new affordable housing, much of it in mixed-income communities like Regent Park. In 2010 the city council adopted a new ten-year plan that was projected to provide an additional 257,000 households with affordable housing, including the conversion of the athletes village at the West Don Lands into a socially mixed community following the conclusion of the Pan Am Games. But in Toronto, as in New York, the definition of affordable—100 percent of the citywide average—points to the desired demographic makeup of the future city. And just like in New York, questions as to why those particular ratios, as well as opposition to proposals to change them, revolve around the economic needs of the city.

Against this backdrop, fault lines began to emerge over who this new Toronto was being built for: the city's existing residents, regardless of their social status, or the globally oriented creative class that Florida and others argued were its future? Ongoing debates about waterfront infrastructure spending associated with the Pan Am Games, for example, centered on whether it made more sense to build light-rail systems for shuttling athletes and spectators between venues or new water treatment plants that would be needed for the eventual influx of long-term residents. Questions also were raised about who was going to foot the bill for the billion-dollar athletes village and whether in 2015 there would still be the necessary demand for waterfront housing. Adding to the controversy was a proposed $34 million Canadian Port Lands Sports Centre complex, complete with four National Hockey League–sized ice "pads," indoor running track, community meeting rooms, and requisite parking. Condemned by many as a single-use destroyer of neighborhood dynamism and diversity that Jacobs would have battled to the bitter end, the complex's inclusion in waterfront redevelopment plans provoked Greenberg to resign his position as a design consultant and in May 2010 threw the twelve-member Waterfront Design Review Panel into open revolt.

As much as anything, the ongoing turmoil surrounding the Toronto waterfront highlighted the continuing rift between the urban visions of Jacobs and Moses and suggested the difficulties of bridging that lasting impasse. In 2007 in a review of the three-part Moses exhibition, *Toronto Star* urban affairs columnist Christopher Hume asked if in light of Toronto's "weak leadership and fractured bureaucracy," it might not be time for a "Great Synthesis," in which "the new champions of urbanity will have to chart a course between Jacobs and Moses." Hume touted the potential of thinking on a human scale, protecting heritage, and strengthening the fabric of neighborhoods while still thinking big and planning for the future (Hume 2007). Almost three years later, at the height of the waterfront battles, in May 2010, Hume suggested that he had found an answer: "If the decade-old waterfront revitalization program is any indication, the city has lost its ability to think big and act accordingly" (Hume 2010).

9

Design as Civic Virtue

In New York City, the "Great Synthesis" that some in Toronto pined for in 2010 already had been under way for the better part of a decade. With Dan Doctoroff, Bloomberg's deputy mayor for economic development, providing the vision for a slate of ambitious projects designed to reshape New York City on a Moses-like scale—and engendering comparisons, both positive and negative, to the power broker as a consequence (Wells 2007; Brash 2006)—the task of infusing the Bloomberg redevelopment agenda with just enough human scope to make it amenable to a city still enamored of Jane Jacobs fell to Amanda Burden, the socialite and civic activist-turned-planner who was appointed director of the Department of City Planning and chair of the New York City Planning Commission following the mayor's election in 2002.

Born into one of postwar New York City's prominent families, Burden came to planning relatively late.[1] After earning a degree in environmental sciences from Sarah Lawrence College in Yonkers, New York, at the age of thirty-four she joined the Street Life Project, urban sociologist William "Holly" Whyte's observation-based effort to provide a detailed analysis of how people use public spaces. She then worked at the New York State Urban Development Corporation, and from 1983 to 1990 was in charge of planning and design for Battery Park City while pursuing a graduate degree in urban planning at Columbia University. Prior to becoming New York City's chief planner early in Bloomberg's first term, she spent more than a decade as one of the City Planning Commission's appointed members.

From the beginning, however, Burden's tenure in the Bloomberg administration was marked by a contentious relationship with Doctoroff. Initially, that animosity stemmed from Burden's support of Bloomberg rival Mark Green during the 2001 mayoral race, and following Bloomberg's victory, Doctoroff actively advocated for Alexander Garvin to lead the City Planning Department. Garvin was then chief planner for the Lower Manhattan Development Corporation, one of the architects of the city's 1969 Master Plan, and a partner in the preparation of the city's 2012 Olympics bid. Like Doctoroff, Garvin was a vocal proponent of transforming New York City through large-scale redevelopment, and he helped conceive the administration's Hudson Yards plan. He was also an outspoken admirer of Robert Moses's ability to get things done, arguing that "nobody, not even Baron Haussmann in 19th-century Paris has ever done more to improve a city" (Jackson 2007, 71).

While Doctoroff eventually acquiesced and Burden assumed the city's planning reins, the rift between the pair only widened as Doctoroff sought to assert control over major development decisions.[2] "She is in a tough position in this administration," said Kent Barwick, the past president of the Municipal Art Society and a long-time Burden acquaintance. "Typically the director [of City Planning] is a sort of physical secretary of state to the mayor. In the Bloomberg administration, Doctoroff was in between" (Barwick 2008b).

Whereas Doctoroff represented the administration's technocratic corporatism and desire to transform the city on a Moses-like scale, Burden brought to her position an aesthetic imperative, a distinctly high-brow sense of what constitutes good design merged with an appreciation for the Jacobsian notion of street vitality and a commitment to enhancing the vibrancy of New York City's streets and open spaces. Still, Burden's sense of design—and its role in enhancing the city's stature as a top-tier global city—as well as her planning experience conform to the greater development orientation of the Bloomberg agenda. Her biography on the Department of City Planning website describes her as spearheading the mayor's "economic development initiatives with comprehensive urban design master plans designed to catalyze commercial and residential development throughout the city and to reclaim its waterfront" (New York City Department of City Planning 2012b). Speaking at the American Institute of Architect's Center for Architecture in May 2009, Burden emphasized that good design can help drive development by adding "value to the neighborhood" (Burden 2009). "Great architecture keeps the city young, vibrant and competitive," she argued, drawing on the clear association of certain terms and notions—neighborhood vitality, economic health—with Jacobs to reinforce a theme that has become a trademark of the Department of City Planning's articulation of the Bloomberg narrative (Burden 2009). In January 2007, not long after Jacobs's death and in the wake the launching of the Moses revisionist effort, Burden told the *New York Times*, "You can measure the health of the city in the vitality of the street life" (quoted in Caldwell 2007, 1).

Perhaps equally important, however, Burden's interest in fashioning a certain kind of city through its physical form and public spaces was reflective of a broader class-based planning ideology that she shared with Bloomberg and Doctoroff.[3] In a profile written not long after her appointment as planning commissioner and just eight months after 9/11—a pivotal moment in New York City redevelopment politics—*New York* magazine described Burden as the quintessential "Bloomberg-era civil servant": well-connected, well-off, and like the mayor, Doctoroff, and others in the administration, someone who does not need the job but is "motivated to make a difference" (Gardner 2002).

Indeed, after taking New York City's planning reins, Burden emerged as one of the key members of the administration, the face of a newly aggressive planning department, and therefore a major figure in the implementation of its urban development agenda—as well as a power broker in her own right. During Bloomberg's first term, Burden championed the revitalization of the dilapidated High Line elevated rail line even after the mayor initially opposed it, arguing that plans to turn the abandoned railway into a park were not just about creating an "iconic" and "world-class" public space in keeping with New York City's ambitions as a global city but also about enhancing real estate values and catalyzing development along Manhattan's Far West Side (Burden 2009). By March of 2008—a full year before the High Line's planned opening—thirty projects were either planned or in construction nearby (Burden 2008a), including a luxury apartment tower at Eleventh Avenue and Nineteenth Street designed by the internationally celebrated Jean Nouvel and a planned fourteen-floor condominium tower adjacent to the park at Twenty-Third Street by another noted architect, Neil Denari.[4]

In 2008 the *New York Observer* ranked Burden fifth on its list of the one hundred most powerful people in New York real estate, behind Bloomberg and a trio of developers and property owners—Jerry Speyer, chair and CEO of Tishman Speyer; Stephen Ross, chair and CEO of Related Companies; and Marc Holliday, CEO of SL Green, New York City's largest commercial landlord. In explaining that ranking, the newspaper noted, "Any major land-use change in the city must pass over Ms. Burden's desk—if it didn't originate there in the first place . . . and to date, she is the shining star of the Bloomberg administration's still-incomplete development legacy" (Medchill 2008). In 2009, with the city's real estate market in retreat because of the onset of the economic crises in 2008, the newspaper dropped her to number eight, explaining, "New condo towers used to sprout wherever Ms. Burden would point.... Those days are over, of course, but as the empress of zoning and public approvals of large-scale development in this city, she still holds a very strong hand, especially if any private developer ever wants to build again" (Acitelli 2009).

Burden also became the administration's main voice as it attempted to mobilize and synthesize the seemingly disparate if not irreconcilable visions of Jacobs and Moses in support of its goals. Aside from participating at the Gotham Center forum—and subsequently publishing her presentation in the *Gotham Gazette* (Burden 2006b)—Burden regularly articulated the direct ideological links between certain of Jacobs's and Moses's foundational precepts and the administration's development philosophy. The concept of diversity, for instance, was made material through rezoning initiatives that included a Jacobsian commitment to creating a deliberate mix of working, living, shopping, leisure, and cultural uses to return life to the city while still making room for Moses-scale creative destruction. "Big cities need big projects," Burden argued, because they "are a necessary part of the diversity, competition and growth that both Jacobs and Moses fought for" (Burden 2006a). But the goal of city planners, she insisted,

> is no longer the broad brush, the bold strokes, the big plan. Although, make no mistake about it, we have an enormous need to build thousands of units of affordable housing, we must create a broad spectrum of jobs for our rapidly expanding population, we need to reclaim and revitalize our waterfront and we must lay the foundations to support the growth that is to come and which we welcome. But it is just not acceptable, or wise, or even possible, to undertake these challenges without espousing Jacobs' principles of city diversity, of the rich detail or urban life and to build in a way that nourishes complexity. (Burden 2006a)

Some observers suggest that Burden was not disingenuous or insincere when she talked of building like Moses but with Jacobs in mind. For instance, in an effort to generate sidewalk vitality at the proposed Jets stadium on midtown Manhattan's Far West Side, Burden argued for building parks on all four sides and advocated for retail and public uses at its street level. Likewise, supporters suggest that her efforts to improve initial plans for Atlantic Yards by insisting on more public space were fundamentally consistent with Jacobs's principles, even as the scale of those megaprojects and the means by which they were approved "overwhelmed any discussion of a possible relationship" to Jacobs's thinking (Barwick 2008a).

In the Shadow of "Holly" Whyte

Yet while Burden trumpeted Jacobs's influence on contemporary planners and urban form, that influence played an ancillary role in her personal approach to urban design. Instead, her inspiration stemmed from a long and close relationship with William "Holly" Whyte, the trained planner who also served as a mentor to Jacobs, and like the latter, was a keen observer and promoter of the dynamism and diversity of city spaces. Whyte casts a long shadow over more than half a century of urban design development in New York City, having served as senior editor at *Fortune* magazine in 1956, when Jacobs penned her earliest critique of urban renewal before, as noted earlier, going on to play an instrumental role in the evolution of the city's zoning regulations and influencing a number of high-profile people and projects through the Street Life Project. Whyte mentored Fred Kent, who, like Burden, worked on the Street Life Project and then went on to found the Project for Public Spaces, an urban nonprofit organization that incorporates the observational techniques pioneered by Whyte as it aspires to help "citizens transform their public spaces into vital places" through "placemaking" (Project for Public Spaces, n.d. a).[5] In addition, Whyte conceived and wrote the 1980 plan for the restoration of midtown Manhattan's Bryant Park as well as the rezoning/redevelopment of Times Square—two projects critics often cite as emblematic of the homogenized, highly disciplined pseudo-public spaces that result from neoliberalism's public-private approach to urban redevelopment.

To be sure, Whyte shared many of Jacobs's foundational ideas, and his prescriptions for revitalizing city centers and creating dynamic public spaces drew on her concepts of small blocks oriented to pedestrian traffic, street vitality, and a mix of old and new buildings (Whyte 1989, 334), as well as the underlying belief that urban redevelopment equals economic development. Though in certain ways at odds with traditional development practices in New York City—he rejected the "belief that major office projects are the prime source of new jobs" (Whyte 1989, 334), for instance—Whyte embraced the notion that, in general, what is good for business is good for the city; therefore, the city should understand what amenities attract successful companies, both large and small, and encourage the provision of them.

Writing in the late 1980s against the backdrop of the failures of the liberal urban policies of previous decades, and under cover of the ascendant rollout neoliberalism of the Reagan-Bush years, Whyte offered an explicit defense for the active and deliberate promotion of gentrification, suggesting the only way for cities to draw people back to their abandoned centers was to promote the rehabilitation of substandard housing as an alternative to the "bleak new utopias" of federal Title I redevelopment projects (Whyte 1989, 326). Drawing from Jacobs's cogent observation of the difficulties residents in blighted neighborhoods face in improving their physical living conditions, Whyte lauded the 1969 *Plan for New York City*, which included proposed loans and mortgage guarantees for one- and two-family homes, loans for renovation work, and temporary tax abatements on home improvements. "If brownstoners have done what they have done in the face of major difficulties," Whyte wrote, quoting the *Plan for New York City*'s description of Park Slope's transformation from a rundown, crime- and drug-infested neighborhood in the mid-1970s into a model of upwardly mobile—though almost exclusively white—urban regeneration, "it is staggering to think of what could be done if the difficulties were removed" (Whyte 1989, 327).

How much of Whyte's embrace of gentrification informed the Bloomberg agenda by way of Burden is hard to tell. However, Whyte's influence on the Burden Department of City Planning emerged explicitly in a number of distinct ways. Most important, perhaps, was in the steadfast belief that diversity and other "desirable pieces of the urban fabric" can be achieved through planning (Catharine Ingraham, quoted in Whyte 1989, 330). Even Whyte, however, warned of the pitfalls of creating diversity from scratch, and, echoing Jacobs, he foreshadowed a number of critiques that would come to frame debates over the Bloomberg administration's plans for Hudson and Atlantic Yards: "Cities-within-cities, alas, are still being built," Whyte wrote. "They are usually very large—often on clear tracts, such as obsolete freight yards, that give architects and developers the blank slate they would be better off for not having . . . for services the projects provide bits and pieces within: a gourmet food shop, a simulation of a raffish pub" (Whyte 1989, 329–330).

Whyte was an early proponent of downzoning as a means of preserving existing neighborhood character (Gilbert 2001, 8). Likewise, his belief—conceived in the context of the incentive zoning debacles of the 1960s and 1970s—that good design can be decreed by adherence to basic formulas lives on in a series of increasingly narrow prescriptions that have become entrenched in New York City Planning Commission design guidelines for privately owned public spaces. These include precise mandates, based on his Street Life Project's detailed—if not obsessive—observations regarding sidewalk and building widths, building setbacks, ground-floor retailing requirements, and rules regarding the planting of street trees, all as a means of re-creating in modern city centers "places to meet and talk" and "a convenient focus for city life" reminiscent of the agora of ancient Greece. Summarizing the Street Life Project's findings, Helen Gilbert, a lecturer in land economics at the University of Technology in Sydney, Australia, notes:

It was observed that the amount of "sittable" space (places where people can sit) is directly related to how much a public space is used. The location of the space is also important—it should be in the heart of the downtown area, preferably on a major corner, as people need to be able to walk to it easily. At least 80% of users are likely to come from a radius of three blocks. Other points the team noted were that the shape of the space is not crucial (one of the most popular spaces in New York was a long narrow indentation in a building) and that the supply of spaces creates demand. A good new space induces people to use it and creates new habits in them—eating outdoors, walking etc. Interestingly, it was observed that people like to position themselves in well-defined spaces—near steps or the border of a pool. The finding that people rarely choose the middle of a large space also supports Sitte's principle that irregular shaped public plazas work best. Finally, the relationship of the location of the space and the street is important—if the space is physically close and visually accessible to the public street it becomes almost instinctive that people enter it. Where the street functions as part of the plaza or public space, the social life of both spaces flows back and forth. (Gilbert 2001, 8)

Burden, it seems, derived much of her sense of planning from this strain of detail-driven design thinking. One example is a series of "seating standards" for public plazas adopted by the City Planning Commission on September 19, 2007, and approved by the city council one month later as part of a broader set of design guidelines for privately owned public spaces. According to these standards, "There shall be a minimum of one linear foot of seating for each 30 square feet of public plaza area"—a holdover from Whyte's earlier guidelines—and seating arrangements should "provide ample opportunity for social seating as a basic seating type that consists of seats that are placed in close proximity and at angles to one another or in facing configurations that facilitate social interaction" (New York City Department of City Planning 2007, 43). Additionally, "seating requirements may be satisfied by the following seating types: moveable seating, fixed individual seats, fixed benches with and without backs, and design-feature seating such as seat walls, planter ledges, or seating steps. All public plazas shall provide at least two different types of seating" (Department of City Planning 2007, 43). Trees are another prescribed feature. According to the design guidelines, all public plazas must have at least four trees (Department of City Planning, 2007, 45).

In this way, Whyte's sense of agora and Jacobs's notion of community and street life filtered through Burden's Department of City Planning to emerge as the vague, but often-articulated principle "design matters"

(Burden 2006a). This focus on the way things look quickly became a trademark of Burden's tenure at the Department of City Planning, and over time she used her growing influence to define and enforce a singular vision of what "quality" or "great" design might be (Gardner 2002). "As director of the City Planning Department, she has built her reputation on a concern for aesthetics: how a building looks, how it relates to the street, how it serves the people who use its public spaces," journalist Robin Pogrebin wrote. "Compared with a Robert Moses . . . Burden might be considered an aesthetic watchdog" (Pogrebin 2004, E1). Robert Yaro of the Regional Plan Association, meanwhile, referred to her as "the design conscience of New York" (Pogrebin 2004, E1).

A Fixation with the Way Things Look

Yet far from being a neutral activity or a mere expression of creativity or imagination, design functions as a powerful tool in determining the profitability and salability of a product (Forty 1992). In the case of the Bloomberg administration, the product to be sold was the city itself and with Burden leading the charge, design became a critical element in the marketing of the administration's larger redevelopment narrative. Arguing that "good architecture is good economic development," Burden prodded developers to employ "starchitects" in designing their projects (Burden 2007a) so as to deliver iconic symbols of the city's global cultural and economic appeal. In overseeing the master planning process for a new East River waterfront in Lower Manhattan, for example, she insisted that the architect Richard Rogers be involved (Burden 2007a), and she regularly touted projects designed by renowned figures like Frank Gehry, Jean Nouvel, Neil Denari, and Alf Naman (Burden 2009).

Among developers and the design community, however, Burden became a lightning rod for criticism not only for that unyielding opinion about what constitutes "good" design but for imposing it through an imperious approach to her position. That imperiousness extended inside the walls of the Department of City Planning, where staff referred to her as the "Chair," never by name, and throughout the design community, where she was dubbed "the city's interior designer" and less flatteringly, "Demanda," for her insistence on personally vetting minute public project details. Developers complained that Burden's preference for starchitects unnecessarily increased project costs (Municipal Art Society 2007b), while architects and design professionals spoke of participating in meetings and approval processes in which Burden held up projects, "micro-managing" details (Caldwell 2007, 1) and causing costly delays to insist that benches be rearranged, specific types of paving stones be used, or that seat heights, depths, and widths conform to exacting measurements. Others contended that the formulas prescribed in the city's zoning criteria stifled innovation. At the panel discussion "The Oversuccessful City: Developers' Realities," developer Carlton Brown of Full Spectrum NY complained that zoning regulations in New York City had become so restrictive they "limit[ed] creativity" (Brown 2007).

Burden's unyielding belief in the superiority of her own sense of design also contributed to her strained relationship with Doctoroff, in particular over the design of the proposed Jets stadium on midtown Manhattan's Far West Side. And in September 2009 it led her to lop 200 feet off the top of Jean Nouvel's design for a 1,250-foot skyscraper next to the Museum of Modern Art (MoMA) on Fifty-Third Street in midtown Manhattan, on the grounds that its peak did not meet the city's aesthetic standards.[6]

Burden's supporters counter that such criticisms of her approach to design, especially given its context within the administration's development agenda, are unwarranted. Kent Barwick, for instance, contends that while major planning decisions were made by Doctoroff, Burden spent much of her time "trying to ameliorate the worst aspects, from the street point of view," of these projects, including the planning of public spaces around the original Frank Gehry–designed arena to be built for the New Jersey/Brooklyn Nets at Atlantic Yards (Barwick 2008b). But others question whether the role of the city's planning commissioner should involve such a hands-on approach to the way things look. One architect, whose working relationship to Burden spans three decades, described her as "a planning figurehead" and "an unqualified social appointee capable of holding hearings and getting votes" but whose own views on planning are "academic," "who throws architects at problems," and whose own design ideas "really have to do with open space."

Regardless, under Burden a focus—some say fixation—on the way things look became an integral component not just of the Department of City Planning's mission but the administration's overall approach to redevelopment.[7] In 2006 Burden hired New York City's first-ever chief urban designer, Alexandros Washburn, whose job was to oversee "citywide policy development and design review of scores of new urban design projects that are now being planned to accommodate a million more New Yorkers in a period of rapid climate change," according to a promotional flyer for an American Institute of Architects (AIA) one-day conference (American Institute of Architects 2008). As Washburn told conference participants, he received a call from Burden, who suggested that with Bloomberg as mayor and herself as director of the Department of City Planning, New York City was entering a unique moment in history and in city government, "a time to bring design to the front." His position was created to help seize that moment, one that he acknowledged was likely to disappear, along with his post, when a new mayor took office.

True to the Bloomberg administration's narrative, Washburn pursued his mission with the stated intention of producing, in his words, "the quantity of Robert Moses with the quality of Jane Jacobs." An important element of that job, he acknowledged, was to get projects "up to snuff" so that they met Burden's design criteria and won her approval. "Don't even think about coming in until it's great," he said, paraphrasing Burden.

A frequent spokesman for the city at design-related events, Washburn regularly touched on the Bloomberg administration's belief in "civic virtue by design" (Washburn 2008a). Defining civic virtue as "the cultivation of habits important for the success of the community," he described the Bloomberg planning agenda as a "paradigm shift . . . nothing short of a new compact with nature." To express it, he insisted,

> we must transform the rigidities of architecture into the adaptations of nature. The stone column crumbles and is replaced by the growing stalk. Networks of green signify community in ways that the architecture of the past no longer can. City-initiated rezonings center around new public spaces or streetscape improvements and each is crafted in consultation with the community it serves. (Washburn 2008a)

To the administration, and the people like Burden and Washburn who were chosen to determine the city's future face and sell that vision to the public, New York City was a "transformative city. . . . Every project has a transformative or positive or negative effect," Washburn said at the AIA conference (Washburn 2008b). It is not always possible to predict what that effect will be, Washburn acknowledged. Nonetheless, "It's cumulative. It's iterative . . . building upon itself to propel forward a comprehensive sense of what the city should look like" and "setting the pattern for the greatest wave of urbanization that the world has ever seen." New York City, Washburn trumpeted, "is at the pinnacle of urban thinking" (Washburn 2008b).

In the eyes of the administration, for example, the provision of "world-class" design in public amenities was to be a driver of redevelopment of Manhattan's Far West Side, enhancing real estate values along select streets and avenues, thereby providing the "armature" for attracting additional private investment that would transform whole neighborhoods along designated corridors (Burden 2009, 2008a, 2007a). "Well-designed, well-used public open spaces" can "be a catalyst for the economic and social well being of a city, and actually change the entire perception of a city," Burden declared in a video interview with the Urban Land Institute. Such spaces, she continued, can be "very transformative in how people feel about making private investment" (Krueger 2011).

In Hell's Kitchen, for instance, certain streets were to be disappeared by eminent domain to make way for a proposed "grand boulevard" reminiscent of the Haussmann-built thoroughfares of Paris (Burden 2008a). Additional streets radiating from that proposed boulevard were up-zoned to allow for greater residential densities of market-rate apartments and condominiums, with height variances added on for ensuring 20 percent of the total number of units remained "affordable." Other streets were rezoned to allow the arrival of commercial tenants and office buildings.

Still, perhaps the best example of "how design can be an amazing catalyst for private investment," Burden suggested, is the High Line. While the first section of the elevated park cost nearly $100 million to build, it "triggered 34 projects worth $2 billion to the city" in nearby neighborhoods. Since opening to the public in 2009, it also had attracted 6.9 million visitors. "Just think what that has done for tourism, for New York City," Burden enthused (Krueger 2011).

In essence, then, Burden's insistent championing of design excellence had two fundamental effects. On one hand, it played a vital role in the city's ability to market itself as a livable, global urban enclave amenable to the creative economy and the discerningly upscale workers that populate it. On the other, it was a strategic mechanism that served to make the economic development at the heart of the Bloomberg administration's redevelopment agenda palatable to a broad segment of native New Yorkers. "Great architecture is very important to the energy and vitality of our cities," she told an international audience during the Urban Age South America Conference in São Paulo, Brazil, in 2008. "It makes them young. It makes them competitive. You have Frank Gehry. You have Helmut Jahn," she continued, referencing two starchitects who designed new buildings in Lower Manhattan in the wake of 9/11. "And then that triggers new office development. You have Norman Foster, Richard Rogers" (Burden 2008b).

Beyond the obvious boosterism though, the administration's approach to design proved more mundane, reflecting the currency of urban policy mobility practices under a technocratic, corporately inclined mayor.[8] While touted as transformative and at the forefront of urban design, the plans for public spaces that resulted from it were more often modified versions of model concepts from other cities, and zoning regulations were conceived as the necessary safeguards "to prevent bad developers and designs from ruining" them, according to Alexandros Washburn.[9] Urban spaces were approached as if there was a single, universally recognized sense of street aesthetic, of what constitutes good design, which could only be ensured by the creation of design standards intended to impose it. Critics contend that such slavish devotion to prescriptive guidelines and formulas inevitably led to its own form of homogeneity, a city of preplanned public spaces scrubbed clean of innovation or sense of place in their own right, just more plazas, streetscapes, and stamped-out parks culled from a template. The result was control of the public realm through design, or heavily prescribed, rigidly disciplined public spaces designed to encourage normative activities—sitting and talking while consuming the products from nearby cafés, for instance—while actively discouraging anything that might run counter to those purposes.

In this way, much as the Bloomberg planning narrative—like the Moses narrative before it—rested on the notion that planning is value neutral and that the administration was acting only in the best interests of the city; the articulation of design as a civic virtue served to naturalize and normalize the class-based values inherent in the administration's larger redevelopment agenda. Through its constant celebration of the transformative potential of the parks, plazas, streetscapes, and buildings planned and constructed as part of the production of a global capitalist city, the administration insisted its overriding interest was in ensuring New York City had the means to compete in a set, immutable future. What the administration's plans actually did, however, was set in motion a series of infrastructure improvements, public works projects, and redevelopment initiatives that ever more tightly embedded the logic and assumptions of capital accumulation in the urban landscape. When Burden and Washburn spoke of the civic virtue of design, what they really described was the process—aided by rezoning and the related critique and control of private sector design—of making the city more marketable. To the administration, then, design's true civic virtue was its ability to make real estate worth more and to valorize a specific, class-oriented notion of quality of life.

10

Building Like Moses with Jacobs in Mind

> As the Mayor says, "If you want to solve the problem of gentrification, you should have crime go up, the schools get worse, the parks dirtier." Gentrification is a natural product of market forces.
>
> —Dan Doctoroff, quoted in Acitelli 2007

For as long as the New York City economy boomed, powered by a raging real estate market and easy access to credit, the Bloomberg camp enthusiastically charged ahead with plans for building a global capital and creative city amenable to the expansion of the financial sector and its ancillary services. But by the fall of 2007 the administration's narrative of a city ascendant had begun to collapse under the weight of its own contradictions and a looming worldwide financial crisis.

The same debt explosion and speculative housing bubble that generated huge profits, as well as enormous salaries and bonuses, within the financial industry in turn drove up real estate values, filling New York City's and New York State's tax coffers and propelling further speculative development in the city. Ultimately, however, the self-generating nature of the bubble proved unsustainable, triggering the sub-prime mortgage crisis and prompting the collapse of three of the world's largest investment banks. As the financial sector unraveled and the global recession deepened, access to credit dried up, and by late March 2008 an estimated $20 billion in prominent development projects across the city—many designed by world-renowned architects and promoted by Burden and other Bloomberg administration figures—had been canceled or delayed. Among the projects most drastically impacted were Atlantic Yards and the proposed redevelopment of Willets Point, which saw essential funding mechanisms disappear. Meanwhile, a plan to replace midtown Manhattan's outdated Penn Station with the new Moynihan Station fell apart, stalling expansion of the Jacob Javits Convention Center and Hudson Yards (see Chapter 3).

In addition, scores of smaller-scale private construction projects ground to a halt—forty-eight in the Brooklyn neighborhood of Bushwick alone, according to the community services organization Make the Road (Lopez 2009)—rendering New York City a patchwork of "cranes on pause."[1]

Even as the crisis was unfolding, however, members of the Bloomberg administration and its allies within the city's growth coalition sought to reinforce the mayor's vision for refashioning the city. On September 18, 2008, just days after the collapse of New York–based financial services firm Lehman Brothers, in the largest bankruptcy in U.S. history, Seth Pinsky, the president of the New York City Economic Development Corporation (NYCEDC), delivered an update on New York City's economic development at a joint gathering of the American Institute of Architects and the American Planning Association at the Center for Architecture in Manhattan.[2] Pinsky opened by noting that "just a few short years ago people were wondering if anything would ever get built in New York" (Pinsky 2008).[3] Citing the $2 billion earmarked for the expansion of the No. 7 subway line, he touted the progress being made in laying the groundwork for establishing the Far West Side as the city's "newest" business district, and the planned development of an East River Science Park as "the flagship" of the city's effort to become a center of biotech research. But he quickly shifted gears to seize on the growing economic uncertainty to echo the Bloomberg administration's narrative regarding the risks ahead. Now, not only was New York City in danger of losing its position as "the economic capital of the world," Pinsky said, but looming budget deficits imperiled the mayor's redevelopment agenda and the then-still emergent crisis within global financial networks was threatening to send the world economy into a sustained tailspin (Pinsky 2008).

Unlike in the 1970s, when the city cut services to make up for the dwindling tax revenues that accompanied that particular municipal crisis, Pinsky maintained that the emphasis this time should be to continue to "build the city, maintain the quality of life" (Pinsky 2008). For the final sixteen months of Bloomberg's second—and at the time seemingly final—term, he insisted, the mayor would focus on pushing forward the various projects already under way or envisioned in his plan. Peppering his talk with boosterish phrases like "bullish on the long-term prospects," "moving forward," and "planning for the future," Pinsky argued that the "frontiers of development" were "virtually limitless" and that "every project is a priority" (Pinsky 2008). However, he warned, in a difficult economic environment the city would be forced to ask for even less from the private sector and instead need to "entice" it with additional subsidies, tax credits, and favorable zoning changes to provide the "necessary improvements." Regardless, Pinsky assured, the mayor's legacy as a great builder in the can-do tradition of Robert Moses "would become clear as the conditions for future growth continue[d] to bear fruit" (Pinsky 2008).

From a different point of view, though, the global financial crisis and its local ramifications offered a valuable lesson in the fallacies and limits of the underlying logic of real estate–driven redevelopment and of the role of capital accumulation in the processes of urbanization as imagined by the Bloomberg administration. Given that the administration's basis for invoking Jacobs and Moses in its development discourse was grounded on the pair's ideological justification for just such an approach to urban regeneration (see Chapter 7), it suggests an opportunity to question the relationship of their legacies to those processes as well.

The Narrative Collapses

In November 2007 the Institute for Urban Design hosted a public forum called "New York 2030: New York's Green and Just Future," at which city officials, policy makers, and urban designers discussed the Bloomberg administration's sustainability initiative, PlaNYC 2030.[4] Following a series of presentations by administration representatives, including Parks Director Adrian Benepe and Chief Urban Designer Alexandros Washburn, an audience member rose to ask, if design was a civic virtue and diversity—which she noted was a hallmark of Jane Jacobs—a goal, how did the city reconcile its support for Columbia University's expansion into West Harlem in spite of significant community opposition and "the inherent contradictions between short-term actions and long-term impacts?" Rohit Aggarwala, as the director of the New York City Office of Long-Term Planning and Sustainability and one of the chief authors of PlaNYC 2030, chose to respond: "The city is full of contradictions, so the plan is too." Arguing that there are trade-offs in any plan, he insisted that Columbia University's expansion was "economically important to the city" and that it was representative of "the necessary trade-off of Jacobs versus Moses." Jacobs, he continued, "wasn't against large-scale development but rather poorly conceived development. She wasn't out to destroy growth but to figure out how to do it right" (Aggarwala 2007).

Aggarwala's suggestion that Jacobs was not necessarily the enemy of large-scale redevelopment could be, as we have seen, debated. Thus, it underscores the degree to which her legacy—just like that of Robert Moses—remains contested, open to a range of readings, interpretations, and adaptations. Yet at the same time it raises, once again, questions about how—and to what purpose—the administration mobilized those legacies in articulating its plans for ongoing transformations of New York City's built environment. For instance, the administration's promotion of design as a civic virtue was a notion that would presumably cause Jacobs to turn in her grave. To Jacobs, art was "arbitrary, symbolic and abstracted." It was selective and limited in its ability to represent the endless intricacies of urban life (Jacobs 1992, 373). "A city," she emphasized, "cannot be a work of art. . . . To approach a city, or even a neighborhood, as if it were a larger architectural problem, capable of being given order by converting it into a disciplined work of art, is to make the mistake of attempting to substitute art for life" (372–373). To Jacobs, previous paradigms in planning—from the City Beautiful and Garden City movements to the Radiant City of Le Corbusier—register as "primarily architectural design cults" (375). And while she agreed that that too much intensity and diversity is overwhelming, the closest she came to providing prescriptions for enforcing visual order was in her discussion of trees and pavements ("with strong, simple patterns") and possibly awnings as street unifiers (390).

Thus, the administration's sense of design as a civic virtue capable of fostering urban dynamism represented just one of the distortions of Jacobs's ideals that was incorporated into the Bloomberg administration's redevelopment agenda. There these distortions were synthesized with choice aspects of Moses's legacy as a means of reconciling fundamental differences between the two figures and making the case for building like Moses with Jacobs in mind. This synthesis, it turns out, was not only selective but interpretive as well. For just as City Planning commissioner Amanda Burden insisted her understanding of the value of urban street life drew direct inspiration from Jacobs, Burden's celebration of diversity, mixed uses, neighborhood vitality, and citizen participation in the planning process represented a highly problematic misuse of Jacobs's ideals. In fact, within the administration, one could argue, those ideals were often secondary, adoptable rather than foundational, and applicable only when they meshed with or could be adapted to fit the broader intentions of the administration's plans. What mattered most to the administration was producing an ascendant global city whose quality of life was a selling point and an object of consumption. When Jacobs and Moses could be bent to serve those purposes, they were.

For example, if Jacobs had been writing of low-economic land uses in 2009, as she did in 1961 in *The Death and Life of Great American Cities*, she might well have chosen to describe the New York City neighborhoods of Manhattanville in West Harlem and Willets Point, Queens, where sixty-two acres of industrial uses, including row after row of small-scale, flood-prone auto repair shops, sat within an epic home run's reach of Citi Field, the then-new $700 million home of Major League Baseball's New York Mets.[5] In fact, powerful forces in the administration and New York City's growth coalition used Jacobs's failed city district argument to have Willets Point and Manhattanville designated blighted and rezoned to make way for more vital, "successful" land uses—the proposed $3 billion redevelopment of Willets Point, including office buildings, a hotel and convention center, parks, retail stores, and fifty-five hundred apartments, and the $6.2 billion Columbia University campus expansion in West Harlem.

Of course, there is another view of these places—that of the people who called the neighborhoods home or owned and worked at the businesses located there. In their view these areas provided low-cost housing, and jobs—some seventeen hundred in Willets Point—and judging from their persistent existence, services that a significant portion of the New York City population deemed essential.

One can only assume that the economic environment Columbia University and the Bloomberg administration wished to "cultivate" in such "failed" districts did not involve those already living and working there at the time. Instead, the revitalizations inherent in their plans seemed destined to make room for a whole new class of folks with the skills and resources likely to dislodge significant numbers of existing inhabitants. One can make that assumption because nowhere in Columbia University's plans or the administration's objectives in Willets Point—or by extension, in *The Death and Life of Great American Cities*—were there provisions to guarantee any other outcome. Just as Jacobs naively conflated geographic proximity of mixed primary uses with jobs for neighborhood residents (Jacobs 1992, 174–175), one of the key points made by the Bloomberg administration in rationalizing its vision of the benefits to be derived from an expanded Columbia University and a rezoned, deindustrialized Willets Point was the jobs that redevelopment would bring. To be sure, there were to be jobs building, maintaining, and operating the new research laboratories or hotels and convention centers. And as part of the administration's plan to transform the area, Willets Point workers were offered free training to "learn to use a computer, wait on tables, keep books, fix cars or simply speak English" through a $2.5 million program known as Willets Point Worker Assistance (Santos 2009, A21). But would the autoworkers of Willets Point in 2009 become the bellboys and service staffs at the hotels and convention centers of the future? And even if they did, would the minimum-wage paychecks those jobs offer keep pace with the rising rents that increasing property values and speculation would likely generate, regardless of the administration's promise to add one thousand or so units of "affordable" housing through inclusionary zoning? Just like the working-class members of Jacobs's Greenwich Village neighborhood, many existing residents of Manhattanville and Willets Point would likely be forced to seek new neighborhoods in which to live. Some of them argued that the money for the worker assistance program would be better spent helping relocate the businesses they already work for and the jobs they already had. "I don't see the point in training people who can't work if there's no guarantee they'll ever find jobs," Marcos Neira, a Colombian immigrant who owned Master Express Deli and Restaurant on Willets Point Boulevard, told the *New York Times* (quoted in Santos 2009, A21).

Masking the Contradictions

In one sense, then, by paying lip service to elements of Jacobs and Moses that did not conform to its agenda, the Bloomberg administration, through its own version of the mainstreaming of recent urban history, masked the contradictions inherent within its redevelopment narrative. To Burden's Department of City Planning, for instance, the promotion of diversity and mixed use through the forced rezoning of "blighted" neighborhoods while scores of firmly middle-class to upper-middle-class communities had the luxury of requesting their streets, lined with single-family homes, be down-zoned to preserve their character translated as a "fine-grain," block-by-block (read Jacobsian) appreciation for the differences between New York City's many neighborhoods. Of course, at its heart selective downzoning also could be read as a not-so-thinly veiled euphemism for defending real estate, and by extension class, values.

And despite the administration's steady rhetoric of working with communities in crafting its plans, the nature of public participation it actually engaged in was hardly the kind envisioned by Jacobs. As community experiences surrounding projects like Columbia University's expansion and the redevelopment of the Atlantic Yards and Hudson Yards rail cuts suggested, neighborhood concerns and priorities for development were taken seriously only when they conformed to the administration's preestablished agenda.

Alexandros Washburn, the administration's chief urban designer, meanwhile, identified where the real participatory influence rested. Asked at his presentation to the American Institute of Architects how developers, designers, and related interest groups could have input in proposed zoning changes, Washburn responded that "most decisions are made in [internal] meetings, meetings that are on your calendar but you may not have thought are important. So, if your point of view isn't in the room, it won't be heard" (Washburn 2008a). The larger point, of course, was that the general public was not invited to participate in these meetings. Instead, even as Doctoroff, Burden, and other city officials publicly insisted community input was a necessary and valued part of the planning process, the reality is that within the Bloomberg framework, plans and decisions integral to their creation were made in closed meetings and only taken to the public for comment once the details were in place. Those who proved critical of these plans were then painted—very much in the Moses tradition—as naysayers, rabble-rousers, and petulant opponents of progress or change (Brash 2006). In one particularly resonant example, during the 2006 Gotham Center forum, Burden dismissed opposition to the proposed new arena at Atlantic Yards as "childish" (Burden 2006a). As a result, New Yorkers—with Jacobs leading the charge—may have won the right to participate in the production of their city through the creation of community boards, the drafting of 197-a plans, and input at public hearings, but that right proved to be an empty one.

In another sense, the administration's effort at synthesis allowed it to incorporate select lessons from both Moses and Jacobs to promote its own big-build strategy. As Doctoroff contended, the administration learned from past experiences with the Olympics, the proposed stadium for the New York Jets, and the redevelopment of Hudson Yards to cherry-pick aspects of Jacobs's and Moses's ideals—to assemble a set of best practices—as it single-mindedly pursued its vision of the city. In this way, the selective repackaging of Moses and Jacobs and the subsequent mobilization of them to support the administration's redevelopment agenda was far from a subjective attempt to reexamine a fixed history, but rather, as we have seen, an ongoing act of representational creative destruction that materialized from the spatial and temporal evolution of the city itself. Over time, Jacobs and Moses were made to serve as ideological bookends, framing debates over development in New York City.

To the members of the Bloomberg administration, then, the concept of building like Robert Moses with Jane Jacobs in mind translated to a fundamental conviction that the promotion of the private market and free enterprise was the best means for solving the intractable urban issues of poverty, homelessness, rising income inequality, and blight. By adopting specific, signature aspects of each figure, the administration constructed a narrative in which urbanism became economic development, or, in the words of Amanda Burden, the "diversity, competition and growth that both Jacobs and Moses fought for" (Burden 2006a).

From Jacobs the administration drew the pretense, at least, of community involvement in the planning process. It promoted her foundational precepts of density, mixed land use, and diversity. That it did so at a citywide scale was complemented by the use of a Moses-like mechanism—zoning—even as that tool was shaped by a Jacobsian devotion to the preservation of neighborhood character. From Moses came a steadfast—and some might claim cynical—commitment to using public funds, in the form of subsidies and tax breaks to developers, to advance the mayor's market-friendly agenda. Moses served as the administration's model for determination and efficiency, and city officials learned valuable lessons from him about marginalizing opposition, dominating discourse, and leveraging the city's resources. Moses's legacy also lay at the heart of the administration's emphasis on expanding the city's network of parks, orienting development to transportation, and reinvigorating prestigious cultural and academic institutions.

A Convergence of Class Politics

Ultimately, whether one thinks Robert Moses saved New York City by positioning it for the future or sparked its decline by orchestrating the ascendance of urbanism as the mainstay of the capitalist economy, whether one believes his force-fed modernism was responsible for situating the city for a new life or hastening its death, depends not only on one's views of planning and how cities work but on one's situation in time and space.

Yet if Moses was a man of his times, Jacobs was certainly a woman of hers, and as much as she has come to represent a fix-it-up ethos that inspires neighborhood diversity and dynamism, her notion of the livable city can be read as just another accumulation strategy, kinder and gentler on the surface but nevertheless paving the way for a block-by-block gentrification that leaves little room for people of lesser means and people of color (Smith and Larson 2007; see also Jameson 1995). By the first decade of the twenty-first century, gentrification was being cited as a key contributor to ending white flight in New York City: in Manhattan, between 2000 and 2005, the number of white children younger than the age of five grew 40 percent, and by 2009 whites made up 51 percent of the population, making them a majority in the borough for the first time since the mid-1970s; meanwhile, between 2000 and 2006, the five boroughs experienced a net loss of forty thousand African Americans.

While, like Jacobs and Moses, the Bloomberg administration envisioned a future of economically vibrant cities without slums, its redevelopment policy neither questioned nor addressed the root cause of blight and slum creation. Instead, it drew from the Moses and Jacobs legacies to promote quality-of-life policies that would attract creative and innovative industries and their sophisticated, highly compensated workers to position New York City at the top of a competitive global city marketplace. When these policies were examined through a class lens, the poor once again became the problem, and the answer to that problem lay in disciplining underperforming neighborhoods by fixing them, rezoning them, or bulldozing them completely to make room for new iconic boulevards, office towers, high-rise condominiums, waterfront parks, and other twenty-first-century amenities that feed real estate values and conform to existing aspirational-city orthodoxy.

It was here, then, in this convergence of class politics, that Amanda Burden's suggestion of a Bloomberg administration that built like Moses but with Jacobs in mind became an essential and extremely powerful tool within the city's greater redevelopment narrative.

It was also here, in New York City's class dynamics and the politics surrounding them, that the very act of reengaging with the legacies of Jacobs and Moses emerged as inherently problematic. For what were at issue were not specific historical events or social conditions but how they were selectively aligned to reflect certain ideologies. While the legacies of Robert Moses and Jane Jacobs continued to be viewed in the context of their antagonisms, those struggles represented battles among the privileged. In the end Moses and Jacobs did not disagree with each other's grander ambition—the exaltation of an America of means—so much, as they did with how best to get there. In this regard, casting Moses and Jacobs as ideological opposites can become a mechanism for intentionally and artificially constraining the debate over urbanism to a narrow band that blindly accepts and promotes the logic of capital accumulation, reinforcing the very social and economic dynamics—poverty, lack of affordable housing, and segregation along class and racial lines—that continue to vex today's cities.

From this vantage point, one can ask whether the argument between today's Moses resurrectionists and Jacobs defenders turns on a question of scale. Where the two sides meet is in the politics of gentrification. Both are for it, just by different means, and far from representing the source of a truly aspirational city—or at least a model of urbanism that subordinates development to social justice—neither Jacobs nor Moses serves as a useful model. Likewise, the Bloomberg administration's reliance on remobilizing their ideas in support of neoliberalism's growth-oriented ideology only perpetuated existing inequalities, encouraging "accumulation through dispossession" (Harvey 2008a) and exacerbating the physical conditions Jacobs, Moses, and New York City's billionaire mayor claimed to want to address. Only by recognizing this reformulation for what it is—a justification for urban class engineering—and moving beyond Jacobs and Moses can we confront the normative logic at the heart of the Bloomberg agenda and begin what urbanist Henri Lefebvre conceived as the struggle to gain command and control over urban spaces to construct a city for all its inhabitants.

Notes

CHAPTER 1

1. In 1995 *The Death and Life of Great American Cities* was named one of the one hundred most influential books "since the war" by the *Times Literary Supplement*, a list that included Antonio Gramsci's *Prison Notebooks*, Carl Jung's *Memories, Dreams, Reflections*, Michel Foucault's *Madness and Civilization: A History of Insanity in the Age of Reason*, and Milton Friedman's *Capitalism and Freedom* ("The 100 Most Influential Books" 1995).
2. The forum, held on October 11, 2006, was called "Jane Jacobs vs. Robert Moses: How Stands the Debate Today?"
3. One reference is in an explanatory footnote; three others come on a single page (Jacobs 1992, 360). By comparison, she mentions other urban thinkers worthy of critique just as often, if not more: the Swiss-French architect Le Corbusier ten times (and his concept of the Radiant City dozens more), Lewis Mumford six times, and Ebenezer Howard fifteen times (with multiple additional mentions of his concept of the Garden City).
4. The following is the full contents of the blunt missive addressed to Bennett Cerf at Random House and dated November 15, 1961: "I am returning the book you sent me. Aside from the fact that it is intemperate and inaccurate, it is also libelous. I call your attention, for example, to page 131. Sell this junk to someone else. Cordially, Robert Moses" (Moses 1961).
5. In doing so, Jacobs drew the ire of others in the planning and urban design communities besides just Robert Moses. Asked for his thoughts on *The Death and Life of Great American Cities*, urbanist Lewis Mumford responded, "In asking for a comment, you are in effect suggesting that an old surgeon give public judgment on the work of a confident but sloppy novice, operating to

remove an imaginary tumor to which the youngster has erroneously attributed the patient's affliction, whilst over-looking major impairments in the actual organs. Surgery has no useful contribution to make in such a situation, except to sew up the patient and dismiss the bungler. Cordially yours, Lewis Mumford. P.S. This note is not, of course, for publication" (Mumford 1961).

6. In 1929 the Committee on a Regional Plan of New York and Its Environs published its first plan, *A Regional Plan for New York and Its Environs*. At that time, the committee was made permanent and incorporated as the Regional Plan Association.

7. For more on Sitte and his influence on Jacobs, see Lilley 1999.

CHAPTER 2

1. Before writing *The Death and Life of Great American Cities*, Jacobs published freelance articles in *Vogue* and the *New York Herald Tribune*, among others. She also worked as an editor at *Architectural Forum*.

2. For a complete list and detailed description of Moses's projects, see the "Catalog of Built Work and Projects in New York City, 1934–1968," in Ballon and Jackson 2007b.

3. For a more detailed discussion of the transition to modernity and the resulting cultural, social, architectural, and economic transformations, see Harvey 1990a and Berman 1982.

4. Moses took particular aim at Walter Gropius, founder of the Bauhaus School and one of modernism's most prominent architects. Gropius, Moses wrote, was a foreigner intent on introducing alien ideas to the United States and who advocated an architectural philosophy that "offers nothing more novel than the lally column and the two-by-four timber" (Moses 1944, 16).

5. For more on the planning debate that pit Moses against Mumford, see "City Planning" 1943.

6. As editor at *Fortune*, Whyte commissioned Jacobs to write an article for the magazine's series "The Exploding Metropolis" in 1958, based on her work for *Architectural Forum*. That article would catch the attention of the Rockefeller Foundation and ultimately result in *The Death and Life of Great American Cities*.

7. For a more comprehensive discussion of early criticism of Moses, see Fishman, 2007.

8. Moses's achievements, Jackson declared at the time, are best put in perspective when measured against New York City circa 1988: "Since Moses lost power in 1968, New York City has built no new bridges, no new highways, virtually no new public housing projects, no new performing arts centers, and no new beaches. Its parks have deteriorated, and its infrastructure is crumbling. The sewage treatment plant on the west side of Manhattan, which was under construction when I moved to New York in 1968, is still unfinished, twenty years and a billion dollars later. Similarly, the Second Avenue sub way and the third water tunnel threaten to drag into the next century" (Jackson 1989, 30).

9. Even earlier, in a speech delivered to the New York State Motorbus Convention in November 1958, Jacobs singled out Mumford for criticism, sug-

gesting that "the greatest menace to downtown today" did not come from suburbanization or economic decentralization, as he held, but rather from "well-meant attempts at traffic stopgap expediencies" (Jacobs 1958).

10. Other early and subsequent reviewers of *The Death and Life of Great American Cities* shared Mumford's reaction to Jacobs's focus on the neighborhood and safety. Writing in the *New Statesman*, Jonathan Miller suggested that Jacobs "mourns not so much the death of the American city as the disappearance of the Village—Greenwich and otherwise. In the advance of the great American Metropolis, the preservation of a vital street culture is a necessary but hardly sufficient condition of a safe and pleasant life. Mrs. Jacobs has varnished over the huge social patterns which determine the texture of city life" (Miller 1962, 497). See also Richard Sennett's comments on the impact of *The Death and Life in Great American Cities* in his 1970 review of *The Economy of Cities* (Sennett 1970) and Gottlieb 1989.

11. In February 2007 the Rockefeller Foundation announced the creation of the Jane Jacobs Medal, an annual prize "to recognize visionary work in building a more diverse, dynamic and equitable city through creative uses of the urban environment." The award honors individuals "whose accomplishments represent Jacobsian principles and practices in action in New York City" (Rockefeller Foundation, n.d.).

12. Whyte's given name was William.

13. The year 1961 was also when *The Death and Life of Great American Cities* was published. In February of that year, New York City's Housing and Redevelopment Board (HRB) sought a $300,000 planning grant to study the potential for urban renewal in Greenwich Village. The request was the outgrowth of meetings among the HRB, New York University, and two neighborhood community organizations—the Greenwich Village Association and the Middle-Income Co-operators of Greenwich Village—which were promoting the need for low- and middle-income housing. But the funding request was made public two days before it was to be voted on, and residents, fearing "that an Urban Renewal study [would] inevitably lead to a destructive Urban Renewal project" (Rich, n.d., 5), formed the Committee to Save the West Village. The committee operated out of Jacobs's house and employed a range of tactics to force withdrawal of the request for funds nine months later. These ranged from engaging in twelve-hour filibuster sessions at public hearings and attracting local and national media coverage to, on one occasion, Jacobs's shredding of meeting minutes to render the session invalid. The West Village Committee then developed its own urban renewal plan using funds from the Mitchell-Lama act, for the construction of the West Village Houses, which were 475 units of affordable housing in five-story buildings built on six vacant lots. Drawn up in 1962, the plan was approved in 1969, and the first tenants took up residence in 1974. Their stay was brief, however. Just one year after opening, the development was forced into foreclosure by "market pressures," and today the units are privately held cooperative apartments. (See also Flint 2009.)

14. PlaNYC 2030 is the first comprehensive master plan proposed for New York City since 1969. Based on Department of City Planning projections that show the city's population swelling by more than one million by the year 2030,

the plan calls for a range of land use initiatives, including the construction of 265,000 new housing units and vastly expanding the city's open-space network. It was announced, symbolically, on Earth Day, April 22, 2007.

15. In 2009 Lander was elected to the New York City Council, representing the Thirty-Ninth District in Brooklyn.

16. For example, writing in *City Journal*, the quarterly journal of the conservative Manhattan Institute for Policy Research, in 1994, Howard Husock argued that Jacobs's opposition to urban renewal was based on economics, not design or planning. Her objection to the construction of public housing in East Harlem in the 1950s, Husock insisted, had as much and perhaps more to do with the use of public funds—some $300 million—as with the displacement of 1,300 Puerto Rican businesses and the residents they served. "Jacobs still has much to offer us, but not what is commonly assumed. Though culturally associated with the Left, Jacobs dared to follow the logic of her own observation in ways that lead her to oppose much that the Left stands for. The real Jane Jacobs not only enjoys busy city blocks, but deplores high levels of welfare spending that inhibit urban economies. The real Jane Jacobs not only enjoys the great variety of small businesses which cities offer, but questions the public operation of services such as transit that preempt the formation of private competitors" (Husock 1994, 111).

17. For a critical review of *The Economy of Cities*, see Sennett 1970.

18. In the introduction to *Jane Jacobs: Urban Visionary*, Alice Sparberg Alexiou credits the Burns documentary for providing the "germ" for her project (Alexiou 2006, ix).

19. Indeed, the device is a central element of Anthony Flint's 2009 accounting of Jacobs's rivalry with Moses, *Wrestling with Moses: How Jane Jacobs Took On New York's Master Builder and Transformed the American City*. While Flint acknowledges that in 1961 Moses was no longer in a position to directly command the Committee for Slum Clearance bulldozers, he asserts that Moses must have lobbied for urban renewal in Jacobs's neighborhood as an act of revenge (Flint 2009). The apocryphal tale, with a special emphasis on Moses's subsequent defeat, also appears early in Zukin's *Naked City: The Death and Life of Authentic Urban Places* (Zukin 2010, 14).

CHAPTER 3

1. The Metropolitan Transportation Authority is the public benefit corporation responsible for overseeing public transportation in New York City's five boroughs and its suburban counties.

2. I consulted Julian Brash's Ph.D. dissertation for the information cited in this book; however, the dissertation was later published as *Bloomberg's New York: Class and Governance in the Luxury City* by University of Georgia Press (2011).

3. On February 16, 2010, Senator Charles Schumer announced that the federal government had awarded $83 million in stimulus funds for phase 1 of the two-phase project.

4. The ESDC is a New York State public benefit corporation that was founded as the Urban Development Corporation (UDC) in 1968, primarily to

finance the construction of public housing. In 1995 the UDC and several other New York State economic development agencies were consolidated and began doing business as the ESDC. Its mission, according to the agency website, is "to promote business investment and growth that leads to job creation and prosperous communities across New York State" (see http://www.empire.state.ny.us/AboutUs.html). The ESDC can issue bonds without public referendum and has the power of eminent domain. Over time, the ESDC/UDC has overseen projects ranging from the construction of Battery Park City and the Jacob Javits Convention Center to the revitalization of Forty-Second Street in Manhattan.

5. In September 2009, in a bid to generate more cash for Atlantic Yards, Ratner sold an 80 percent stake in the Nets and a 40 percent share of the arena to Russian mogul Mikhail Prokhorov.

CHAPTER 4

1. Ballon's statement at the forum was "We are perhaps now coming out of a prolonged period of cynicism about large-scale government planning efforts, and Moses's dilemmas are instructive" (Ballon 2006).

2. Doctoroff officially stepped down as Deputy Mayor in December 2008 to return to the private sphere and become president of Bloomberg L.P., the information services and media company founded by the mayor. Even so, Doctoroff continued to advise the administration and remained intimately involved in many of the bigger development projects begun on his watch.

3. The notion of recapturing New York City's waterfront from industrial uses is not new; members of the Dinkins administration advocated such a redevelopment strategy in the early 1990s.

4. For a positive comparison, see Halle 2006. For more critical commentary, see Fainstein 2005a and Wells 2007.

5. Mitchell Moss, professor of urban planning at New York University and chair of the Group of 35, touted the games' transformative potential (Applebome 1996).

6. As part of New York City's land use approval process (ULURP), local communities are empowered to propose their own neighborhood redevelopment plans, which are known as 197a plans. These community-generated plans are nonbinding and are required to pass through the same multistep approval process as other plans.

7. Two prominent examples are Rohit Aggarwala, who in 2006 was named director of New York City's Office of Long-Term Planning and Sustainability, and Vishaan Chakrabarti, director of the Manhattan office of the New York City Department of City Planning from 2002 to 2004. Aggarwala, who, before joining the Bloomberg administration, worked in the U.S. Department of Transportation under Clinton and as a consultant at McKinsey and Company, earned a Ph.D. in history at Columbia University, where Kenneth Jackson served as the faculty adviser for his dissertation, "Seat of Empire: New York, Philadelphia, and the Emergence of an American Metropolis, 1776–1837." Chakrabarti helped develop the city's plans for the redevelopment of Hudson Yards before leaving to join Related Companies, the private firm in charge of that

redevelopment. In the summer of 2009 he left Related Companies to become the director of the real estate development program at Columbia University's School of Architecture and Planning. Since leaving the administration, he has become an enthusiastic proponent of private sector involvement in redevelopment and an urban intellectual, "talking and writing about what he sees as misguided ideas about city planning, particularly the notion that big is automatically bad. Call it the Jane Jacobs effect" (Starita 2008, 28).

CHAPTER 5

1. Another "crucial" project referenced by Butzel was Consolidated Edison's unsuccessful proposal to build a hydroelectric plant at Storm King Mountain on the Hudson River in 1966.

2. Robert Yaro, the president of the Regional Plan Association and coauthor of *A Region at Risk*, jokes of having a "Death of New York bookcase" in his office, anchored by Caro's *The Power Broker*, with its assertion that Moses had engineered the "Fall of New York" (Yaro 2009).

3. It would not be the last time that the narrative would revolve around scenarios of projected population growth and the threats, or at least challenges, associated with it. Writing in the *Municipal Review* in 1948, at the height of the Moses era, Paul Windells, then president of the Regional Plan Association, estimated that by 1970, two million additional people would reside in the New York metropolitan region. "This may be the best, it may also be the last, opportunity for an effective decision as to our future," he concluded (Windells 1948, 373).

A late-1962 edition of the Pratt Planning Papers, published from 1962 to 1968 by the Pratt Institute's Department of City and Regional Planning, relied on that same prediction to argue that those additional residents would "settle" more than fifteen hundred square miles of undeveloped land in the New York metropolitan region while an equal number of inner-city residents would migrate from the city center to its outskirts and "1½ million minority group members [would] be added to the region's as yet unassimilated two-and-one-half millions" (Pratt Institute Department of City and Regional Planning 1962, 1). Exactly one year later, another editorial warned that because of a lack of room for expansion in an already dense city center, "by 1985, it is expected that the surrounding communities will have to absorb the entire forecast 6 million population growth" (Pratt Institute Department of City and Regional Planning 1963, 2). At the time, the metropolitan region's population was already at sixteen million. "The six million extra people will be here by 1985, whether we like it or not. They will need homes," the editorial warned, and it went on to argue for the "channeling of growth" by regulating development and passing state legislation that would allow "the establishment of public development corporations empowered to acquire land—by eminent domain, if need be—and to build all public facilities, streets, and utilities needed by the future population of the town" (Pratt Institute Department of City and Regional Planning 1963, 2–4).

Then in 2007 Mayor Bloomberg would launch his PlaNYC 2030 on the basis of projections that New York City's population would grow by another one million people by 2030 (see Chapter 4).

4. Among those critics was Lewis Mumford, who questioned the notion that population growth was inevitable and argued for restricting development and deconcentrating the urban core (Yaro and Hiss 1996, 1).

5. The name "Greensward" was drawn directly from Olmsted (Yaro and Hiss 1996, 83).

6. For instance, the report noted that federal funding for communities in New York and New Jersey to meet the goals of the federal Clean Water Act fell from $600 million in 1972 to $235 million in 1987, and that this funding came in the form of low-interest loans rather than direct grants (Yaro and Hiss 1996, 64).

7. Creating one hundred new parks and recreation areas in "underserved neighborhoods" alone was projected to cost $195 million; to maintain them would require an additional $20 million annually, according to the New York City Parks Council (Yaro and Hiss 1996, 110).

8. Two examples highlighted in *A Region at Risk* were the New York City Department of City Planning's use, in the 1990s, of the Intermodal Surface Transportation Efficiency Act (ISTEA) to fund the rebuilding of a hiking and biking trail along the Shore Parkway in Brooklyn and to acquire the abandoned North Shore Staten Island Railroad right of way for extension of its greenway plan (Yaro and Hiss 1996).

9. For a detailed discussion of uneven development, see Smith 2008. For a more focused discussion as it relates to gentrification, see Smith 1996, 77–92.

10. For a complete discussion of issues surrounding the rebuilding of the World Trade Center, see Mollenkopf 2004. As Lynne Sagalyn wrote in her chapter in *Contentious City*, "Early in the rebuilding dialogue, some advocated for a powerful rebuilding czar, a modern-day Robert Moses, who could overcome the conflicting imperatives and incessant pressures to show quick progress in the effort" (Sagalyn 2004, 26).

CHAPTER 6

1. In advertisements for *The Power Broker* that appeared in the *New York Times Book Review*, for instance, Jacobs enthusiastically trumpeted author Robert Caro's work: "What a great thing Caro has done! I could hardly put it down. I had to force myself to ration it in order to continue my own work. Apart from being so good as biography, as city history, as sheer good reading, *The Power Broker* is an immense public service" (*New York Times Book Review* 1974, 11).

2. In keeping with its ongoing celebration of the Jacobs spirit, the Municipal Art Society hosted a book launch celebration on June 16, 2009.

3. FARs are multipliers for determining a building's size; for example, 15, the median FAR for commercial use at the time, meant a developer could build a building that has an overall square footage equal to the square footage of the lot multiplied by 15.

4. At the time of the survey, the remaining 4 percent were under construction or being renovated (Kayden 2000).

5. Jacobs was writing *The Death and Life of Great American Cities* as the 1961 zoning changes were being considered. Of them she wrote, "There are

several dozen use categories, each differentiated most carefully and thoughtfully—and all of them are irrelevant to the real life problems of use in diverse city districts" (Jacobs 1992, 235).

6. In *The Death and Life of Great American Cities* she wrote, "In city downtowns, public policy cannot inject directly the entirely private enterprises that serve people after work and enliven and help invigorate the place. Nor can public policy, by any sort of fiat, hold these uses in a downtown. But indirectly, public policy can encourage their growth by using its own chessmen, and those susceptible to public pressure, in the right places as primers," (Jacobs, 1961, 167).

7. The meeting occurred June 11, 2008, at PS 51 Elias Howe School, 530 West Forty-Fifth Street.

8. In June 2007 Develop Don't Destroy Brooklyn, a nonprofit community group founded in 2004 to fight the proposed redevelopment of Atlantic Yards, calculated that Forest City Ratner was slated to receive $2.11 billion in public subsidies of one form or another for the redevelopment of Atlantic Yards, including $650 million for the proposed Frank Gehry–designed events arena (Develop Don't Destroy Brooklyn 2007). An April 2006 report by the City of New York Independent Budget Office estimated construction of a new stadium for the New York Mets baseball franchise would cost New York City approximately $177 million—and the state of New York an additional $89 million—over forty years, while New York City would provide $220 million for parking facilities, waterfront parkland, and other work related to a new ballpark for the New York Yankees (City of New York Independent Budget Office 2006).

9. In 2004 the area's median income was $50,000 for a family of four (New York City Department of Housing Preservation and Development 2002).

CHAPTER 7

1. In 2000, of the forty-eight owner-occupied units in Census Tract 173—an area bounded by Amsterdam Avenue, Ninetieth Street, Central Park West, and Eighty-Sixth Street—thirty-six had values of $1 million or more. The median family income for the area was $124,000 (U.S. Bureau of the Census, 2000b).

2. Jaffe also appears in *The Death and Life of Great American Cities*, though in a modestly revised role.

3. In 2000, 30.2 percent of New York City residents owned their own homes, compared with 53 percent for New York State and 68.9 percent for the United States. The median value of owner-occupied housing in the city was $211,900, while citywide median household income was just $38,293. In comparison the median value of owner-occupied housing statewide was $148,700 and median household income was $43,393. Slightly more than one in five—21.2 percent—of New York City residents lived below the poverty line, compared with 14.6 percent statewide (U.S. Bureau of the Census 2000a).

4. In his unfinished contribution to *Robert Moses and the Modern City*, contributor Joel Schwartz contends that Jacobs's interest in diversity had less to do with economic growth or the creation of jobs and more with the construction of "a varied 'ambience'—a carnival atmosphere in the West Village, an array of delights and attractions for the flâneur, the casual observer, and the middle-

class café idler. Note that she applauded changes from factories to services and residences, never the reverse. . . . She supported blue-collar jobs only when they sustained the ambience of middle-class residential neighborhoods (Schwartz 2007, 132–133).

5. Here, Jacobs adopts a notion—not to mention language—culled straight from Adam Smith's discussion of primitive accumulation and the origins of capitalism: "Long, long ago there were two sorts of people; one, the diligent, intelligent and above all frugal elite; the other, lazy rascals, spending their substance, and more, in riotous living" (Sites 2003, 13).

6. Jacobs herself bears the characteristics of an early gentrifier. A "middle-class girl from the working class city" of Scranton, Pennsylvania, upon moving to New York City, she and her husband bought a "tiny old rowhouse" on Hudson Street—at the time a predominately Irish working-class part of Greenwich Village—and renovated it, transforming it into a "middle class rowhouse" (Gans 2006, 213). Still, Gans argues that Jacobs has been unfairly "blessed and blamed for inspiring or encouraging" a greater "gentrification boom" (Gans 2006, 214). Likewise, Klemek argues that a close reading of Jacobs's chapter on preservation in *The Death and Life of Great American Cities* and her advocacy for older, less up-to-date structures as economically viable sources of affordable housing complicates her position in relation to gentrification (Klemek 2008a).

7. For more on Jacobs's relationship to South Street Seaport, see Zuccotti 1974.

8. At the end of the first decade of the twenty-first century, a similar approach was being taken regarding the redevelopment of Governors Island, the 172-acre former military base just off the tip of southern Manhattan in Upper New York. There, a multimillion-dollar park, designed by the Dutch landscape architecture firm, West 8, was being built in part to attract development interest.

9. The arrangement also included a loophole, however, allowing New York City to divert those funds to maintain existing municipal services. Over time, this loophole became a budgeting crutch, and off-site housing programs were suspended in 1990 as a consequence of budget shortfalls. All told, the initiative generated pledges of $1 billion, but the actual amount spent on housing was far less, and the number of units created was limited: there was the rehabilitation of 1,557 units and community facilities in vacant city-owned buildings and the renovation of 14 abandoned buildings with 893 units in the South Bronx and an additional 40 vacant buildings and 664 units in Central Harlem. Another 2,128 units were generated through the sale of empty buildings to nonprofit developers in the South Bronx (Gordon 1997). In 2006 an agreement was reached whereby $130 million in Battery Park City revenues would be used to create the New York City Housing Trust Fund and provide seed financing for the New York Acquisition Fund, an initiative to preserve and construct 30,000 units of off-site affordable housing over ten years (New York City Department of Housing Preservation and Development 2008).

10. During his tenure, from 1949 to 1960, as chair of the Mayor's Committee on Slum Clearance, Moses obtained thirty-two planning grants, saw seventeen redevelopment/renewal projects completed, and helped New York access $65.8 million in federal Title I resources (Ballon 2007).

11. Moses located twelve of his seventeen Title I projects near existing public housing projects; in two cases Title I projects were built in conjunction with public housing projects (Ballon 2007).

CHAPTER 8

1. For instance, for a discussion of Jacobs's legacy and its relationship to redevelopment policies in Chicago, as well as to New Urbanism and Richard Florida's concept of the creative city, see Bennett 2010.

2. Within policy mobility literature, Moses, by traveling to Portland from New York City to "impart knowledge," operated as an "incoming policy consultant" (McCann 2011, 114).

3. By 1950 Portland's metropolitan population had practically doubled from its prewar levels, reaching 705,000 inhabitants. By 1990 it had grown to 1.8 million, and, by year's end 2009, according to Portland State University estimates, Portland alone had a population of 582,130, while the greater metropolitan region ballooned to 2.2 million (Portland State University 2009).

4. To some, at least, Portland once had such a figure—although perhaps more enlightened—in Glenn Jackson, one-time CEO of Pacific Power and Light and chair of the Oregon Highway Commission, who, according to a 2007 editorial in the *Portland Oregonian* could "conjure bridges and highways from discrete-but-forceful conversations with key players in business and government" (Editorial 2007, C6). In response, a blogger on the website *Portland Transport* referred to Jackson as "the closest Oregon ever had to a Robert Moses-type character" ("Pining for Glenn Jackson" 2007).

5. Her second book, *The Economy of Cities*, was published in 1970; her third, *Cities and the Wealth of Nations*, in 1984.

CHAPTER 9

1. Burden is the daughter of Stanley Mortimer, heir to the Standard Oil fortune, and Babe Paley, the New York City socialite and fashion icon.

2. Publicly, Doctoroff denied any rift with Burden and has played down any inference that she was an alternative choice to serve as planning director. In a 2002 interview with *New York* magazine Doctoroff noted that he interviewed Burden three times and conducted "extensive due diligence and what I found was somebody who was strikingly substantive, passionate about her work, passionate about New York City, and had a sense of where she wanted to take the City Planning Commission. I was very comfortable" (Gardner 2002).

3. In July 2004 Bloomberg announced the creation of a Design and Construction Excellence (D+CE) initiative as a means of demonstrating the administration's "commitment to fostering good design in our City" and expanding New York City's "pre-eminence as the design capital of the world." Administered through the city's Department of Design and Construction (DDC), the program's "hallmark" involves the adoption of a quality-based selection process "for procurement of design services" (Bloomberg 2004).

4. On October 19, 2009, the same day the New York City Council approved the rezoning of the western half of Hudson Yards, Burden announced that the city would move ahead with plans to purchase the remaining northern-most section of the High Line, which runs along the southern and western edges of Hudson Yards (for more information, see Chaban 2009).

5. The Project for Public Spaces includes both Whyte and Jacobs among its select group of "pioneer placemakers." According to the project's website, "The Placemaking movement was born over forty years ago, when pioneers like Jane Jacobs and William H. Whyte published their groundbreaking ideas about Americans and the urban experience. Back then there was no name for their way of thinking—they simply showed us that cities should be designed for people, with walkable streets, welcoming public spaces, and lively neighborhoods" (Project for Public Spaces, n.d. b).

6. If built as originally designed, the building would have been as tall as the Empire State Building.

7. Like Burden, New York City Parks Director Adrian Benepe also takes a "hands-on" approach to the way projects under his purview look, and he too "reviews all designs at the final schematic stage" (Benepe 2008a, 57).

8. To be sure, the administration participated in both directions of the policy mobility process. Burden, with members of her staff, not only traveled the world in search of best practices to adapt to New York City's particular circumstances, but she, Doctoroff, and the mayor were frequent speakers at international events where they positioned New York City as being at the forefront of contemporary urban innovation and design.

9. For example, in an effort to capture and re-create Copenhagen's lively street café scene, Burden and Washburn traveled to Denmark, where they paced off the exact dimensions of a waterfront café in Copenhagen. Washburn, in his presentation to the American Institute of Architects, included a photograph of Burden riding a bicycle through the city.

CHAPTER 10

1. In 2008 local public radio host Brian Lehrer launched a website that allowed New York residents to list stalled projects, "cranes on pause," as part of the radio station WNYC's "Your Uncommon Economic Indicators" series. The site can be accessed at http://maps.google.com/maps/ms?msa=0&msid=1025206 26049988660817.00046e3703b8126b12edb&ie=UTF8&ll=40.700422%2C-73 .970947&spn=0.057262%2C0.077248&z=13&source=embed.

2. The NYCEDC is a nonprofit, public-private agency whose mission is to "encourage economic growth in each of the five boroughs of New York City by strengthening the City's competitive position and facilitating investments that build capacity, generate prosperity and catalyze the economic vibrancy of City life as a whole" (New York City Economic Development Corporation 2012). The NYCEDC has been intimately involved in the planning and execution of Mayor Bloomberg's development agenda, working closely in an "iterative process" on major projects, including the revitalization of 125th Street in Harlem and Willets

Point (Pinsky 2008). The NYCEDC is controlled by the mayor through his direct appointment of seven of twenty-seven board members, including the chair, who nominates ten additional members. The remaining ten board positions are selected by the city's five borough presidents, each of whom appoints one, and the speaker of the city council, who appoints five. In its 2007–2008 budget, the NYCEDC reported that it received nearly $589.9 million in reimbursements and grants from New York City. That accounted for almost 70 percent of the NYCEDC's $848.8 million total operating revenues for the year. Another $122.6 million (14.4 percent) in operating revenues was generated by real estate sales and property rentals.

3. Prior to taking the reins of the NYCEDC in February 2008, Pinsky, a real estate lawyer, served as the corporation's executive vice president, codirecting the Financial Services Division. He administered many of the New York City's discretionary incentive programs and helped negotiate a number of major development projects, including Atlantic Yards. Even earlier he had helped coordinate the NYCEDC's efforts at Hudson Yards.

4. The Institute for Urban Design is a New York–based nonprofit that aims to provide a "central platform for debate over issues related to urban planning, development and design" by "creating a common territory for architects, planners, policy-makers, developers, academics, journalists, and urban enthusiasts" (Institute for Urban Design 2012).

5. Opened in April 2009, the forty-five-thousand-seat stadium was built with more than $160 million in city and state subsidies and $540 million in tax-exempt financing.

References

Abbott, Carl. 1983. *Portland: Planning, Politics, and Growth in a Twentieth-Century City*. Lincoln: University of Nebraska Press.
———. 2010a. E-mail exchange with the author, October 25.
———. 2010b. E-mail exchange with the author, November 15.
———. 2010c. "Robert Moses in Portland." *Urban West*, July 7. Available at http://theurbanwest.com/page/2.
Acitelli, Tom. 2007. "Doctoroff on Moses Comparisons: 'Always a Little Odd.'" *New York Observer*, December 7. Available at http://observer.com/2007/12/doctoroff-on-robert-moses-comparisons-always-a-little-odd.
———. 2009. "The Power 100: The Most Powerful People in New York Real Estate." *New York Observer*, June 3. Available at http://observer.com/2009/06/the-power-100-the-most-powerful-people-in-new-york-real-estate.
Aggarwala, Rohit. 2007. Remarks at "New York 2030: New York's Green and Just Future," Cooper Union, New York, November 17.
Alexiou, Alice Sparberg. 2006. *Jane Jacobs: Urban Visionary*. Piscataway, NJ: Rutgers University Press.
American Institute of Architects. 2008. Flyer for "Ecotones: Mitigating NYC's Contentious Sites" conference, New York, May 22.
Anderson, Martin. 1964. *The Federal Bulldozer*. Cambridge, MA: MIT Press.
Angotti, Tom. 2005. "Atlantic Yards: Through the Looking Glass." *Gotham Gazette*, November 15. Available at http://www.gothamgazette.com/article/landuse/20051115/12/1654.
———. 2007. "Plan NYC 2030." *Gotham Gazette*, February 6. Available at http://www.gothamgazette.com/article/landuse/20070206/12/2095.

Applebome, Peter. 1996. "So You Want to Hold an Olympics." *New York Times*, August 4. Available at http://www.nytimes.com/1996/08/04/weekinreview/so-you-want-to-hold-an-olympics.html.

Atlantic Yards. n.d. "Community Benefits Agreement." Available at http://www.atlanticyards.com/community-benefits-agreement (accessed December 11, 2012).

August, Martine. 2008. "Social Mix and Canadian Public Housing Redevelopment: Experiences in Toronto." *Canadian Journal of Urban Research* 17 (1): 82–100.

Bagli, Charles. 2009a. "M.T.A. and Developer Agree to Delay $1 Billion Railyard Deal." *New York Times*, February 2. Available at http://www.nytimes.com/2009/02/03/nyregion/03yards.html?ref=westsiderailyardsnyc.

———. 2009b. "New Design Unveiled for Atlantic Yards Arena." *New York Times*, September 9. Available at http://cityroom.blogs.nytimes.com/2009/09/09/new-design-unveiled-for-atlantic-yards-arena/?ref=charlesvbagli.

———. 2009c. "New Nets Arena Wins Another Court Challenge." *New York Times*, December 1. Available at http://www.nytimes.com/2009/12/02/nyregion/02yards.html?ref=charlesvbagli.

———. 2010. "Development at Railyards Is Delayed." *New York Times*, February 1. Available at http://www.nytimes.com/2010/02/02/nyregion/02railyards.html?ref=charlesvbagli.

Ballon, Hilary. 2006. Remarks at "Jane Jacobs vs. Robert Moses: How Stands the Debate Today?" Gotham Center for New York City History, City University of New York, New York, October 11.

———. 2007. "Robert Moses and Urban Renewal." In *Robert Moses and the Modern City: The Transformation of New York*, edited by Hilary Ballon and Kenneth Jackson, 94–115. New York: Norton.

———. 2008. Presentation to Masters of Urban Planning Program, Robert F. Wagner Graduate School of Public Service, New York University, New York, February 19.

Ballon, Hilary, and Kenneth Jackson. 2007a. Introduction to *Robert Moses and the Modern City: The Transformation of New York*, edited by Hilary Ballon and Kenneth Jackson, 65–66. New York: Norton.

———. 2007b. *Robert Moses and the Modern City: The Transformation of New York*. New York: Norton.

Barbanel, Josh. 2004. "Remaking, or Preserving, the City's Face." *New York Times*, January 18. Available at http://www.nytimes.com/2004/01/18/realestate/remaking-or-preserving-the-city-s-face.html?pagewanted=all&src=pm.

Barbaro, Michael. 2008. "As Bloomberg's Time Wanes, Titans Seek Mayor in His Mold." *New York Times*, July 7. Available at http://query.nytimes.com/gst/fullpage.html?res=9806E0D9103FF934A35754C0A96E9C8B63&ref=michaelbarbaro.

Barwick, Kent. 2008a. E-mail exchange with the author, November 25.

———. 2008b. Interview with the author, November 4.

Beauregard, Robert. 1989. "Between Modernity and Postmodernity: The Ambiguous Position of U.S. Planning." *Environment and Planning D: Society and Space* 7 (4): 381–395.

Beckelman, Laurie. 2007. Remarks at "The Future Face of New York," Hunter College, New York, October 18.
Benepe, Adrian. 2007. Remarks at "New York 2030: New York's Green and Just Future," Cooper Union, New York, November 17.
———. 2008a. "Friday in the Park with Adrian." By Linda McIntyre. *Landscape Architecture* 98 (2): 50–59.
———. 2008b. Remarks at "Civic Talk: Battles of Development," Museum of the City of New York, New York, July 17.
Bennett, Larry. 2010. *The Third City: American Urbanism*. Chicago: University of Chicago Press.
Berman, Marshall. 1982. *All That Is Solid Melts into Air: The Experience of Modernity*. New York: Simon and Schuster.
Bernstein, Adam. 2006. "Jane Jacobs, 89: Writer, Activist, Spoke Out against Urban Renewal." *Washington Post*, April 26. Available at http://www.washingtonpost.com/wp-dyn/content/article/2006/04/25/AR2006042501026.html.
Bianco, Martha. 2001. "Robert Moses and Lewis Mumford: Competing Paradigms of Growth in Portland, Oregon." *Planning Perspectives* 16:95–114.
Bloomberg, Michael. 2004. "Mayor Michael R. Bloomberg Announces the 22nd Annual Art Commission Awards for Excellence in Design." Available at http://www.nyc.gov/portal/site/nycgov/menuitem.c0935b9a57bb4ef3daf2f1c701c789a0/index.jsp?pageID=mayor_press_release&catID=1194&doc_name=http%3A%2F%2Fwww.nyc.gov%2Fhtml%2Fom%2Fhtml%2F2004b%2Fpr191-04.html&cc=unused1978&rc=1194&ndi=1.
———. 2007. Keynote address, "Thinking Big for New York City," Manhattan Institute Center for Rethinking Development, New York, November 1.
———. 2008. "Mayor Bloomberg Delivers 2008 State of the City Address." Available at http://www.nyc.gov/portal/site/nycgov/menuitem.c0935b9a57bb4ef3daf2f1c701c789a0/index.jsp?pageID=mayor_press_release&catID=1194&doc_name=http%3A%2F%2Fwww.nyc.gov%2Fhtml%2Fom%2Fhtml%2F2008a%2Fpr018-08.html&cc=unused1978&rc=1194&ndi=1.
———. 2009. "Statements of Mayor Bloomberg and Governor Patterson on Final Public Approval of General Project Plan for Columbia University Expansion." Available at http://www.nyc.gov/portal/site/nycgov/menuitem.c0935b9a57bb4ef3daf2f1c701c789a0/index.jsp?pageID=mayor_press_release&catID=1194&doc_name=http%3A%2F%2Fwww.nyc.gov%2Fhtml%2Fom%2Fhtml%2F2009a%2Fpr233-09.html&cc=unused1978&rc=1194&ndi=1.
Boudreau, Julie-Anne, Roger Keil, and Douglas Young. 2009. *Changing Toronto: Governing Urban Neoliberalism*. Toronto: University of Toronto Press.
Boyer, M. Christine. 1992. "Cities for Sale: Merchandising History at South Street Seaport." In *Variations on a Theme Park: The New American City and the End of Public Space*, edited by Michael Sorkin, 181–204. New York: Hill and Wang.
Brash, Julian. 2006. "The Bloomberg Way: Urban Development Politics, Urban Ideology, and Class Transformation in Contemporary New York City." Ph.D. dissertation, Graduate Center, City University of New York.
Brenner, Neil and Nik Theodore. 2002. "Cities and the Geographies of Actually Existing Neoliberalism." *Antipode* 34 (3): 349–379.

Brown, Carlton. 2007. Remarks at "The Oversuccessful City: Developer Realities," New York Times Center Stage Auditorium, New York, November 27.

Buettner, Russ, and Ray Rivera. 2009. "A Stalled Vision: Big Development as the City's Future." *New York Times*, October 29, A1.

Burden, Amanda. 2006a. Remarks at "Jane Jacobs vs. Robert Moses: How Stands the Debate Today?" City University of New York, New York, October 11.

———. 2006b. "Jane Jacobs, Robert Moses, and City Planning Today." *Gotham Gazette*, November 6. Available at http://www.gothamgazette.com/article//20061106/202/2015.

———. 2007a. "Shaping the City: A Strategic Blueprint for New York's Future," presented at the Department of Urban Affairs and Planning, Hunter College, New York, November 5.

———. 2007b. Remarks to Crain's New York Business Breakfast, New York, February 14.

———. 2008a. "Shaping the City: A Strategic Blueprint for New York's Future," presented at the School of Architecture, City College of New York, New York, March 27.

———. 2008b. "Amanda Burden Negotiating City Design." Urban Age South America Conference, São Paulo, Brazil, December 3–5. Available at http://www.youtube.com/watch?v=JiCgFZvNIC4.

———. 2009. "Shaping the City: A Strategic Blueprint for New York's Future/The Five Borough Economic Plan," presented at the American Institute of Architects, New York Chapter, Center for Architecture, New York, May 26.

Butler, Stuart. 1981. *Enterprise Zones: Greenlining the Inner Cities*. New York: Universe Books.

Butzel, Albert. 2008. Remarks at "Civic Talk: Battles of Development," Museum of the City of New York, New York, July 17.

Caldwell, Diane. 2007. "Once at Cotillions, Now Reshaping the Cityscape." *New York Times*, January 15, 1.

Caro, Robert. 1975. *The Power Broker: Robert Moses and the Fall of New York*. New York: Vintage Books.

Chaban, Matt. 2009. "Planning Ahead: Amid Flurry of Approvals, New York Moves Forward on the High Line." *Architect's Newspaper*, October 20. Available at http://www.archpaper.com/e-board_rev.asp?News_ID=3944.

Chan, Sewell. 2007. "Panel Rejects Columbia's Expansion Plan." *New York Times*, August 16. Available at http://cityroom.blogs.nytimes.com/2007/08/16/panel-rejects-columbias-expansion-plan/?ref=sewellchan.

City of New York Independent Budget Office. 2006. "Double Play: The Economics and Financing of Stadiums for the Yankees and the Mets." Available at http://www.ibo.nyc.ny.us/iboreports/doubleplay.html.

———. 2009. "The Proposed Arena at Atlantic Yards: An Analysis of City Fiscal Gains and Losses." Available at http://www.ibo.nyc.ny.us/iboreports/AtlanticYards091009.pdf.

City of Portland Bureau of Planning. 2008. "Urban Design Assessment: Central Portland Plan." Available at http://www.portlandoregon.gov/bps/article/218810.

City of Toronto. 2002. "Regeneration in Kings: Directions and Emerging Trends." Available at http://www.toronto.ca/planning/kings_execsum.htm.

———. 2003. "Culture Plan for the Creative City." Available at http://www.toronto.ca/culture/brochures/2003_cultureplan.pdf.

"City Planning: Battle of the Approach." 1943. *Fortune* 18:164–168, 222–223.

Coalition for a Livable Future. 2007. *The Regional Equity Atlas: Metropolitan Portland's Geography of Opportunity.* Portland, OR: Coalition for a Liveable Future and Portland State University. Available at http://www.equityatlas.org/chapters/EquityAtlas.pdf.

Columbia University. n.d. "Manhattanville in West Harlem." Available at http://neighbors.columbia.edu/pages/manplanning/index.html (accessed November 11, 2007).

Congress for the New Urbanism. 2001. "Charter of the New Urbanism." Available at http://www.cnu.org/charter.

Cooper, Alexander. 2009. Interview with the author, January 13.

Dear, Michael. 1989. "Survey 16: Privatization and the Rhetoric of Planning Practice." *Environment and Planning D: Society and Space* 7:449–462.

Debord, Guy. 1983. *Society of the Spectacle.* Detroit: Black and Red.

Develop Don't Destroy Brooklyn. 2007. "Documents Show More Than Half of the Financing for Forest City Ratner's Atlantic Yards Project Is Government Backed." Available at http://dddb.net/php/press/070606Subsidies.php.

———. 2009a. "About the Ratner Plan." Available at http://dddb.net/php/aboutratner.php.

———. 2009b. "New Atlantic Yards Lawsuit Slams Empire State Development Corporation; Could Doom Project." Available at http://www.dddb.net/php/latestnews_Linked.php?id=2398.

———. 2010. "Eminent Domain." Available at http://www.developdontdestroy.org/eminentdomain.

Doctoroff, Daniel. 2009. Remarks at "Plan NYC: Innovation and Legacy," Museum of the City of New York, New York, April 15.

Dolowitz, D., and D. Marsh. 1996. "Who Learns What from Whom: A Review of the Policy Transfer Literature." *Political Studies* 44:343–357.

Dotan, Hamutal. 2009. "Following in Jane's Footsteps." *Torontoist*, May 1. Available at http://torontoist.com/2009/05/following_in_her_footsteps.

Dreier, Peter. 2006. "Jane Jacobs's Legacy." *City and Community* 5 (3): 227–231.

Duncan, James, and Nancy Duncan. 2001. "The Aestheticization of the Politics of Landscape Preservation." *Annals of the Association of American Geographers* 91 (2): 387–409.

Dunlap David. 1988. "At 50, Planning Commission's Influence Is Diminishing." *New York Times*, November 30, B1.

———. 1992. "The Quest for a New Zoning Plan." *New York Times*, August 12, 101.

Editorial. 2007. *Portland Oregonian*, January 5, C6.

Fainstein, Susan. 2005a. "The Return of Urban Renewal: Dan Doctoroff's Grand Plans for New York City." *Harvard Design Magazine* 22:1–5.

———. 2005b. "Cities and Diversity: Should We Want It? Can We Plan For It?" *Urban Affairs Review* 41 (3): 4–19.

Finder, Alan. 1989. "Council Land-Review Role Increased." *New York Times*, August 2, B3.
Fishman, Robert. 2000. "The Death and Life of American Regional Planning." In *Reflections on Regionalism*, edited by Bruce Katz, 107–123. Washington, DC: Brookings Institution Press.
———. 2007. "Revolt of the Urbs: Robert Moses and His Critics." In *Robert Moses and the Modern City: The Transformation of New York*, edited by Hilary Ballon and Kenneth Jackson, 122–129. New York: Norton.
Flint, Anthony. 2009. *Wrestling with Moses: How Jane Jacobs Took on New York's Master Builder and Transformed the American City*. New York: Random House.
Florida, Richard. 2002. *The Rise of the Creative Class and How It's Transforming Work, Leisure, Community, and Everyday Life*. New York: Basic Books.
Flyvberg, Bent. 2005. "Design by Deception: The Politics of Megaproject Approval." *Harvard Design Magazine* 22:50–59.
Forty, Adrian. 1992. *Objects of Desire: Design and Society Since 1750*. London: Thames and Hudson.
Freeman, Joshua. 2000. *Working-Class New York: Life and Labor since World War II*. New York: New Press.
Furman Center for Real Estate and Urban Policy. 2010. "How Have Recent Rezonings Affected the City's Ability to Grow?" Available at http://furmancenter.org/files/publications/Rezonings_Furman_Center_Policy_Brief_March_2010.pdf.
Garber, Judith, and David Imbroscio. 1996. "The Myth of the North American City Reconsidered: Local Constitutional Regimes in Canada and the United States." *Urban Affairs Review* 31 (5): 595–624.
Gans, Herbert. 2006. "Jane Jacobs: Toward an Understanding of 'Death and Life of Great American Cities.'" *City and Community* 5 (3): 213–215.
Gardner, Ralph, Jr. 2002. "Social Planner." *New York*, May 13. Available at http://nymag.com/nymetro/news/politics/newyork/features/6005.
Gelfand, Mark. 1975. *A Nation of Cities*. New York: Oxford University Press
Gilbert, Helen. 2001. "A Case Study in Contemporary Development: How Does It Measure Up to the Principles of Classic Urban Design Theorists?" Paper presented at the Seventh Annual Pacific Rim Real Estate Society Conference, Adelaide Australia, January 21–24.
Goldberger, Paul. 2007a. "Eminent Dominion: Rethinking the Legacy of Robert Moses." *New Yorker*, February 5. Available at http://www.newyorker.com/arts/critics/skyline/2007/02/05/070205crsk_skyline_goldberger.
———. 2007b. "Commemoration." In *Block by Block: Jane Jacobs and the Future of New York*, edited by Timothy Mennel, Jo Steffens, and Christopher Klemek, 12. Princeton, NJ: Princeton Architectural Press.
Gordon, David. 1997. *Battery Park City: Politics and Planning on the New York Waterfront*. Amsterdam: Gordon and Breach.
Gottlieb, Martin. 1989. "Climbing Jacobs' Ladder." *The Nation*, June 5, 772–776.
Grant, Kelly. 2010. "Province Approves Reducing Queens Quay to Two Lanes." *Globe and Mail*, April 20. Available at http://www.theglobeandmail

.com/news/toronto/province-approves-reducing-queens-quay-to-two-lanes/article4315595.
Gratz, Roberta Brandes. 2010a. Remarks at "Jane Jacobs, Robert Moses and the Automobile," Museum of the City of New York, New York, May 17.
———. 2010b. *The Battle for Gotham: New York in the Shadow of Robert Moses and Jane Jacobs*. New York: Nation Books.
Greenberg, Ken. 2010. Interview with the author, June 29.
Hackworth, Jason. 2000. "The Third Wave." Ph.D. dissertation, Rutgers University.
Haley, Gregory. 2007. "Balancing Great American Cities: Its Form AND Content." *E-Oculus*. Available at http://www.aiany.org/eOCULUS/newsletter/?p=203.
Halle, David. 2006. "Who Wears Jane Jacobs' Mantle in Today's New York City?" *City and Community* 5 (3): 237–241.
Harvey, David. 1990a. *The Condition of Postmodernity: An Enquiry into the Origins of Cultural Change*. Oxford: Blackwell.
———. 1990b. "Between Space and Time: Reflections on the Geographical Imagination." *Annals of the Association of American Geographers* 80 (3): 418–434.
———. 1997. "The New Urbanism and the Communitarian Trap." *Harvard Design Magazine* 1 (Winter/Spring): 1–3.
———. 2008a. "The Right to the City." Fifth Annual Lewis Mumford Lecture on Urbanism, Graduate Program in Urban Design, School of Architecture, City College, New York. April 3.
———. 2008b. "The Right to the City." *New Left Review* 53:23–40.
———. 2010. *The Enigma of Capital: And the Crises of Capitalism*. Oxford: Oxford University Press.
Hess, Paul. 2010. Interview with the author, June 28.
Hume, Christopher. 2007. "Is It Time for the Great Synthesis?" *Toronto Star*, October 6. Available at http://www.thestar.com/article/264146--is-it-time-for-the-great-synthesis.
———. 2010. "How Toronto Plans for Failure." *Toronto Star*, May 8. Available at http://www.thestar.com/news/insight/article/806539--how-toronto-plans-for-failure.
Husock, Howard. 1994. "Urban Iconoclast: Jane Jacobs Revisited." *City Journal*, Winter: 110–114.
Institute for Urban Design. 2012. "About Us." Available at http://www.ifud.org/about-us.
Jackson, Kenneth. 1989. "Robert Moses and the Planned Environment: A Re-evaluation." In *Robert Moses, Single-Minded Genius*, edited by Joann Krieg, 21–30. Interlaken, NY: Heart of the Lakes.
———. 2007. "Robert Moses and the Rise of New York: The Power Broker in Perspective." In *Robert Moses and the Modern City: The Transformation of New York*, edited by Hilary Ballon and Kenneth Jackson, 67–71. New York: Norton.
Jacobs, Jane. 1958. Speech to the New York State Motorbus Convention, November 10. MS1995-29, box 25, folder 8, Jane Jacobs Papers Archives and Manuscripts, John J. Burns Library, Boston College.

———. 1962. "The Citizen in Urban Renewal: Participation or Manipulation?" Unpublished manuscript, Jane Jacobs Papers Archives and Manuscripts, John J. Burns Library, Boston College.

———. 1969. *The Economy of Cities.* New York: Vintage Books

———. 1992. *The Death and Life of Great American Cities.* New York: Random House.

———. 2005. "Letter to Mayor Bloomberg and the City Council." *Brooklyn Rail.* Available at http://www.brooklynrail.org/2005/05/local/letter-to-mayor-bloomberg.

———. n.d. "Public Life, at Sidewalk Scale." Unpublished manuscript, Jane Jacobs Papers Archives and Manuscripts, John J. Burns Library, Boston College.

Jameson, Fredric. 1996. "City Theory in Jacobs and Heidegger." In *Anywise,* edited by Cynthia Davidson, 32–39. Cambridge, MA: MIT Press.

Kayden, Jerold S. 2000. *Privately Owned Public Space: The New York City Experience.* New York: Wiley.

Kennicott, Philip. 2007. "A Builder Who Went to Town." *Washington Post,* March 1, NO1.

Kidder, Paul. 2008. "The Urbanist Ethics of Jane Jacobs." *Ethics, Place and Environment* 11 (3): 253–266.

King, John. 2007. "He May Not Be PC, but He Sure Could Plan a City." *San Francisco Chronicle,* April 20, E6.

Klemek, Christopher. 2007. "Jane Jacobs and the Future of New York." In *Block by Block: Jane Jacobs and the Future of New York,* edited by Timothy Mennel, Jo Steffens, and Christopher Klemek, 7–11. Princeton, NJ: Princeton Architectural Press.

———. 2008a. "From Political Outsider to Power Broker in Two 'Great American Cities': Jane Jacobs and the Fall of Urban Renewal Order in New York and Toronto." *Journal of Urban History* 34 (2): 309–332.

———. 2008b. Interview with the author, October 6.

Krueger, Robert. 2011. "Amanda Burden on Creating Value with Urban Open Space." *Urban Land,* November 23. Available at http://urbanland.uli.org/Articles/2011/Fall11/KruegerBurdenVid.

Lander, Brad. 2006. Remarks at "Jane Jacobs vs. Robert Moses: How Stands the Debate Today?" City University of New York, New York, October 11.

Lefebvre, Henri. 1996. *Writings on Cities.* Edited by Eleonore Kofman and Elizabeth Lebas. Oxford: Blackwell.

———. 2003. *The Urban Revolution.* Translated by Robert Bononno. Minneapolis: University of Minnesota Press.

Lemon, James. 1996. *Liberal Dreams and Nature's Limits: Great Cities of North America Since 1600.* Toronto: Oxford University Press.

Lilley, K. D. 1999. "Modern Visions of the Medieval City: Competing Conceptions of Urbanism in European Civic Design." *Environment and Planning B: Planning and Design* 26:427–446.

Lopez, Jose. 2009. Remarks at "Radical Urbanism: A Conference on the Right to the City," Graduate Center, City University of New York, New York, December 11.

Mandelbaum, Seymour. 1991. "Telling Stories." *Journal of Planning Education and Research* 10 (3): 209–213.
Martin, Douglas. 2006. "Jane Jacobs, Urban Activist, Is Dead at 89." *New York Times*, April 25, A1.
"Mayor Bloomberg and Speaker Quinn Announce Final Rezoning for Redevelopment of Hudson Yards Area." 2009. NYC.gov. Available at http://www.nyc.gov/portal/site/nycgov/menuitem.c0935b9a57bb4ef3daf2f1c701c789a0/index.jsp?pageID=mayor_press_release&catID=1194&doc_name=http%3A%2F%2Fwww.nyc.gov%2Fhtml%2Fom%2Fhtml%2F2009b%2Fpr545-09.html&cc=unused1978&rc=1194&ndi=1.
McCann, Eugene. 2004. "'Best Places': Interurban Competition, Quality of Life, and Popular Media Discourse." *Urban Studies* 41 (10): 1909–1929.
———. 2011. "Urban Policy Mobilities and Global Circuits of Knowledge: Toward a Research Agenda." *Annals of the Association of American Geographers* 101 (1): 107–130.
McGeehan, Patrick. 2011. "The High Line Isn't Just a Sight to See; It's Also an Economic Dynamo." *New York Times*, June 5, A18.
Medchill, Lisa. 2008. "The 100 Most Powerful People in New York Real Estate." *New York Observer*, May 14. Available at http://observer.com/2008/05/the-100-most-powerful-people-in-new-york-real-estate.
Merrifield, Andy. 2006. *Henri Lefebvre: A Critical Introduction*. New York: Routledge.
Miles, Malcolm. 2000. "After the Public Realm: Spaces of Representation, Transition and Plurality." *Journal of Art and Design Education* 19 (3): 253–261.
Miller, Jonathan. 1962. "In Praise of Hudson Street." *New Statesman*, October 12, 496–497.
Mollenkopf, John. 2004. *Contentious City: The Politics of Recovery in New York City*. New York: Russell Sage Foundation.
Montgomery, Roger. 1998. "Is There Still Life in *The Death and Life*?" *Journal of the American Planning Association* 64 (3): 269–274.
Moran, Tim. 2006. "ESDC Approves Atlantic Yards." *Real Deal*, December 8. Available at http://therealdeal.com/blog/2006/12/08/esdc-approves-atlantic-yards.
Morrone, Francis. 2008. "Battery Park City: A New Neighborhood Rises." Municipal Art Society walking tour, September 21.
Moses, Robert. 1942. "What Happened to Haussmann?" *Architectural Forum* 77:57–66.
———. 1943. "Director's Report." In *Portland Improvement*, 7–16 (Portland, OR: City of Portland). Available at http://blogtown.portlandmercury.com/images/blogimages/2009/09/30/1254339381-portland_improvement_-_robert_moses_1943.pdf.
———. 1944. "Mr. Moses Dissects the 'Long-Haired' Planners." *New York Times Magazine*, June 25, 16–17, 38–39.
———. 1961. Letter to Bennett Cerf. Jane Jacobs Papers Archives and Manuscripts, John J. Burns Library, Boston College.
Mumford, Lewis. 1939. Introduction to *Regional Planning in the Pacific Northwest*. Portland, OR: Northwest Regional Council.

———. 1959. "The Skyway's the Limit." *New Yorker*, November 14, 181–191.

———. 1961. Letter to Mr. Wensberg. Jane Jacobs Papers Archives and Manuscripts, John J. Burns Library, Boston College.

———. 1962. "Mother Jacobs' Home Remedies." *New Yorker*, December 1, 148–179.

Municipal Art Society of New York. 2007a. *Jane Jacobs and the Future of New York*. Urban Gallery, Municipal Art Society, New York.

———. 2007b. "The Oversuccessful City: Developers' Realities," New York Times Center Stage Auditorium, New York, November 27.

———. n.d. a. "Jane Jacobs Forum 2011: Women as Intellectuals." Available at http://mas.org/programs/jane-jacobs-forum/jj11 (accessed November 25, 2012).

———. n.d. b. "Livable Neighborhoods Program." Available at http://mas.org/programs/livable-neighborhoods (accessed November 25, 2012).

Muschamp, Herbert. 1998. "Critic's Notebook: Barking at the Barricades in a City of Twilight Zoning." *New York Times*, January 8, E2.

Museum of the City of New York. 2007. "Robert Moses and the Modern City: Remaking the Metropolis." Available at http://www.mcny.org/exhibitions/past/robert-moses-and-the-modern-city-remaking-the-metropolis.html.

Nelson, Arthur, Rolf Pendal, Casey Dawkins, and Gerrit Knapp. 2002. "The Link between Growth Management and Housing Affordability: The Academic Evidence." Brookings Institution Discussion Paper. Available at http://www.brookings.edu/es/urban/publications/growthmang.pdf.

Nelson, James. 2011. "449 Washington Street—Rezoning Gives a $1M Boost in Value." *National Real Estate Investor*, September 14. Available at http://blog.nreionline.com/the-full-nelson/2011/09/14/449-washington-street---rezoning-gives-a-1m-boost-in-value.

Newman, Oscar. 1996. *Creating Defensible Space*. Washington, DC: U.S. Department of Housing and Urban Development, Office of Policy Development and Research. Available at http://www.huduser.org/portal/publications/def.pdf.

New York City Department of City Planning. 2007. "Privately Owned Public Plazas: Text Amendment." Available at http://www.nyc.gov/html/dcp/pdf/priv/101707_final_approved_text.pdf.

———. 2012a. "Borough Waterfront Plans." Available at http://www.nyc.gov/html/dcp/html/pub/waternyc.shtml#contents.

———. 2012b. "Chair: Amanda M. Burden, FAICP." Available at http://www.nyc.gov/html/dcp/html/about/amandaburden.shtml.

———. 2012c. "Hudson Yards." Available at http://www.nyc.gov/html/dcp/html/hyards/hymain.shtml.

———. 2012d. "Privately Owned Public Space." Available at http://www.nyc.gov/html/dcp/html/pops/pops.shtml.

New York City Department of Housing Preservation and Development. 2002. "The New Housing Marketplace: Creating Housing for the Next Generation, 2004–2013." Available at http://nyc.gov/html/hpd/downloads/pdf/10yearHMplan.pdf.

———. 2008. "Mayor Bloomberg's Affordable Housing Plan." Available at http://www.nyc.gov/html/hpd/downloads/pdf/New-Housing-Market-Place-Plan.pdf.

New York City Economic Development Corporation. 2012. "Mission Statement." Available at http://www.nycedc.com/about-nycedc/mission-statement.

New York City Planning Commission. 1993. *Shaping the City's Future: New York City Planning and Zoning Report for Public Discussion.* New York: New York City Planning Commission.

New York Times Book Review. 1974. Advertisement for *The Power Broker*, October 13, 11.

"The 100 Most Influential Books Since the War." 1995. *Times Literary Supplement*, October 6, 39.

Orloff, Chet. 2010. E-mail exchange with the author, October 27.

Ouroussoff, Nicolai. 2006a. "Outgrowing Jane Jacobs." *New York Times*, April 30, C1.

———. 2006b. Remarks at "Jane Jacobs vs. Robert Moses: How Stands the Debate Today?" Gotham Center for New York City History, City University of New York, New York, October 11.

Peck, Jamie, and Nik Theodore. 2010. "Mobilizing Policy: Models, Methods, and Mutations." *Geoforum* 41:169–174.

Peck, Jamie, and Adam Tickell. 2002. "Neoliberalizing Space." *Antipode* 34 (3): 380–404.

Perrine, Jerilyn. 2008. Remarks at "First Annual Jane Jacobs Forum: Housing New Yorkers in the 21st Century," New York University Law School, New York, November 5.

"Pining for Glenn Jackson." 2007. *Portland Transport*, January 8. Available at http://portlandtransport.com/archives/2007/01/pining_for_glen.html.

Pinsky, Seth. 2008. "Update on New York City's Economic Development," presented at "Dialogue between Planners and Architects" meeting, American Planning Association Economic Development Committee, American Institute of Architects, New York, September 18.

Pogrebin, Robin. 2004. "An Aesthetic Watchdog in the City Planning Office." *New York Times*, December 29, E1.

———. 2007. "Rehabilitating Robert Moses." *New York Times*, January 23, 28.

Portland State University. 2009. "Certified Population for Oregon and Oregon Counties." Available at http://www.pdx.edu/sites/www.pdx.edu.prc/files/media_assets/2009CertPopEst_web3.pdf.

Portland State University College of Urban and Public Affairs. 2010. "Learning Portland: Expert's Guide to Where to Find It and How It Happened." Promotional brochure.

Pratt Center for Community Development. 2009. "Protecting New York's Threatened Manufacturing Space." Available at http://prattcenter.net/issue-brief/protecting-new-yorks-threatened-manufacturing-space.

Pratt Institute Department of City and Regional Planning. 1962. Editorial. *Pratt Planning Papers* 1 (3): 1.

———. 1963. Editorial. *Pratt Planning Papers* 2 (3): 2–4.

Project for Public Spaces. n.d. a. "About: Placemaking for Communities." Available at http://www.pps.org/info/aboutpps/about (accessed November 20, 2012).

———. n.d. b. "Placemaker Profiles." http://www.pps.org/reference-categories/placemaker-profiles (accessed November 20, 2012).

Ravitch, Richard. 2008. Remarks at "The Fate of the Far West Side: New York Neighborhoods, Development, and Preservation," Museum of the City of New York, New York, January 29.

Regional Plan Association. 2012. "Mission." Available at http://www.rpa.org/mission.html.

Rich, Damon. n.d. "Big Plans and Little People, or Who Has the Keys to the Federal Bulldozer?" Unpublished manuscript in the author's possession.

Roberts, Sam. 2006. "Bloomberg Administration Is Developing Land Use Plan to Accommodate Future Populations." *New York Times*, November 26, 39.

Rochon, Lisa. 2007. "New Ideas Require New Buildings." In *Block by Block: Jane Jacobs and the Future of New York*, edited by Timothy Mennel, Jo Steffens, and Christopher Klemek, 40–42. New York: Princeton Architectural Press.

Rockefeller Foundation. n.d. "Jane Jacobs Medal." Available at http://www.rockefellerfoundation.org/what-we-do/where-we-work/new-york-city/jane-jacobs-medal (accessed December 11, 2012).

Sagalyn, Lynne. 2004. "The Politics of Planning the World's Most Visible Urban Development Project." In *Contentious City*, edited by John Mollenkopf, 23–72. New York: Russell Sage Foundation.

———. 2008. Remarks at "The Fate of the Far West Side: New York Neighborhoods, Development and Preservation," Museum of the City of New York, New York, January 29.

Santos, Fernanda. 2009. "Preparing Workers for Jobs after the Junkyards Go." *New York Times*, May 27, A21.

Schumer, Charles. 2005. "West Side Site Isn't Downtown's Foe." *Newsday*, May 25.

Schwartz, Joel. 1993. *The New York Approach: Robert Moses, Urban Liberals, and the Redevelopment of the Inner City*. Columbus: Ohio State University Press.

———. 2007. "Robert Moses and City Planning." In *Robert Moses and the Modern City: The Transformation of New York*, edited by Hilary Ballon and Kenneth Jackson, 130–133. New York: Norton.

Sennett, Richard. 1970. "An Urban Anarchist," review of *The Economy of Cities*. *New York Review of Books* 13 (12): 22–24.

Shiffman, Ron. 2007. Remarks at "Interpreting and Misinterpreting Jane Jacobs: New York and Beyond," Museum of the City of New York, New York, March 3.

Sites, William. 2003. *Remaking New York: Primitive Globalization and the Politics of Urban Community*. Minneapolis: University of Minnesota Press.

Smith, Neil. 1996. *The New Urban Frontier: Gentrification and the Revanchist City*. New York: Routledge.

———. 2002. "New Globalism, New Urbanism: Gentrification as Global Urban Strategy." *Antipode* 34 (3): 427–450.

———. 2008. *Uneven Development: Nature, Capital, and the Production of Space.* 3rd ed. Athens: University of Georgia Press.

Smith, Neil, and James DeFilippis. 1999. "The Reassertion of Economics: 1990s Gentrification in the Lower East Side." *International Journal of Urban and Regional Research* 23 (4): 638–653.

Smith, Neil, and Scott Larson. 2007. "Beyond Moses and Jacobs." *Planetizen*, August 13. Available at https://www.planetizen.com/node/26287.

Sorkin, Michael. 2006. Remarks at "Jane Jacobs vs. Robert Moses: How Stands the Debate Today?" Gotham Center for New York City History, City University of New York, New York, October 11.

———. 2007. "Can Robert Moses Be Rehabilitated for a New Era of Building?" *Architectural Record* 195 (3): 23.

———. 2008. Interview with the author, June 3.

South, Walter. 2007. "Columbia University's Planned Expansion," presented at Department of Urban Affairs and Planning, Hunter College, New York, September 17.

Starita, Angela. 2008. "Profiles in Courage: Building in Uncertain Times." *Architect's Newspaper* 6 (13): 28.

Sternberg, Ernest. 2000. "An Integrative Theory of Urban Design." *Journal of the American Planning Association* 66 (3): 265–278.

Stolarick, Kevin. 2010. Interview with the author, July 15.

Sutton, Stacey. 2008. Remarks at "Radical Urbanism: Critical Discourse on the Right to the City," Center for Place, Culture, and Politics, Graduate Center, City University of New York, New York, December 12.

Throgmorton, James. 1992. "Planning as Persuasive Storytelling about the Future: Negotiating an Electric Power Rate Settlement in Illinois." *Journal of Planning Education and Research* 12:17–31.

U.S. Bureau of the Census. 2000a. Summary File 1: Demographic profile.

———. 2000b. Summary File 3: Income profile.

Vitullo-Martin, Julia. 2008. "Rezone the Rockaways—They've Waited Long Enough." Manhattan Institute, June. Available at http://www.manhattan-institute.org/email/crd_newsletter06-08.html.

Wallace, Mike. 2006. Remarks at "Jane Jacobs vs. Robert Moses: How Stands the Debate Today?" City University of New York, New York, October 11.

Washburn, Alexandros. 2008a. "Civic Virtue by Design: The Meaning behind Mayor Bloomberg's Vision for New York City." Unpublished manuscript in the author's possession.

———. 2008b. Remarks at "Ecotones: Mitigating NYC's Contentious Sites" conference, American Institute of Architects, New York, May 22.

Wells, Richard. 2007. "A Moses for Our Time." *Brooklyn Rail*, March. Available at http://www.brooklynrail.org/2007/03/express/a-moses-for-our-time.

Whyte, William. 1989. *City: Rediscovering the Center.* New York: Doubleday.

Wickersham, Jay. 2001. "Jane Jacobs's Critique of Zoning: From Euclid to Portland and Beyond." *Boston College Environmental Affairs Law Review* 28 (4): 547–564.

Windells, Paul. 1948. "Metropolis at the Crossroads." *National Municipal Review* 37 (7): 371–376.

Winsa, Patty. 2010. "Queens Quay Ready for Its Makeover." *Toronto Star*, April 19. Available at http://www.thestar.com/news/gta/article/797710--queens-quay-ready-for-its-makeover?bn=1#article.

Wintrob, Suzanne. 2010. "GTA Waterfront Properties in Great Demand." *National Post*, June 18. Available at http://www.nationalpost.com/waterfront+properties+high+demand/3172238/story.html.

Yaro, Robert. 2008. Interview with the author, November 11.

———. 2009. Remarks at "New Urbanism for New Yorkers," Museum of the City of New York, New York, February 25.

Yaro, Robert, and Tony Hiss. 1996. *A Region at Risk: The Third Regional Plan for the New York–New Jersey–Connecticut Metropolitan Area*. Washington, DC: Island Press.

Zuccotti, John. 1974. "How Does Jane Jacobs Rate Today?" *Planning*, June, 23–27.

Zukin, Sharon. 1987. "Gentrification: Culture and Capital in the Urban Core." *Annual Review of Sociology* 13:129–147.

———. 2006. "Jane Jacobs: The Struggle Continues." *City and Community* 5 (3): 223–236.

———. 2010. *Naked City: The Death and Life of Authentic Urban Places*. New York: Oxford University Press.

Index

Abbott, Carl, 118, 122–124
Abrams, Charles, 19
affordable housing: and Battery Park City, 109, 163n9; and the Bloomberg administration, 2, 13, 17, 39–42, 90, 93–96, 136, 143, 153; and inclusionary zoning, 94–95, 143, 149; and Jane Jacobs, 13, 56, 98–99, 104, 157n13, 163n6; and Portland, Oregon, 124; and *A Region at Risk*, 75; and Toronto, 130–132
Aggarwala, Rohit, 81–82, 147, 159n7
Alexiou, Alice Sparberg, 9, 16, 158n18
Anderson, Martin, 27
Atlantic Yards redevelopment, 2, 24, 38–40, 55, 136, 138, 141, 145, 150, 159n5 (ch. 3), 166n3; and affordable housing, 38, 40; and eminent domain, 38–39; opposition to, 38–40, 43, 151, 162n8

Bagli, Charles, 37, 95–96
Ballon, Hilary, 9, 30, 46, 78, 97, 122; on Jane Jacobs and role of government in urban planning, 26; on Robert Moses and role of government in urban planning, 26; and Robert Moses's legacy, 9, 13, 20–22, 25, 28, 30, 60, 98, 104, 125, 159n1
Barclays Center, 38
Bartholomew, Harland, 119

Barwick, Kent, 76; and Bloomberg administration redevelopment agenda, 45, 52, 57, 76, 134, 141; and Jane Jacobs's legacy, 24–25, 30, 52; and Robert Moses's legacy, 30, 52
Battery Park City, 26, 37, 47, 56, 74, 94, 100, 106–110, 133, 158–159n4, 163n9
The Battle for Gotham: New York in the Shadow of Robert Moses and Jane Jacobs (Gratz), 9
Benepe, Adrian, 78–79, 82, 147, 165n7
Bennett, Edward, 119
Berman, Marshall, 7, 21, 61
Birch, Eugenie, 95–96
Bloomberg, Michael: legacy of, 54, 135, 146–147; reelection to third term as mayor, 54, 81, 88
Bloomberg administration: and planning as economic development, 42, 50, 55, 80, 134, 143, 151; and the rebirth of long-term planning, 17, 33, 50–54, 78; and the rehabilitation of Robert Moses, 13, 45, 46, 52, 56; and the synthesis of Jane Jacobs and Robert Moses, 3, 5, 10, 12, 13, 45, 46, 78, 133, 148, 151–152
Bloomberg administration redevelopment agenda, 2, 3, 8, 10–11, 13, 16–17, 30–46, 50–52, 54–57, 75–83, 87–94, 97, 102, 133–136, 139–153; and affordable

Bloomberg administration redevelopment agenda (*continued*)
  housing, 2, 17, 39–42, 75, 90, 92–96, 136, 149, 163n9; and architecture/iconic spaces, 38, 51, 74, 134–135, 140–144; and community input, 35, 150–151; and global competitiveness, 16, 51–52, 75, 79–80, 134–135, 140, 143–145, 148, 152, 165n9; and the greater public good, 57, 144; and incentives and subsidies for private development, 31, 37, 81–82, 89, 92, 94–95, 146, 151, 162n8, 166n5; and inclusionary zoning, 88, 92, 94–96, 149; influence of *A Region at Risk* on, 12, 62, 75–76; influence of Jane Jacobs on, 11–13, 17, 46–47, 51, 78, 98, 131, 133, 135–136, 142, 146–153; influence of Robert Moses on, 11–13, 17, 31, 46–47, 52, 78, 98, 102, 131, 133, 136, 139, 142, 144, 146–153; and manufacturing, 91–94, 96; and narrative of risk/threat, 75, 79–80; opposition to, 33–35, 38–43, 57, 79, 90–91, 143–144, 147, 151, 162n8; and parks and public spaces, 13, 17, 51, 75, 78–80, 82, 95, 135–136, 139–144, 149, 151–152; and quality of life, 75, 80, 144, 146, 148, 152; and real estate–based redevelopment, 10, 13, 75, 91, 93, 130, 135, 142, 144, 147, 150, 152; and sustainability, 25, 51, 54, 75, 80–81, 147, 157–158n14, 160n3 (*see also* PlaNYC 2030); and waterfront redevelopment, 17, 35, 51, 55, 71, 74–75, 78, 80–82, 91–93, 96, 134, 136, 140, 152, 159n3; and zoning, 2, 12, 35–36, 41–42, 53–57, 80, 82–83, 87–96, 136, 141–144, 165n4; and zoning and real estate values, 93, 142–144, 150, 152
Brash, Julian, 35, 52–53, 158n2
Bryant Park, 69, 137
Burden, Amanda, 2, 36, 133–142, 164n1 (ch. 9), 165n4; and affordable housing, 95; and the Bloomberg administration's redevelopment agenda, 2–3, 10, 17, 51, 75, 78–81, 83, 87–88, 92, 97, 135–136, 138, 150, 152, 165n9; and design, 13, 51, 134, 140–145, 165n9; and Jane Jacobs's legacy, 17, 77, 98, 134–136, 139, 148–151; and Robert Moses's legacy, 78, 81, 136; and "Shaping the City: A Strategic Blueprint for New York's Future," 51, 79, 88; and the synthesis of Jane Jacobs and Robert Moses, 2–3, 10, 46, 79, 136, 151, 152; and zoning, 83, 87–90, 93, 95, 150
Burnham, Daniel, 5, 119
Burns, Ric, 28–29, 158n18
Butzel, Albert, 61, 160n1

Caro, Robert, 9, 13, 161n1; and Robert Moses's legacy, 19–21, 25, 29, 31, 61, 104, 125
Chakrabarti, Vishaan, 36, 159n7
Cheney, Charles, 119
City Beautiful movement, 5, 82, 119, 148
City of New York Independent Budget Office, 40, 162n8
Coalition to Preserve Community, 42
collapse of planning and development, 12, 47–50
Columbia University expansion, 21, 24, 40–43, 75, 81, 147, 149; and eminent domain, 2, 41–42; and gentrification, 42–43; opposition to, 11, 41–42, 43, 150; and zoning, 41
Committee on a Regional Plan of New York and Its Environs, 5, 156n6 (ch. 1)
community benefits agreement, 39, 42
Community Board 4 (CB4) of Manhattan, 90–91
comprehensive planning, 51
Cooper, Alexander, 26, 56, 100, 106. *See also* Battery Park City
creative destruction, 18, 30, 81, 111, 136, 151
creative economy/creative class, 27–28, 100, 110, 123–124, 132, 143
Cross, Jay, 36
"Culture Plan for the Creative City," 128

The Death and Life of Great American Cities (Jacobs), 1, 155n1, 156n1, 162n2, 163n6; influence of, 3, 7, 15–16, 25, 43, 69, 77, 107, 123; and Jacobs's critique of planning, 3, 5, 23, 47; response to, 4, 23, 26, 155n4, 155–156n5, 157n10; and urban form, 7–8, 25, 98, 107, 123, 161–162n5, 162n6. *See also* Jacobs, Jane
Dinkins, David, 34, 48, 52, 86, 159n3
displacement, 18, 31, 103, 131, 158n16
Doctoroff, Daniel, 34–36, 135, 159n2; and Amanda Burden, 134–135, 141, 164n2 (ch. 9); and the Bloomberg redevelopment agenda, 46–47, 50–52, 56–57, 76, 78, 82, 90, 133, 150–151,

165n8; comparisons of, to Robert Moses, 51–52, 76, 133; and gentrification, 145; and NYC2012, 34–35, 55
Duany, Andrés, 26. *See also* New Urbanism
Durst, Douglas, 95

Eckstut, Stanton, 26, 56, 100, 106. *See also* Battery Park City
The Economy of Cities (Jacobs), 27, 157n10, 158n17, 164n5
eminent domain, 2, 24, 31, 39, 41–42, 55, 74, 81, 143, 158–159n4, 160n3
Empire State Development Corporation (ESDC), 38, 39
enterprise zones, 27

"Far West Midtown: A Framework for Development," 35
Far West Side redevelopment, 2, 11, 33, 36–37, 75, 81, 87, 135–136, 142, 146; opposition to, 90–91; rezoning of, 35, 54–55, 80, 90
financial (sub-prime mortgage) crisis of 2008, 13, 37, 40, 43, 54, 106, 113, 145–147
fiscal crisis of the 1970s, 10, 21, 37, 54, 76, 106, 113, 146, 152; and the collapse of planning, 47–48, 52, 85
Flint, Anthony, 9, 13, 77, 158n19
floor-area ratios (FARs), 83–86, 161n3
Florida, Richard, 27–28, 100, 116, 128, 132, 164n1 (ch. 8)
Forest City Ratner, 38, 162n8
Fortune (magazine), 19, 137, 156n6 (ch. 2)
Furman Center for Real Estate and Urban Policy, 93

Garden City movement, 23, 148, 155n3
Garvin, Alexander, 34, 56, 134
Gehry, Frank, 2, 38, 40, 74, 140–141, 143, 162n8
gentrification: and the Bloomberg administration, 12, 42, 75, 94, 145, 152; and Jane Jacobs, 10, 12, 73, 107–110, 152–153, 163n6; phases of, 72–74, 161n9; and Portland, Oregon, 124; as public policy, 71, 73–75; and *A Region at Risk*, 71, 73–75; and Robert Moses, 10, 12, 110–113, 153; and Toronto, 130; and William "Holly" Whyte, 137–138
Giuliani, Rudolph, 34, 48, 50, 55
Goldberger, Paul, 17, 33

Goldstein, Daniel, 40
Goldstein et al. v. Empire State Development Corporation, 39. *See also* Atlantic Yards redevelopment: opposition to
Goldstein v. Pataki, 39. *See also* Atlantic Yards redevelopment: opposition to
Gotham Center for New York City History, 1, 3–4, 26, 28, 30–31, 46, 91, 95–96, 136, 151
Gratz, Roberta Brandes, 9, 13
greater public good/public interest, 29, 42, 57, 144; and Robert Moses 6, 22, 57, 60, 144
Greenberg, Ken, 127, 131–132
Greenpoint/Williamsburg rezoning, 55–57, 81
Greenwich Village: and gentrification, 110, 149, 163n6; and Jane Jacobs 15, 23, 99–101, 105; proposed urban renewal of, 25, 157n13
Group of 35, 55, 61, 75, 159n5 (ch. 4)

Harvey, David, 111, 113, 121–122
Haussmann, Baron von, 35, 76, 111, 113, 134, 143
Hess, Paul, 130
High Line, 81, 87, 92–93, 129, 135, 143, 165n4
Hiss, Tony, 62, 64. *See also A Region at Risk: The Third Regional Plan for the New York–New Jersey–Connecticut Metropolitan Area* (Yaro and Hiss)
Housing Act of 1949, 112
Howard, Ebenezer, 5, 23, 155n3
Hudson Yards redevelopment, 33–37, 43, 55–56, 87, 106, 134, 145, 150–151, 159–160n7, 166n3; opposition to, 35, 90–91; and rezoning, 36, 90, 92, 94, 165n4
Hume, Christopher, 132

industrial business zones (IBZ), 91–92

Jackson, Kenneth, 9, 13, 159–160n7; and calls for a new Robert Moses, 31; and Robert Moses's legacy, 9, 20–22, 25, 28, 78, 97–98, 122, 125, 156n8
Jacob Javits Convention Center, 34–35, 37, 145, 158–159n4
Jacobs, Jane: activism and community organizing by, 12, 16, 24–25, 32, 99, 123; and affordable housing, 56, 99, 104, 153, 157n13, 163n6; and the built

Jacobs, Jane (*continued*)
  environment, 99–107; and catastrophic money, 10, 103–104; and cities as processes, 8; and critique of planning, 4, 5, 7, 15, 23, 26, 50, 103–104, 110, 128, 137, 155n3; critiques of, 23, 27, 50, 99, 110, 130, 155–156n5, 158n17, 159–160n7; and design, 84, 100, 101, 147–148; and diversity, 2, 8, 15, 17, 26–29, 46, 79, 87, 99–102, 105–106, 109–110, 116, 127–128, 136, 147–152, 162–163n4; and enterprise zones, 27; and "eyes on the street," 27, 50, 69, 103; and failed city districts, 102; and gentrification, 10, 12, 73, 103, 106–110, 152–153, 163n6; legacy of, 1–13, 15–18, 22–31, 42–43, 45–47, 50–52, 56–57, 60–62, 69–71, 75, 77–80, 99–100, 106–107, 147–153, 164n1 (ch. 8); and localism, 10, 97; and "low economic" uses, 102, 105, 148; and neighborhood regeneration, 9, 25, 27, 56, 73, 81, 103–105, 107, 109–110, 112; and precepts for livable cities/principles for urban design, 8, 15, 25–26, 99, 106, 108, 123, 126–128, 151; and private enterprise, 27, 102–104, 151, 158n16, 162n6; and real estate–based redevelopment, 104; and the role of government in urban planning, 10, 25–27, 80, 101–103; and Toronto, 125–128, 130–132; and unslumming, 27, 105–106, 109; use/misuse of ideas of, 10, 12, 26–28, 79–80, 86, 101, 106–108, 110, 130, 147–153; and zoning, 84–85. *See also The Death and Life of Great American Cities* (Jacobs)
Jane Jacobs and the Future of New York (exhibit), 9, 17, 19, 22–23, 95, 99
Jane Jacobs: Urban Visionary (Alexiou), 9, 16, 158n18

Kennicott, Philip, 20, 30, 125
Kent, Fred, 137
King, John, 125
Klemek, Christopher, 24–25, 27, 30, 126, 163n6
Koch, Ed, 34, 38, 52
Kriegel, Jay, 34, 36, 56

Lander, Brad, 158n15; and the Bloomberg administration's redevelopment agenda, 91–92, 96; and Jane Jacobs's legacy, 26–28, 31; and Robert Moses's legacy, 31
"Learning from Moses," 46

Le Corbusier, 5, 8, 84, 148, 155n3
Lefebvre, Henri, 99, 102, 153
Lemon, James, 130–131
Levin, Anna Hayes, 90

Madison Square Garden, 34, 37
Mandelbaum, Seymour, 78
Melrose Commons, 25
Metropolitan Transportation Authority (MTA), 22, 33, 36–38, 158n1
modernism, 5–7, 10, 18–21, 27, 29, 60, 80, 152, 156nn3–4; and Portland, Oregon, 117, 121, 123; and Toronto, 126, 128; and urban planning, 5–7, 8, 12, 18–21, 27, 43, 47, 61, 79, 81, 83, 103, 110–111, 117, 121, 123, 126, 128
Morris, Robert, 7
Moses, Robert: and affordable housing, 13, 104; build-big urbanism, 11, 16, 33, 45–46, 78, 79, 117; and the built environment, 3, 6, 70, 102–103, 115, 121; calls for a new, 29–31, 113; and civic institutions and redevelopment, 10, 104, 112; and debt financing, 113, 121; and federal policy/programs, 5, 6, 16, 22, 47, 63, 104, 111–112; and gentrification, 10, 12, 110–113, 153; and infrastructure and redevelopment, 6, 12, 17, 30–31, 156n2; legacy of, 1–6, 8–13, 16–22, 25–26, 28–31, 34–35, 42–43, 45–47, 51–52, 56–57, 60–62, 69–71, 110–113, 114, 116–125, 132, 136, 144, 147–148, 150–153, 158n19, 160n2, 163n10, 164n11; and the middle class, 6, 21, 71, 104, 110–112; and modernism, 5–7, 10, 18–21, 29, 60, 80, 83, 103, 111, 117, 121, 123, 152, 156n4; and narratives of planning, 52, 60, 61, 79, 120, 144; and parks, 10, 12, 17, 20, 67, 79, 82, 119, 122, 151–152, 156n8; and Portland, Oregon, 12, 117–125; and real estate–based redevelopment, 104; rehabilitation/revisionist readings of, 9, 13, 20–22, 25, 28, 30–31, 45, 52, 56, 122; and role of government in urban planning, 10, 26, 30, 47, 57, 103–104, 118, 120; and role of market in urban planning, 22, 103–104, 112–113, 151; and slum clearance, 16, 28–29, 47, 79, 103, 158n19, 163n10; and Title I, 6, 103–104, 111–112, 138, 163n10, 164n11; and urban renewal, 6, 9, 10, 16–17, 28–29, 71, 78, 98, 103–104, 111–112, 121–122, 158n19

Moynihan Station, 37, 81, 145
Mumford, Lewis, 23, 155n3, 155–156n5, 161n4 (ch. 5); and critique of Jane Jacobs, 23, 155–156n5, 157n10; and critique of Robert Moses, 19, 156n5 (ch. 2); and planning in Portland, Oregon, 119–120, 123
Municipal Art Society of New York, 9, 22, 24–25, 28, 30, 76, 84, 95–96, 134, 161n2
Museum of the City of New York, 28, 37, 61, 78

narratives in planning, 12, 13, 28–29, 59–61, 76, 78, 104, 116, 160n3; and the Bloomberg administration, 13, 46, 51, 55, 57, 75, 78–83, 88, 135, 140–142, 144–146, 150–152; and Robert Moses, 52, 60–61, 79, 120, 144; of threat, 60, 79–82
neighborhood regeneration, 9, 25, 27, 56, 73, 81, 103–105, 107, 109–110, 112, 138, 142
neoliberalism, 63, 68, 72, 137; and urbanism/redevelopment, 12, 27, 77, 96, 116, 131, 137, 153
New Housing Marketplace Plan, 94
New Urbanism, 11, 26, 70, 100, 106–108, 110, 123, 131, 164n1 (ch. 8)
New York: A Documentary Film (1999), 28–29, 158n18
New York Charter Revision Commission, 48–49
New York City Board of Estimate, 47–49, 85
New York City Department of City Planning, 35–36, 42, 50, 84, 86, 88, 133–134, 138–141, 150, 157–158n14, 159–160n7
New York City Department of Parks and Recreation, 78
New York City Economic Development Corporation, 146, 165–166n2
New York City Housing Authority, 19
New York City Housing Trust Fund, 94, 163n9
New York City Office of Long-Term Planning and Sustainability, 54, 81, 147, 159–160n7
New York City Planning Commission, 2, 17, 19, 34, 36, 41, 47–88, 90, 133, 138–139, 164n2 (ch. 9); history and evolution of, 47–50, 85
New York Jets stadium proposal, 34, 36, 45, 136, 141, 151

9/11, 76, 135, 143
1969 Master Plan, 47, 56, 134, 138
No. 7 subway line expansion, 35, 37, 75, 81, 146
Nos Quedamos, 25
NYC2012, 33–35, 56, 106

Office of Industrial and Manufacturing Business (OIMB), 91–92
Olmsted, Frederick Law, 67, 79, 119, 161n5 (ch. 5)
Olmsted, John Charles, 119
Olympic Games (Summer 2012), 2, 11, 34–36, 55–56, 92, 134; as a "forcing mechanism" for development, 55, 159n5 (ch. 4)
Orloff, Chet, 122–123
Ouroussoff, Nicolai, 30, 38

Peck, Jamie, 116
Pinsky, Seth, 146–147, 166n3
Plan for New York City, 47, 138. *See also* 1969 Master Plan
PlaNYC 2030, 25, 51, 54, 75, 81, 90, 147, 157–158n14, 160n3
policy mobility/policy transfer, 12, 115–117, 143, 164n2 (ch. 8), 165n8
Portland Area Postwar Development Committee, 117
Portland Improvement, 118–122
The Power Broker: Robert Moses and the Fall of New York (Caro), 9, 19, 21, 25, 29, 125, 160n2, 161n1
Pratt Center for Community Development, 26, 28, 41, 91, 96
public-private partnerships, 72; and redevelopment 10, 73, 98, 129, 137

Radiant Cities, 5, 8, 84, 148, 155n3
Ravitch, Richard, 37
real estate–based redevelopment, 53, 72–75; and the Bloomberg administration redevelopment agenda, 10–11, 13, 91, 93, 135, 142–144, 147, 150–152; and Jane Jacobs, 10, 12–13, 104, 130, 147; and *A Region at Risk*, 71; and Robert Moses, 10, 13, 104, 147; and Toronto, 130
recession of 1989–1992, 62, 64, 66
Regent Park, 128, 130–131
Regional Plan Association (RPA), 11–12, 62–71, 73–76, 78–79, 100, 110, 129, 140, 156n6 (ch. 1), 160n2. *See also A Region at Risk: The Third Regional*

Regional Plan Association (*continued*)
Plan for the New York–New Jersey–Connecticut Metropolitan Area (Yaro and Hiss)
A Region at Risk: The Third Regional Plan for the New York–New Jersey–Connecticut Metropolitan Area (Yaro and Hiss), 11–12, 61–71, 73–76, 129, 160n2, 161n8; and "centers campaign," 70–71; and gentrification, 71, 73–75; and global economy, 62, 64–67, 71; and "Greensward" initiative, 67–69, 161n5 (ch. 5) ; influence of, on Bloomberg administration redevelopment agenda, 12, 62, 75–76; influence of Jane Jacobs's legacy on, 62, 69–70, 71, 75; influence of Robert Moses's legacy on, 62, 64, 67, 70–71, 75; and manufacturing, 64, 66; and mixed-use development, 69–70, 75; and parks and public spaces, 67–70, 72, 75; and public-private model of redevelopment, 68–69, 71, 73, 75; and quality of life, 62, 65–67, 71, 74–75; and real estate–oriented development, 71, 75; and the three *E*s, 64–65; and transit-oriented development, 68, 70–71, 75; and waterfront redevelopment, 65, 68–69, 71, 75
Related Companies, 36–37, 135, 159–160n7
Remaking the Metropolis (exhibit), 20
rhetoric, 12, 79; and the Bloomberg administration, 8, 12, 17, 78, 150; and the greater good, 27, 52; and planning, 12, 13, 60
Rich, Damon, 28–29
Robert Moses and the Modern City (exhibit), 9, 17, 19–21, 25–26
Robert Moses and the Modern City: The Transformation of New York (Ballon and Jackson), 9, 19–21, 25, 162–163n4
"Robert Moses: Single-Minded Genius" (conference), 21
Robertson, Jacquelin, 56
Rockefeller Foundation, 23–24, 77, 156n6 (ch. 2), 157n11
Rouse, James, 108

Schumer, Charles, 55, 61, 75, 158n3
Schumpeter, Joseph, 18, 110
"Shaping the City: A Strategic Blueprint for New York's Future" (Burden), 79
Silver, Sheldon, 36, 45

Sitte, Camillo, 7–8, 39, 156n7 (ch. 1)
socially mixed housing, 127–128, 131
Sorkin, Michael, 28, 96
South Street Seaport, 107–108, 163n7
Sprayregen, Nick, 41
starchitects, 74, 140, 143
St. Lawrence redevelopment, 127–128, 131
Street Life Project, 85, 133, 137–138
sustainability, 51, 54, 75, 80–81, 147
synthesis of Jane Jacobs and Robert Moses, 12–13, 46, 78, 132–133, 148, 151

Theodore, Nik, 116
Times Square redevelopment, 48, 108, 137
Tishman Speyer, 36, 135
Title I, 6, 103–104, 111–112, 138, 163n10, 164n11

Uniform Land Use Review Procedure (ULURP), 48, 50, 85–86, 90, 159n6
urban renewal, 6, 27, 47–48, 71, 73; and Jane Jacobs, 9–10, 25, 28–29, 71–72, 98, 103–106, 126, 128, 137, 157n13, 158n16; and Portland, Oregon, 121–122; and Robert Moses, 9–10, 16–17, 47, 28–29, 60, 78, 103–104, 111–112, 158n19; and Toronto, 126–127

Wallace, Mike, 1, 4–5
Washburn, Alexandros, 141–144, 147, 150, 165n9
waterfront redevelopment, 74, 107, 159n3; and the Bloomberg administration's redevelopment agenda, 17, 35, 50–51, 55–56, 78, 80–82, 87, 91–93, 96, 134, 136, 140, 152; and Jane Jacobs, 80–82, 107; and New York City, 48; and Portland, Oregon, 119, 121; and *A Region at Risk*, 65, 68–69, 71, 75; and Toronto, 129–130, 132
West Harlem Local Economic Development Corporation, 42
Westside Neighborhood Alliance, 90
Westway, 61, 78
Whyte, William "Holly," 16, 25, 156n6 (ch. 2), 157n12, 165n5; and critique of Robert Moses, 19; and gentrification, 137–138; and public space, 85–86, 133, 137; and the Street Life Project, 85, 133, 137–139; and zoning, 85–86, 137–138
Willets Point redevelopment, 2, 80, 145, 148–150

World Trade Center, 47–48, 55, 76, 161n10

Wrestling with Moses: How Jane Jacobs Took On New York's Master Builder and Transformed the American City (Flint), 9, 77, 158n19

Yaro, Robert, 62, 69–70, 74–76, 110, 140, 160n2. *See also A Region at Risk: The Third Regional Plan for the New York–New Jersey–Connecticut Metropolitan Area* (Yaro and Hiss)

zoning, 83, 100, 102; history and evolution of, in New York City, 11–12, 47–50, 83–87, 108, 137–138, 161–162n5; incentive zoning and public space, 84–86; and Portland, Oregon, 121; and Toronto, 127. *See also* Bloomberg administration redevelopment agenda: and affordable housing; Bloomberg administration redevelopment agenda: and inclusionary zoning; Bloomberg administration redevelopment agenda: and zoning

Zukin, Sharon, 16, 99, 158n19

Scott Larson is an independent scholar who has taught geography and urban studies at Vassar College, Queens College, and Hunter College.